4.00

D1506829

THE CARTER ECONOMY

THE CARTER ECONOMY

George Melloan
Joan Melloan

JOHN WILEY & SONS

NEW   YORK   ·   CHICHESTER   ·   BRISBANE   ·   TORONTO

Library of Congress Cataloging in Publication Data:

Melloan, George, 1927-
  The Carter economy.

  Includes bibliographical references and indexes.
  1. United States—Economic policy—1971-
2. United States. President, 1977-   (Carter)
I. Melloan, Joan, 1926-   joint author. II. Title.

HC106.7.M45   338.973   78-4625
ISBN 0-471-03374-X

Printed in the United States of America

10 9 8 7 6 5 4 3 2 1

To Jim, Missy, and Maryanne

PREFACE

This book is an account of the economic problems confronted by President Carter in his first year in office and of how he attempted to deal with them through presidential programs and policy decisions. The issues will all be familiar ones to the well-informed reader— energy, Social Security, welfare, inflation, government regulation . . . They have been debated and redebated in the press and over the airwaves for the last year and longer, and they will continue to be debated during the coming year and longer. They are the economic issues of our times; for that matter, most of them have been familiar to all times.

Income transfer, the economist's term that is becoming part of the public vocabulary to describe the central function of the welfare state, was a central topic of debate in the Athens of Pericles. The Panic of 33, brought on by misguided government monetary policies and described by the historian Tacitus, was not the Great Depression of 1933 but the economic collapse of Rome in 33 A.D. under the rule of Tiberius Caesar, who had certain perverse limits to growth theories that caused him to sharply curtail the money supply and precipitate one of the great credit crunches of all time. The greatest portraits of mindless, impersonal bureaucracy come not from Milton Friedman or C. Northcote Parkinson but from the surrealistic fiction of Franz Kafka, writing at the turn of the century from middle Europe.

We would hope in this book not to complicate the debate further but to simplify it, giving it some of the perspective of recent (and occasionally, ancient) history that is so often lacking in the press reports from Washington or "Meet the Press" types of encounter on television. We have no illusion that public issues are simple—else why would history be so full of error and contention?—but we suspect that their complexities derive more from the politics that surround them than from the economics. We deal here mostly with the economics, fully recognizing that economics and politics are inseparable in the real world, but also recognizing that the rightness or wrongness of public policies is usually easier to analyze in economic terms than in political terms. As we said, we are seeking to simplify.

In such an analysis it is difficult to be uncritical of political leaders. But we would note that our criticisms are not intended in a personal way, even when we might speculate on how the personal attitudes of Mr. Carter and other leaders might have played a role in shaping policy judgements.

Mr. Carter and his principal advisers are estimable, even admirable individuals, seeking to serve the nation to the best of their abilities. They are subject to limitations on what even the best intentions can achieve in government, operating as they are in a political milieu that subjects them to hundreds of competing claims and dozens of conflicting theories.

Although they are charged with leadership roles, they also are faced with the vital political task of adjusting competing claims and mediating between the warring elements of a complex and pluralistic society. That task is by no means an easy one, and we recognize its difficulties.

Nor are we cynical about the American political process, that great and complex competition of groups and individuals to influence Congress and the executive branch and thus gain advantage, or protection, or redress from the state. It is capable of serious error, we suspect, perhaps the most serious in the long run being its tendency to expand and encompass problems that once were solved more efficiently without governmental intervention. But it is not easy in politics to distinguish between error and necessary political accommodation.

The very competition of voices that makes the political process in the United States so raucous and confusing also contributes to its strength, by balancing interests and assuaging disaffection. As great bazaars through history have demonstrated—the New York Stock Exchange, for example—the noisier it is the more likely it is to be serving its purpose. The United States political process responds in its own complex and cumbersome way to the mood of the nation. It may have saved Mr. Carter, an inexperienced President afflicted with the overconfidence that imperils most White House newcomers, from serious errors in economic policy in his first year; it is harder than most people think to legislate change, and that is very often a good thing.

We recognize that ours is a particular, although by no means unorthodox, view of the world. There is much eighteenth century liberalism in our make-up, a la Adam Smith and Thomas Jefferson. Despite our respect for the American political process, we are not much enamored of the idea of using the state to regulate or manipulate economic processes—how much a man or woman should charge for his or her labor, how much a merchant should charge for bread, where an individual's savings should be invested, how much return he should earn, how he should put his land or other property to use. We prefer the "unseen hand" described by Adam Smith—the assumption that if people are free to make their own economic choices, they will make them efficiently and innovatively, with benefits to the total society. The quality of their lives will be enhanced by their political and economic freedoms. The state, on the other hand, is likely to be inefficient, repressive, and destructive as it expands its role in economic choices.

Now we are not so naive as to believe that anything so pure as a *free market* either exists or is likely to come about. Indeed, the trend throughout the world may well be in the opposite direction, with national governments taking an increasingly more active and powerful role in attempting to manipulate economic processes.

But we think the United States would benefit from a relatively greater faith in the market process. We doubt the arguments of the new "consumerists" that the market "doesn't work," or victimizes consumers. When it doesn't work the reason is usually that it isn't being allowed to work, and government usually has a hand in the trouble. And it should be remembered that demands for governmental intervention in the market usually are made by producers, seeking protection from the cruelties of market competition, rather than consumers, who reap the benefits of that competition. Of course, most people are producers as well as consumers, which is why the free-market argument often sounds cruel. But we would side with the Milton Friedmans and Adam Smiths of the world and their argument that maximum freedom yields the most good for the most people in both economic and political terms.

Indeed, we are not sure there is any way of discussing economics other than in market terms, or that markets can ever be destroyed even when state dogma demands it. Even in the Soviet Union, we have noticed, there seems to be a tendency of individuals to strike bargains with each other, often in sordid or antisocial ways and very often outside the law. We wonder if the cruelty of subjecting individuals to the rigors of markets and competition can really be half as bad as the cruelty of subjecting them to state repression and forcing them to make their bargains outside the law and in terms other than simple cash. Perhaps John Kenneth Galbraith, who seems to have become an antimarket philosopher, can someday explain himself well enough to overcome our doubts, but the odds are highly unfavorable.

It should also be noted that the authors do not write from a "business" point of view. First of all, we're not sure that there is such a thing. Business is a pursuit, not a philosophy. The president of GUM in Moscow could probably run Macy's, although he would have to learn how to change price tags.

Men and women in business tend to be pragmatists, in that they know that they must deal with the world as it is, not as they would like it to be. And if the world were as they would like it to be, free of business risks, for example, it would not necessarily make for a very efficient or desirable economic system. Some parts of the energy chapters in this book may sound like a defense of the energy corporations, but that is only because the oversimplified rhetoric of politics and Washington journalism has somehow pitted the energy producers against consumers and put government on the side of the consumers. As we will attempt to explain, the energy problem is by no means that simple. At any rate, we don't accept the notion that government helps consumers by disrupting markets. Lest there be any further doubt, we are firmly on the side of the market—and the consumer.

We look with great skepticism on government wage and price controls, tax penalty and incentive systems that attempt to manipulate complex market forces, and political attacks on producers who are willing to take their chances in a free market, as opposed to those who prefer government coddling.

As to other trends in government, we explore some of the concerns that we sense around us over income transfers from producers to nonproducers, for example, the rising Social Security tax bill. We fully understand that compassion for the weak and the poor plays a salutary role in the American political and social process, and we would not like to see that change. But we fear that it might if the economic burden should ever become so large as to produce a strong political reaction. Even aside from this possibility, we do not discount fears among some economists that the disincentives created by income redistribution could eventually retard economic growth. In either case, the weak and poor would suffer most.

Further, we have somewhat more concern than this administration has demonstrated about inflation, for reasons that we also discuss in more detail. The administration's peculiarly casual attitude toward the weakness of the dollar in foreign exchange markets during much of 1977, its difficulties in engendering business confidence and its failures in resisting political pressures for increased government spending all add to our concern.

In short, we hope our analysis and criticism will contribute to the public discussion of the administration's economic policies. We do not believe that economics is an arcane subject understood only by economists. *Everyone* is an economist except, perhaps, for those fortunate few who never had to balance a checkbook and wonder how to equate resources with needs. Economists very often simply offer mathematical proofs of what most people know instinctively, for example, that people spend more for health care when they are insured than when they aren't or that they turn the thermostat down when the price of fuel goes up. The electorate has perceived the confusions and contradictions in many of Mr. Carter's economic policies.

We would hope that this book might serve as an antidote to the confusions and contradictions that remain, that it will shed light on current politicoeconomic problems by tracing them back to their sources and trying to identify the policy errors. If it does that it will have succeeded in its aims.

George and Joan Melloan

Westfield, N.J.
February 1978

CONTENTS

CHAPTER ONE

PROSPERITY AND DOUBT

I think we've addressed all the major problems already. . . . I think most of the major debates now already have been initiated.—Jimmy Carter, at a press conference on October 10, 1977.

JIMMY CARTER, IN HIS FIRST YEAR AS PRESIDENT OF THE UNITED States, did indeed initiate debates—on energy, Social Security, taxation, welfare, labor law, monetary policy, deregulation, and many lesser issues that all have a bearing on the health of the American economy. It is safe to say that the debates will continue through to the end of his four-year term in January 1981, and no doubt beyond.

The debates are steamy, with a considerable disinclination on the part of large segments of the Congress and the electorate to follow the President's leadership. The degree of emotion, and also confusion, that characterizes them says a great deal about the current state of American political and economic processes. That state can best be described as doubt in the midst of prosperity.

By any measure, the United States economy has made a remarkable recovery from the serious recession of 1974 and 1975. In 1978, barring some unforeseen economic disaster, it will produce over $2 trillion in goods and services, or gross national product (GNP). It employs over 92 million civilian workers. That number rose by over 4 million in 1977, more than twice the average gain of the preceding decade.

Average weekly earnings in 1977 rose by almost 8%. Retail sales were vigorous. Housing starts were up sharply from the year before. There were statistics available, although somewhat controversial ones, to indicate that the nation's income-transfer programs, such as welfare and Social Security, had all but eliminated poverty in the statistical sense.

And the economic forecasts for 1978 were, by and large, optimistic. A *Business Week* survey of economists at the end of 1977 (December 26 issue) showed that the average forecast for nine "econometric" models was for a 4.1% "real" growth in the economy this year, after adjusting for inflation. The average for 27 economists working without computerized models was 4.3%. Those are not spectacular growth rates, and are less than the robust advance of 1977, but they are slightly above the post-World War II average of about 4%. And of course, they are applied to an ever larger economic base, which means that they translate into ever larger numbers of additional goods, services, and jobs.

Juxtaposed against this healthy-looking statistical picture are the doubts. That great measure of economic confidence, the stock market, showed mixed results at the end of 1977. The broadest averages, reflecting prices of stocks traded in all significant markets, held up reasonably well. But the Dow Jones industrial average, reflecting the prices of the largest, mainly multinational corporations, dropped by 17% during the year. The broader Standard & Poor index, based on 500 stocks, declined by some 8%.

Another key measurement of business confidence, capital spending, showed gains finally in 1977 after almost no recovery from the recession during 1976. But it was still lagging below the expansion rate that economists feel is necessary to insure continued strong expansion of the general economy in the years just ahead. Of all the indicators of future economic activity, this was the most troubling one. When business decision makers are reluctant to make long-term commitments to build new plants and buy productive machines, it means that they do not see attractive potential yields on such investments.

There can be a variety of reasons for such pessimism, all of them economically important. Growth in technological innovation may be slowing. Innovation opens new profit-making opportunities in two ways: by yielding new products that will be attractive to consumers and by developing new production and distribution processes that will be more efficient and thus will lower costs. Examples of the first would be television tape recorders, of the latter, new computerized glassmaking processes or the wide-bodied jet aircraft with its larger payload. The United States still is a highly innovative country, but research-and-development spending has been declining, and worker productivity, a direct measure of economic efficiency, is not rising as rapidly as in years past.

Still another reason for the difficulty of finding high-yield investments is the tax burden, direct and indirect. The expanding role of government in managing national income and wealth is perhaps the most powerful economic fact of the twentieth century. In the United States the share of that $2 trillion GNP gathered and redistributed by government at all levels now is over 37%, compared with 26% twenty years ago. That is lower than in most of the Western democracies and certainly much lower than in the almost totally socialist states, such as the Soviet Union, but there is no significant sign of reversal of the long-term growth trend. The Social Security bill passed by Congress in 1977, which will add some $227 billion to the total United States tax bill over the next decade, and Mr. Carter's promise of a "national health" program during his administration seem certain to push the percentage upward.

Indirect taxation is more difficult to measure. Rather than raise direct taxes, the federal government at the beginning of this decade began to expand taxation through regulation to achieve social and political goals. The Clean Air Act of 1970 was a primary example. The goals of this form of taxation usually have strong political support—most Americans, for example, feel that clean air and water are goods worth buying through the regulatory process, just as they feel that public education is worth buying through direct tax payments. The problem is that the costs of regulatory taxation are hidden, and there are increasing signs that this may be a highly inefficient way of buying socially desirable goods because of the difficulties of comparing costs to benefits. Economic inefficiency on such a mass scale translates quickly into lower real economic growth and slower improvement, or even a decline, in general living standards.

Associated with this difficulty of comparing costs and benefits is the temptation that regulatory taxation presents to political leaders. It seems like a way to offer their constituents something for nothing, and some seem to believe that is what actually happens. The political rhetoric of the 1970s has been full of talk about how "business" will be made to bear the cost of clean air or cheap fuel, all of it ignoring the fact that "business" is an abstraction, merely something that individuals engage in through various means of organization—for example, through joint stock corporations or, at the other extreme, through selling pink lemonade on the front lawn. Business is a transmission belt, not a cornucopia, and costs dumped onto the transmission belt by government eventually are paid by living, walking, and talking human beings. This transmission belt is not even a very good way to achieve income redistribution, contrary to what some of the more sophisticated politicians suggest, because the costs usually are shared very broadly by rich and poor alike and, if anything, perhaps fall more heavily on the relatively poor.

Mr. Carter fell prey to the cost-hiding temptation in 1977, when he attempted to shift a larger share of the Social Security tax burden to employers in his proposed Social Security amendments. Congress, to its great credit, did not buy this, or more specifically, the House didn't. The final bill maintained the principle of an equal tax on employee and employer.

But of all the concerns of business decision makers and investors, the most serious is inflation. The problems of insufficient innovation and excessive taxation are aggravated by inflation. Inflation raises tax burdens on both individuals and businesses. Individuals are moved into higher tax brackets as inflation moves their dollar incomes higher, and this, under the progressive income-tax system, means that a larger and larger percentage of their incomes goes into taxes. Businesses find that the costs of replacing plant and equipment rise more than the tax-free depreciation allowances they are able to set aside for that purpose, which means that they are both overtaxed and discouraged from modernizing. The steel industry, with its long-lived, costly capital equipment, has suffered particularly. Inventories also appreciate in dollar terms because of inflation, producing "phantom" profits that also are taxed. The pinch on retained earnings makes business less inclined toward capital investment. Research and development is a form of capital investment. Thus innovation is discouraged in two ways.

The results of this inflationary impact on business profits are several. During the first half of this decade, corporations sharply increased their borrowing. Corporate debt climbed 68% to $1.3 trillion. Because of their poor profit performance, corporations chose to raise capital this way rather than attempting to sell stock. The result was that when the 1974–1975 recession hit, corporate balance sheets were top-heavy with debt, and banks were becoming seriously worried about repayments.

A major reason capital spending has not recovered adequately from the recession is that corporations have felt it wise to use their improved earnings to repay some of their debts and put their balance sheets into better order. With the economic recovery three years old in the spring of 1978, many are wondering if it is wise to expand now when another downturn in the economic cycle is likely soon.

The heavy corporate borrowing had another serious effect. It aggravated the very same inflationary pressures that helped bring it about by putting heavy pressures on the banking system—and hence the Federal Reserve Board—to maintain a policy of relatively easy money. Too sudden a clampdown at a time when businesses were heavily in debt and banks overextended could have brought about even more serious bank and business failures in the mid-1970s than those that actually occurred. Add to that the fact that the federal government now consistently runs large deficits, and the pressure on the Fed to expand the money supply is enormous. Too-rapid expansion of the money supply is inflationary.

When business pulled in its horns in 1976 and the federal government also got its borrowing under better control, the Fed was able to follow a more conservative monetary policy, and inflation fell from the dangerous levels of 1974 and 1975. Contrary to neo-Keynesian warnings, this greater conservatism on the part of both business and government did not abort the economic recovery. Rather, it no doubt enhanced it, because the one big fear of businesses, bankers, and the general public—inflation—came under better control. A measure of the improvement was the fact that the Dow Jones industrial average climbed again, going just above the 1000 mark at the end of 1976. Businesses even began to find it possible to sell stock and thus pay off some of their heavy debts.

It was in this generally improving economic climate that Jimmy Carter became President of the United States in January 1977. The country still had serious economic problems, but it was not so close to the brink of economic chaos as it had been in 1975.

The four-year terms of American Presidents are an arbitrary allotment. The natural cycles of the universe—rainfall and drought, mild and severe weather, and, most importantly for the purposes of this book, economic expansion and recession—operate independently of the dictates of the United States Constitution and the American voters.

It is also true, as we discuss in later chapters about Congress and the President's economic "team," that no President can truly dominate economic policymaking in the United States. Congress came to play an ever larger role in all kinds of policymaking during the years 1969 through 1976 when the Congress was dominated by Democrats and a Republican was in the White House. This has not changed under Jimmy Carter. Even the administrative bureaucracy does not always respond the way a President might like, given all the ways that important bureaucrats can find to manipulate policy, by working closely with key Congressmen, for example, or through their control of the information the President receives.

This complex diffusion of power is not necessarily bad. It lends a certain stability to government, albeit a certain inertia as well. It may at times prevent truly serious miscalculations by the President. It gives a large number of interests a role in policymaking, which contributes toward social and political stability.

For all these reasons, no President can receive full credit for the economic fortunes of the country during his tenure. Neither can he be accorded full blame for the misfortunes. This book, for purposes of simplicity, is entitled *The Carter Economy,* but the American economy has never been and never will be one man's economy. As it becomes larger and more complex, that becomes more and more true.

But we can justify the title on grounds that the President is the titular leader of the American nation. And though there is much he cannot do, for either good or ill, to affect the economic processes of the country, there also is much he *can* do, also for good or ill. He must be held accountable, as any chief executive must be, for the quality of economic leadership he supplies, which in turn will rest on the degree of his understanding of the nation's economic life and his skills in managing the government's now central role in the national economy.

It should not be overlooked that the American President also bears a responsibility for the growth and stability of the world economy. The American economy is, of course, the world's largest by far. The United States is the world's foremost capital market. Some 70% of world trade is transacted in United States dollars, which depend upon the wisdom of United States monetary authorities for their value and stability. Large American-based "multinational corporations" are a major source of managerial and technological know-how for the world, but they can only be so as long as the United States government supplies them with a solid political and economic base.

Thus the American President has come to be looked upon as not only the dominant political figure in the world but also its foremost economic manager. Because of the interrelationships of trade and capital movements and because of the role of the United States dollar as an international currency, his decisions, however much subject to the vagaries of natural cycles, random events, and the alterations of Congress and the bureaucracies, have a powerful influence on whether the world's millions eat well or poorly, have adequate or inadequate shelter, and can hope realistically for a better life or must be afflicted with despair.

Most people know this, either explicitly or instinctively, and have come to look upon the American President for economic wisdom as well as for political leadership (if it can truly be said that those two things can be separated, which we doubt). United States economic policy is the center ring of the world's political circus. The ups and downs of the dollar, the Dow Jones Industrials, the United States Consumer Price Index, and the unemployment rate are watched around the world, in Moscow, U.S.S.R. as avidly as in Moscow, Idaho, for signals on how the great industrial giant is doing, whether its government is being managed well or badly. The American President, despite the limitations on his role, is held accountable indeed.

When Mr. Carter stepped onto the world stage in November 1976, a narrow victor over Gerald Ford, to assume this enormous burden of accountability, he brought to the task some attributes that a majority of the voters found attractive. He was a new face in the national politics of a nation grown weary of many of the old faces. He was deeply rooted in the land and its fundamental institutions of family and church, a seemingly constant man in an age of uncertainty and change. He was articulate, intelligent, and possessed of a quick smile and a sense of humor. Although not always consistent in his positions on public issues, he was uncommonly candid for a public figure. He came, as do all men who seek the Presidency, with an enormous confidence in his ability to do the job. He brought along the pragmatism of a career as a farmer-businessman. And after four years as governor of Georgia, he had some understanding of government, particularly those areas of government, such as welfare and public housing, where the states share responsibility with the federal government.

But he also brought, as most Presidents have, only an uncertain grasp of what has come to be called macroeconomics, the study of those large forces of market interactions and responses that affect the daily lives of all of us. Because of the expanded role of national governments in the world economy—their ability to affect the value of money, incentives to production, wealth redistribution, and so many other concerns crucial to the lives of millions—macroeconomic policy and big government are handmaidens.

The lack of a sure grasp of the nation's and the world's economic problems, plus the usual political pressures that a freshman President must face, soon had Mr. Carter tangled in contradictions and confusions. One of his announced goals, and a laudatory one, was to balance the federal budget by 1981 and reduce federal spending as a percentage of gross national product to 21% from 23%. But one of his first policy decisions, an expansion of the fiscal 1978 budget prepared by President Ford, actually raised the projected deficit. The fiscal 1978 deficit will be on the order of $60 billion compared with about $45 billion for fiscal 1977, and the President's projected fiscal 1979 deficit is on a similar scale.

The country has become inured to large federal deficits, but even in the neo-Keynesian theory that Mr. Carter's economic advisers generally espouse, it is assumed that as the economy approaches the peak of a recovery cycle the deficit should fall, not rise. Otherwise, the combined credit demands of a vigorous economy and government are likely to generate inflation.

Still another goal of Mr. Carter was to reduce inflation, getting it down to somewhere close to the 4% level. Such a goal was not only laudable but an economic and political imperative. There is a great preponderance of belief in the United States, shared by everyone from New York cabbies to Milton Friedman, that inflation is the nation's number one problem.

But here again, Mr. Carter's announced goal and his policies diverged. Not only did he expand the federal deficit but by midway in his first year, he and his economic team were applying pressures on the Federal Reserve Board for a more liberal monetary policy. They got it and when the United States dollar's value began to sag in relation to the German mark, the Japanese yen, the Swiss franc, and even the British pound, Treasury Secretary Michael Blumenthal said he was unconcerned. His unconcern further weakened world confidence in the dollar. This crisis of confidence placed a far higher importance than it deserved on whether Mr. Carter would reappoint Arthur Burns as chairman of the Federal Reserve Board. In the summer and fall of 1977 Mr. Burns seemed to be the only one in Washington who cared about the stability of the dollar, even though he wasn't succeeding very well in doing anything about its serious instability.

Mr. Carter, who had been elected in part because he was not a part of the Washington "establishment," also quickly fell prey to some of that city's more intense lobbying pressures. Labor extracted a $21 billion "jobs" bill from Congress and a 45% increase in the minimum wage; we explain the implications of both in a later chapter. Mr. Carter attempted to push through a protective "cargo preference" act for the maritime unions and maritime industry, but Congress would not buy that. It did however, sharply expand subsidies and import protections for agriculture. The President, while espousing free trade, moved toward greater protectionism for steel and other industries late in 1977.

Mr. Carter had stressed his abilities as a manager and had achieved credibility for this claim through his record as a businessman and as governor of Georgia, where he had installed "zero-base" budgeting as a means of forcing department heads to justify better their budget requests. But even those abilities came into question when it became evident that the President was often launching major programs without adequate consultation with appropriate advisers, his Treasury Secretary for example. At midyear 1977 it became evident that the government's chief manager, Office of Management and Budget Director Bert Lance, had been an incredibly bad choice. As everyone now well remembers, Mr. Lance resigned after it came to light that he had used extremely poor judgement in the handling of overdrafts and loans while he was a banker in Georgia.

As a still further evidence of fecklessness, Mr. Carter's major Social Security and welfare reform programs contained conceptual problems. His Social Security program, flawed by its attempts to hide tax costs, was heavily reworked by Congress to remove this and other objectionable features, but nonetheless resulted in the biggest tax increase in United States history, $227 billion over the next decade. His welfare program, which would have presented both a high cost burden and formidable administrative problems, was held up in Congress in 1977 to be pursued further in 1978.

Both the welfare and Social Security programs were products of the Department of Health, Education, and Welfare, presided over by Joseph Califano, a man who could hardly have been more a part of the Washington "establishment." Mr. Califano had been one of the architects of President Johnson's "Great Society" programs of the 1960s and moved afterward to a lucrative Washington law practice. His activist instincts have made him one of the most influential persons in the Carter administration. Mr. Carter's original economic "team"— Treasury Secretary Blumenthal, chief economic adviser Charles Schultze, and the now-deposed Bert Lance—lost influence early under the pressures from other Cabinet members and from leading Congressmen for activist economic policies.

The other major actor in the first year of Mr. Carter's administration was James Schlesinger, who became Secretary of the new Department of Energy. He and the energy program he produced in the first 90 days of the Carter administration became the center of controversy in the young administration. We devote a great deal of attention in a later chapter to the energy problem and why the Schlesinger–Carter program was a badly conceived response to it. Suffice it to say at this point that, here again, Mr. Carter moved too quickly and without adequate consultation with the more conservative voices in his administration and the country at large.

He approached a problem of serious market disruption, most of it caused by the mistakes of past administrations and Congresses, as if it were some great moral issue. His instincts as a moralist and a Southern populist led him badly astray, contributing perhaps the largest component to the totality of confusion that sharply reduced public confidence in his administration during his first year in office.

Mr. Carter's promise in October that he had put his major programs on the table and probably would not offer much more in his four-year term was greeted with an immense sense of relief. The stock market, which had staggered downward during the first 10 months of his administration, even rallied briefly on this news.

By year-end 1977 the Carter energy program had been hacked to pieces in Congress, and even the few parts that Congress could agree upon had not been put to a final vote. Some of the more objectionable features, such as a gasoline tax with a potential cost of $50 billion, were dead, and there no longer seemed to be a threat that Congress would risk shutting the economy down by adding massive energy taxes to the massive Social Security tax program. Mr. Carter was promising a $25 billion tax cut in 1978 to offset some of the tax rise that would be generated by the added Social Security levy and inflation.

The truly serious legacy of Mr. Carter's first year, however, is that he had squandered a unique opportunity to start treating some of the threatening underlying economic problems of the United States and the industrial democracies.

He could have freed the energy industry of the economic controls that, over six years, had put it into such a sorry state. He could have encouraged sound money policies, which would have increased, rather than shattered, worldwide confidence in the dollar and, by extension, United States economic leadership. He could have perceived that chronic inflation in the United States and the Western world stemmed from the same causes from which inflation has almost always arisen: a too rapid expansion of public and private debt. With a little more analysis and a lot less heed to advice from the political left, he could have seen that American industry is not fat with profits and is, in fact, not even in a very healthy state. It is still burdened with inflation, regulation, debt, and unfunded obligations (pension funds, for example) that are increasingly difficult for it to manage. The stock market, far from being some irrational barometer of the emotions of the rich, is a fairly accurate guide to how millions of investors, of whom professionals who manage large funds are the most influential, view the future of American business. A 17% decline in the Dow Jones industrial average in a year in which the economy is otherwise recovering indicates that the future is not viewed with a great deal of optimism.

There was evidence late in 1977 that the President was awakening to some of the confidence problems that his administration had generated. He issued a statement on December 21 suggesting that the United States might intervene in foreign-exchange markets more broadly in support of the dollar to calm "disorderly markets." The assurances brought an immediate response in both the stock market, where the Dow Jones industrial average rose, and foreign-exchange markets, where the dollar strengthened against other currencies.

Intervention in foreign-exchange markets is not the most desirable way to support the dollar. The most desirable way is for the Fed to follow a prudent policy of money creation. But purchases of dollars by the Fed's foreign-exchange desk have much the same effect as the issuance of government securities for dollars by the Fed's open-market desk, which is the fundamental way of controlling the money supply. They mop up liquidity and thus shore up the dollar's value.

The disadvantage of using foreign-exchange intervention as a means of controlling the dollar supply is that it places burdens on foreign central banks. The United States must borrow foreign currencies to use for buying dollars, making use of what is known as the "swaps" network, which complicates the problems of foreign central banks in controlling their own money supplies. It also creates external debt for the United States.

Less significantly, intervention is offensive to many monetary theorists who believe that in a world of "floating" exchange rates, with no established system for maintaining parities among currencies, it is important for central banks to keep hands off the foreign-exchange markets and let currencies find their "true" values. It is believed that if this happens the market will apply discipline to monetary management by the separate central banks. But however valid that theory might be, central banks have not chosen to keep hands off, and it may well be that intervention is a useful secondary way to maintain greater stability in foreign-exchange relationships.

Whatever theory you use, European bankers were grateful for Mr. Carter's December hints of firmer dollar management. And obviously Mr. Carter himself was beginning to have some doubts about the theory, still very widespread in 1977, that a weak currency helps a nation balance low exports and high imports by making exports more expensive and imports cheaper. This may happen to some degree, although there is not much proof of it in countries, such as England, that have been trying to make it work for many years. It may well be, as economists Art Laffer and Robert Mundell theorize, that the weak currency is quickly translated into higher costs, wiping out any hoped-for advantage. It is certainly true that a weak currency is simply another description of inflation, and, whatever trade benefits there might be, inflation is hardly something to be welcomed.

Mr. Carter also gained a few notches in the estimation of business when his proposal for a $25 billion tax cut was revealed in late December. It did not contain some of the more troublesome ideas that the administration had been toying with during the summer, such as elimination of preferential treatment of capital gains under the income-tax laws. This would have meant higher taxes on capital and, even though the administration was talking of offsetting this to some degree with lower taxation of corporate dividends, the whole idea increased concerns about the nation's low rate of capital formation. The impact of the capital gains tax grows worse with inflation, of course.

These objections earlier in 1977 no doubt contributed to Mr. Carter's decision to postpone announcement of a tax "reform" package, which he had originally promised to offer Congress in September. This would have been his fourth major program in 1977, along with his energy, Social Security, and welfare packages. Another reason for postponing it was that both the energy and Social Security packages contained large tax increases, and he wanted to see what Congress would do with them before he offered a tax program. And still another reason was that the President began to understand in the summer of 1977 that his new administration was not winning friends, either in Congress or among the public, with the programs it was producing. Prudence suggested that it was time to back off and think things over.

The Carter tax program in December was a great deal simpler than the trial balloons of the summer. Of the total of $25 billion in proposed cuts, there was a $6 billion to $7 billion reduction for business, mainly through a lowering of the maximum corporate rate to 44% from 48%. Small businesses would get a nice reduction as well, through a new 18% rate on the first $25,000 of corporate earnings and a 20% rate on the second $25,000. Those rates were both down 2 points.

The administration took pains to point out that it was trying to restore business confidence, a healthy sign. But there were a couple of snares for business in the package, too. Corporations would no longer be able to set up tax-sheltered "domestic international sales companies" or DISCS to handle their exports. And earnings of their foreign subsidiaries would be taxed immediately, eliminating a tax-deferral rule in the existing law. The second change was particularly serious, considering the fact that many large American companies derive half or more of their earnings from abroad and try to use the capital they generate there for overseas expansion. This tax change was in response to complaints from organized labor in the United States, which has traditionally claimed that foreign investments by American companies "export jobs." It is a doubtful argument, but the administration had apparently accepted it. (A good case can be made that foreign investments actually create jobs in this country by increasing world demand for United States equipment, parts, and consumer products.)

Another problem with the Carter tax package was that it would increase the progressivity of the personal income tax, which means that as inflation moves more and more Americans into higher tax brackets the tax bite rises more rapidly. The only gainers from the proposed tax cuts were families earning less than $16,000 a year and single workers earning less than $12,000. The proportion of Americans in those categories is steadily shrinking. Taxes would go up for people who earn more. By and large, they are the nation's most productive workers. Many economists feel that rising tax burdens on these middle-class workers reduce their incentives and thus lower the productivity of the total economy.

However you evaluate that problem, even the $25 billion in net reductions would only slow, not reverse, the rising tax burden. Minnesota economist Walter Heller estimated in the *Wall Street Journal* on December 22, 1977, that the 1979 federal tax bill for Americans would be about $40 billion higher than in 1977, mainly as a result of inflation and higher Social Security rates. He proposed a tax cut of at least $35 billion to offset these effects.

Still another imponderable at the end of 1977 was what tax effects there might be in eventual energy legislation. Although Congress ended the year without passing an energy bill and it certainly won't apply the massive taxes and costs Mr. Carter originally proposed, the issue is not dead. There might still be substantial taxes on crude-oil production. Much of this might be absorbed by the oil industry rather than being passed along to consumers, but it would represent a drag on the economy. More seriously, it would impede the United States industry most in need of development: energy.

Another part of Mr. Carter's program that seemed likely to survive was a set of penalties and incentives designed to persuade electric utilities and industries to convert to coal from oil and natural gas. Congressional committees took much of the sting out of this program in 1977 by granting an escape hatch if excessive costs or environmental damage threatened. But passage of this provision would nonetheless be likely to raise electric rates and the cost of some consumer products.

There were some other uncertainties facing the 1978 economy. A renewed rise in business and consumer borrowing, coupled with continued large federal deficits, raised the threat of very heavy demands on the credit markets. Those demands were likely to be translated into heavy pressures on the Federal Reserve Board to expand the money supply. Inflation at an annual rate of some 6% still was high by historical standards, and it was not hard to imagine a new expansion of the money supply triggering a new bout of double-digit inflation.

Mr. Carter had, of course, replaced Arthur Burns as chairman of the Fed, appointing G. William Miller, an obscure business executive, to take charge of the nation's awesome monetary responsibilities. The Fed's record of money management under the eight-year reign of Dr. Burns was hardly awe-inspiring, but at least Dr. Burns was a known quantity and had gained experience at saying "no" to the heavy political pressures for a more rapid rate of money growth. In fact, Mr. Carter's decision not to reappoint him probably had something to do with the criticisms Dr. Burns had directed at the administration's ineptitudes in fiscal and monetary policies during 1977.

Mr. Miller was an unknown quantity. Treasury Secretary Blumenthal, who had been the target of some of Dr. Burns' barbs, had a hand in picking the new chairman. So had Vice President Walter Mondale, a former liberal Senator. Mr. Miller, who had been chief executive of Textron, Inc., a successful conglomerate, was certainly a man of proven abilities. But his inexperience and the enthusiasm with which "easy money" advocates greeted his appointment was a source of disquiet to inflation worriers.

Still another uncertainty for 1978 was the age of the economic recovery. Most economists doubted that recovery could be sustained much beyond 1978, if indeed that long, without recession. Congress had timed the new Social Security taxes to bite after the 1978 Congressional elections, out of concern for its members' survival at the polls, but that only meant that the tax burden and the end of the economic upswing might coincide. If still other taxes and costs were to be inflicted on the economy in 1978, the risks would of course grow.

If the economy should fall into the kind of serious "stagflation" that hit in 1974–1975, President Carter would be under strong pressure to apply wage and price controls. He has declared his opposition to controls, but if adversity strikes, he will find it difficult to resist cries from within his own party to "do something." And about the only thing government knows to do when its policies have misfired is to resort to police powers, which, of course, are the basis for economic controls. There is no reason to expect that the effects of another such experiment will be less serious than those from the experiment of 1971–1973.

Mr. Carter's economic-policy fumbles in the first year of his administration left him with sharply reduced credibility. Opinion polls at the end of the year showed that Americans still admired Mr. Carter for his personal qualities but had substantially reduced confidence in his ability to manage the government. The President himself had admitted that perhaps he had tried to do too much.

At the end of the year, he seemed to be turning more and more to political experts for advice on economic policy: people like Vice President Mondale; Robert Strauss, who had been chairman of the Democratic party before becoming the President's chief trade negotiator; and Stuart Eizenstat, the young Atlanta lawyer who had accompanied Mr. Carter to the White House from Georgia. The President was trying to work out more orderly methods of procedure in policymaking. He was pushing harder on the monumental task of governmental reorganization, for which he had received Congressional authorization in 1977 (one of the few clear-cut legislative victories).

The President had the benefit of a relatively vigorous economy in his first year in office. The American political process had saved him from serious policy excesses. But his big tasks still lay ahead.

The following chapters discuss in detail the economic problems Mr. Carter will be trying to deal with through the remainder of his term and why he, along with past presidents, has had so much difficulty with them. Part of the failure lies in serious misconceptions about the nature of the problems: the notion, for example, that the world is running out of energy was discredited at the very time that sweeping, costly policies were being formulated on that assumption. Part of it lies in simple political dynamics: the seeming inability of Congress to reduce income transfers even though the burdens are becoming excessive. Part lies in a fundamental conflict between the opposing philosophies of those who are willing to trust the nation's economic fate to market forces and those who insist upon ever greater government manipulation of the market in an effort to achieve certain social ends.

The starting point for this discussion is Mr. Carter himself, however, and we now move on to a review of some of the political and economic forces that thrust him into his world leadership role.

CHAPTER TWO

WHY JIMMY CARTER WON

If government is to retain the confidence of the people, it must not spend more than can be justified on grounds of national need or spent with maximum efficiency.—John F. Kennedy, 1961.

Everybody seems to be running against Washington this year . . . .—Frank Reynolds of ABC News, in preface to a question to President Ford during the first Ford–Carter TV debate, September 23, 1976.

JOHN F. KENNEDY'S WARNING OF 1961 WAS APPROPRIATE TO the presidential campaign of 1976. Government had failed to retain the confidence of the people, judging from all the major opinion polls. Unjustifiable or inefficient spending of tax dollars was certainly not the only reason, but it was one reason. There was a perception abroad that the vast amounts of money that had been spent on social programs of all kinds since the beginnings of the Great Society in the mid-1960s had not yielded the promised benefits. The nation had suffered inflation and recession in 1974 and 1975. And the 1976 economic recovery had slowed in September.

As Mr. Reynolds said, everyone was running against Washington. Despite a creditable record of solid, unspectacular management during his two years in office, President Ford was unable to counter this anti-Washington sentiment, nor could the candidates in the primaries who had been associated with the Democratic majority in Congress during the decade preceding the election year. Despite vigorous campaigning, Senators Birch Bayh, Fred Harris, and Henry Jackson and Representative Morris Udall all fell by the wayside well before the Democratic convention in New York in July. Jimmy Carter won 18 out of 26 presidential preference primaries and picked up additional votes by placing second in seven others. The one place where he fared badly was in Massachusetts, the single state George McGovern had won in the 1972 Presidential election. Mr. Carter placed fourth there.

The only Democrat who seemed capable of stopping Mr. Carter in the primaries turned out to be another man new to the national scene: California's Governor Jerry Brown, who defeated Mr. Carter in Maryland on May 18 and in California on June 8. But Mr. Brown issued forth too late, and perhaps too diffidently, to block Mr. Carter from going to the convention with overwhelming delegate strength.

That, of course, is now all familiar history. But it is useful to go deeper into the public attitudes of the spring, summer, and fall of 1976 to ponder what it was that the voters were seeking in their President. It is not enough to say that they wanted a new face. The real question is, *Why?*

Woodrow Wilson had speculated in 1885 in *Congressional Government*[1] that because the Presidency was primarily an administrative office, the best preparation for it might well be serving as governor of a state. There is a compelling logic in that, and some vigorous Presidents have come from state houses, including Grover Cleveland and Theodore Roosevelt, who had both been Governor of New York, and Woodrow Wilson himself, a former Governor of New Jersey. But in part because of the trend in this century toward a more powerful central government and with it a rising prominence for Washington politicians, Americans, before they elected Jimmy Carter, had not turned to a former governor since they elected Franklin D. Roosevelt, a two-term Governor of New York, in 1932.

It would be tempting to suppose that the voters in 1976 were harking back to the Wilson dictum and searching for an experienced executive. Indeed, Jimmy Carter in his campaign made much of the fact that he had reorganized the Georgia government by installing zero-base budgeting, which is designed to compel government agencies periodically to justify their budget requests and their very existence. Mr. Carter promised that he would do the same in Washington while at the same time cutting the number of government agencies and the waste and overlap represented by their profusion, and his promise of more efficient government obviously had political appeal.

It is also tempting to draw a parallel between the election of Jimmy Carter and that of Franklin D. Roosevelt. However, the parallel falls a long way short of perfection. There is certainly no valid comparison to be made between the affluent America of 1976 and the economically depressed and demoralized America of 1932. There was no genuine and acute national emergency of the type that faced FDR. Unemployment was relatively high in 1976 but was cushioned by unemployment compensation and welfare. The 7.5 million listed as out of work were far below the 12 million unemployed in 1932 of a population only about half as large as that of 1976. Every statistic, from ownership of second cars and homes to attendance at the theater and sports events, made it clear that our economic well-being had expanded enormously since the 1930s and that the United States was a very rich country indeed.

But although the problem of public confidence was different in 1976 from 1932 and by no means as acute, it nonetheless existed and was founded in part on government economic mismanagement. A 1976 poll by the Institute for Social Research at the University of Michigan showed that over half of those canvassed expressed a distrust of political authority. A Louis Harris poll in early 1977 showed that public confidence in the executive branch had plummeted to 23% from 41% a decade earlier and that confidence in Congress had dropped even further, to 17% from 42%.

In fact, public confidence in all institutions had declined in the decade preceding 1976. There may be many explanations for this—a more sophisticated population due to the influence of television and sharply expanded higher education, for example; the trauma of defeat in Vietnam; or, of course, the Watergate experience. But a further compelling possibility is that though Americans were still rich in 1976, they weren't as rich as before the recession of 1975. There was a general lack of confidence in economic leadership, whether in Washington, state houses, city halls, corporate boardrooms, or the halls of academia.

As a skillful and perceptive politician, and one who had the good sense to spend a lot of time traveling and listening to what voters had on their minds, Mr. Carter quickly discerned this unease. As with all politicians (both to their credit and occasional discredit), he distilled these concerns into simple terms—problems that could be described, if not fully understood, with a few simple code words.

The statistic that best served this purpose was the one that purported to describe unemployment in the United States. Up until 1975, the highest unemployment had reached in the postwar era had been 6.8% in 1958. In 1975 it averaged 8.5%. By June of 1976 the rate had fallen to 7.6%, but, unfortunately for President Ford, it began to climb slightly in the third quarter of 1976 during the heat of the election campaign.

Historical memories are such that comparison with the 1930s was inevitable and freighted with political emotion. High unemployment figures are worrisome and for perfectly valid reasons, even if the numbers offer only a limited glimpse of the true state of the economy. As we said before, this was not the 1930s. Not only was unemployment better cushioned, but the 8% statistic itself did not represent the amount of hardship it would have then, when it primarily signified male heads of household out of work and thus whole families on "relief."

In trying to counter the Carter attack, Mr. Ford was able to argue, quite accurately, that although unemployment was high by historical standards, so was *employment*. In fact, with over 89 million workers on the job in July and August of 1976, it was at a record level. The high rate of unemployment was due to the fact that rising inflation and declining real income had driven more and more housewives and teenagers to seek jobs. (There is another quirk that we deal with in a later chapter. Quite possibly, a good many people listed as unemployed would not have been counted as recently as 1970.)

Mr. Carter's focus on unemployment, however much based on a doubtful way of measuring economic hardship, obviously touched a responsive chord in the electorate. No doubt that statistic was a touchstone for a complex of public concerns. It is not very hard to perceive what had woven the thatch of doubt and worry. Some elements were economic and some were not, but they all added up to a sense of insecurity and a desire for change.

Perhaps the best measure of those concerns was provided by William Watts, president of Potomac Associates, a Washington-based research organization, and Lloyd A. Free, president of the Institute for International Social Research, which is affiliated with Johns Hopkins University in Baltimore. Watts and Free, two of the country's most respected public-opinion researchers, surveyed a national sampling of 1071 Americans in May 1976, using the technical facilities of the Gallup Organization of Princeton, New Jersey.

The resulting publication, *America's Hopes and Fears—1976,*[2] revealed that the number one fear of Americans was "crime in this country." Crime scored 91 on a scale of 0 to 100 in which problems that worried the respondents "a great deal" were rated 100 and those that worried them not at all were scored zero. Three other problems were directly behind with a score of 90: "the amount of violence in American life," "corruption or law-breaking on the part of government officials," and, significantly, "the rise in prices and the cost of living." Unemployment ranked eighth with a score of 83. Interestingly enough, the survey showed a public recognition that the country had made progress on some of the most seriously rated problems during President Ford's administration, including both inflation and unemployment. That judgment was borne out by economic statistics. But as both the survey and the election suggested, the public was not satisfied with the rate of progress.

In order to understand some of the difficulties that troubled and perplexed the American people in 1976—and still do today—it is necessary to reach back into the 1960s. Much has been made of the public reaction against the pattern of extralegal, illegal, and deceitful practices in Washington roughly categorized as "Watergate." This pattern no doubt played a role in diminishing public confidence in government, but we won't belabor the subject here except to say that the slippage of official standards of conduct was underway long before Watergate and that the situation has since improved under both President Ford and President Carter. Watergate was an exercise in cutting men of power down to size that we suspect will someday be regarded not as a dismal interlude but as a sign that the American democracy was still, in 1974, vital and participatory.

Since this is a book about economic policy, however, it should be noted that former President Nixon has a great deal more to answer to in the history books than the Watergate cover-up. Of more importance, in our view, in terms of the realities of American life, were several economic misjudgements by Mr. Nixon and the Congress during his administration.

We refer particularly to the President's decision, influenced by pressure from the liberal Democrats in Congress and his Treasury Secretary, John Connally, to put the nation under economic controls in August 1971. In essence, this represented massive government interference in the workings of the market economy, the use of state police power to dictate the price at which individuals could sell their labor or manufacturers and retailers their products and the return investors could recover on the use of their money. All this, in the name of containing "inflation," employed an argument governments in trouble have used since the beginning of time, namely, that a weak currency is the fault of the people rather than of government itself. The disincentives and market distortions caused by that two-year exercise in economic dictatorship have still not worked their way out of the American economy.

In fairness to Mr. Nixon, it should be noted that the inflationary pressures the controls were supposed to contain had been building long before August 1971. They were the result of excessive spending generated by the flurry of income-transfer programs initiated by Lyndon B. Johnson under the general heading of the "War on Poverty," and, of course, by the simultaneously high cost of conducting the war in Vietnam. A crucial economic debate in the mid-1960s had revolved around the question of whether the American economy was strong enough to buy both "guns and butter," conduct a space program, and do all the other things an activist administration and Congress wanted to do. Mr. Johnson may have had a few doubts of his own, but his basic position was that the United States was the world's most powerful nation, both militarily and economically, with almost unlimited capabilities. The first part was true. The second part wasn't.

Evidence of that began to show up about 1968 with the beginnings of a breakdown in the world monetary system, for which the United States dollar had been the base since the system was charted at Bretton Woods, New Hampshire, in July 1944 under United Nations auspices. The dollar was pegged to the price of gold at $35 an ounce, with that relationship to be maintained by the United States buying and selling gold from its own substantial reserves. Other national currencies were pegged at a fixed parity to the dollar (four German marks to the dollar, for example), although it was expected that these other currencies would be adjusted (devalued or valued upward) in dollar value as required by economic conditions within the individual nations. Temporary imbalances would be dealt with through the loan facilities of the International Monetary Fund.

The system worked reasonably well through the 1950s and early 1960s, helping to make possible a rapid expansion of international trade and development that brought about a remarkable growth of prosperity in the market economies participating in the system. Trade restrictions designed to protect weak domestic economies from external competition were gradually dismantled through formation of the European Economic Community and through the comprehensive reductions negotiated under the auspices of the General Agreement on Tariffs and Trade (GATT). The GATT negotiations—known as the Kennedy Round, because they had been promoted by President Kennedy before his death—resulted in 1967 in a one-third reduction of all tariffs by 49 countries accounting for some 80% of the world's trade.

But in order for the international monetary system to work properly it was vital for its base, the United States dollar, to remain reasonably stable in relation to gold. With the United States money supply expanding to accommodate federal deficits (gross federal debt climbed 7% in 1968 alone, more than it had in the previous four years), the dollar began to weaken against gold. Foreign countries, France in particular, began to complain that the United States was exporting inflation, by which they meant that all currencies were depreciating, along with the dollar, in relation to gold. By 1968 speculation against the dollar and in favor of gold was depleting the United States gold supply, forcing leading IMF nations to set up a "two-tier" gold system, under which the dollar-gold ratio would be maintained only in official transactions between central banks; gold bought and sold on the open market would be allowed to find its own price, which it did by promptly rising well above the $35-an-ounce official price. This temporarily stemmed the attack on the dollar, but it was the beginning of the end of the Bretton Woods system. The dollar continued to be weak, and finally, in that famous meeting at Camp David in August 1971, the United States "gold window" was closed even to official transactions.

The dollar was, in essence, devalued, and the United States economy was placed under economic controls. Attempts were made thereafter to patch the money system back together by ad hoc agreements on exchange parities, but they proved futile, and in 1973 currencies were allowed to float, meaning that there was no longer any agreement to support parities through central-bank and IMF interventions. However, countries continued to intervene in foreign-exchange markets through informal arrangements or to suit their own needs.

The economic controls in the United States were designed to "protect" Americans from the inflation inherent in the dollar's weakness and the breakdown of the monetary system. They ultimately failed, as any economist worth his salt could have told Mr. Nixon, Mr. Connally, and the controls advocates in Congress they would.

The failure, as has almost always been the case, came in deceptive stages. At first there was the appearance of enormous success. The economy in 1972, fueled by continued federal deficits and a rapid growth in the money supply and with the inflationary effects of those two things temporarily contained by price controls, took on all the aspects of an economic paradise. Prosperity seemed unbounded. There was bumper-to-bumper traffic on interstate highways that summer as Americans set out for beaches, mountains, Disneyland, Disney World, and thousands of other playgrounds to spend their sudden riches. Mr. Nixon, despite his failure to make a dent in the Vietnam war and the mounting level of civil disobedience and discord at home, was swept back into office with a landslide vote over George McGovern in November of 1972.

But the fun could not last. An American President can control, for a time, prices of many products and services produced and sold in this country but he cannot control the price of goods Americans buy abroad. Nor can he effectively control the price of raw farm commodities—and Mr. Nixon didn't attempt to—partly because of the power of the farm lobby, but more importantly because the cost of producing farm commodities is influenced by uncontrollable variables such as the weather. Further, farm products are a big United States export, so when farmers can't get the price they want in the domestic market they have every incentive to try to get it overseas and thus leave the United States with a short supply. When housewives in 1972 began to notice sharp run-ups in the price of meat and other raw foodstuffs there was a brief consideration in the administration of trying to bring them under controls too, but it was written off as impossible.

At the same time, consumers were beginning to notice shortages of some goods based on imported materials. The federal Council on Wage and Price Stability, which had charge of administering controls, was besieged with demands for price relief from manufacturers who said that controls on their end products coupled with rising prices for raw materials from abroad and from United States farms were putting them out of business.

Mr. Nixon began dismantling controls through a series of decontrol "phases," but before he had completely succeeded, the United States was hit by the biggest shock of all. The overheating of the economy under artificially low prices and rapid money growth had created an unprecedented demand for fuel, not the least for that travel binge everyone was enjoying. Price controls had provided further discouragement for United States oil companies from doing exploration and development here, causing them to go abroad, where oil and gas were easier to find at any rate.

Whereas a few years earlier there had been a worldwide surplus of crude oil, brought about by the enormous finds by Western oil companies in Saudi Arabia, Libya, Iran, and elsewhere, the huge American economy, which consumes a third of the world's energy, had gulped the surplus. The dollar was at the same time becoming a less attractive currency to the governments of oil-producing nations. And these governments were extending their control over production by international oil companies.

This situation was putting the Organization of Petroleum Exporting Countries (OPEC) in a stronger and stronger bargaining position vis-à-vis the oil companies serving markets in the industrial world. Since the oil-producing nations had the normal aspirations to improve their own prosperity, they began demanding a larger cut of oil revenues and greater control over the price of crude.

In October 1973 the Arab nations, piqued over our support for Israel in the Yom Kippur war, embargoed oil shipments to the United States. In the surplus days of a few years before, Americans would hardly have noticed and, even in 1973, it was possible to juggle worldwide oil logistics to ease the embargo pressure.

But the embargo exposed the vulnerability the United States had acquired through destruction of the dollar's value in international markets and through discouraging domestic energy development. The embargo didn't last long, but the OPEC nations, with their new-found solidarity and power, began the now-famous sudden sharp boosts in the price of crude oil. The price quadrupled in the space of a few months. No group of producers, cartelized or not, and particularly no group with such frictions and suspicions among themselves as the OPEC nations had, could have accomplished such a thing had it not been for the help received from United States economic mismanagement. Cartels can make rewarding gains, at least temporarily, in a free-market economy, but the combination of reduced demand at cartel prices and the possibilities for substitution of other sources limits that power. The dramatic oil-price boost was not so much a reflection of the strength of the OPEC cartel as it was a belated proof of how weak the United States dollar and United States energy production had actually become.

The United States responded with more mismanagement. Controls on most other products were removed, but the commodity representing the biggest problem, oil, remained under controls. Or at least, domestic sources remained under controls. There was nothing President Nixon could do about the price of imported oil. Thus the possibility for expanded United States production to meet the OPEC challenge was foregone because of the continued belief in controls as a protection for the American public.

Economic controls had another effect that was in many ways as demoralizing as the misallocations and price anomalies that resulted. Political leaders in Washington, perceiving the failure of the controls they had advocated, began to blame the failures on the producers they had subjected to economic restriction. In the familiar inflated rhetoric of politics it was suggested that all of a sudden, in a period that just happened to coincide with a breakdown in the dollar-based monetary system and a sharp curtailment of economic freedom by the United States government, there had been an outburst of human greed.

The "giant oil companies," whose employees and executives could see themselves as no better or worse, in a moral sense, then they had been a decade earlier when prices were low and hardly anyone noticed them, suddenly found themselves under severe political attack. Senator Jackson accused them of earning "obscene profits." The rancor spread beyond the oil companies to businessmen in general as inflation in 1974 and 1975 began to make up for the period in which it was temporarily suppressed.

The rancor was, of course, not confined to politicians and business. It spread throughout American society. Vietnam was still festering. The burden on the American economy of higher oil prices and the resulting transfer of wealth to the OPEC nations was taking its toll of private investment. So were rising tax burdens brought about in large part by inflation's moving individuals into higher tax brackets and overvaluing the taxable earnings of business. So was the hidden tax, paid at the cash register by consumers, represented by expanding federal regulatory mandates calling for more investment in pollution-control and safety equipment—some of it useful, some unnecessary and wasteful of resources.

The destructive social impact of inflation in pitting consumers against producers and generating doubts and uncertainties about government can probably not be overrated. Professors David Meiselman and Gordon Tullock of Virginia Polytechnic Institute have told us they believe that inflation and general political unrest and upheaval go hand in hand. Professor Tullock feels that a fairly close correlation can be made between the level of inflation and general public dissatisfaction with government—in other words, exactly what the polls have been showing in the 1970s.

Professor Meiselman associates inflation with a breakdown of standards of all kinds—in our era, there has been a debasement not only of money but of college grading practices, of law enforcement, of any standards that might exact penalties for insufficient effort or for misconduct, in short, a general breakdown of both imposed discipline and self-discipline. "I'm not sure what causes it but it seems to happen simultaneously," he says.

Such ideas probably are not subject to proof, but there can be little doubt that the early 1970s were a period of turmoil in the United States. They finally culminated in the fall of both a President and Vice President. By September 1974, with Jerry Ford striving mightily to bind up the nation's divisions, this country was moving into an economic condition it had never before experienced (or at least identified), something first called "stagflation" and later "slumpflation."

By 1974, when the Consumer Price Index soared by 11%, the United States economy was suffering from double-digit inflation, unprecedented in the lives of living Americans. The value of a 1967 dollar had dropped to 67.8 cents and that of a 1954 dollar to 54.5. Savings were being eroded, pensioners were finding it hard to live, and stock prices were down, with a resulting impact on such diverse interests as college endowment funds and union pension funds. Americans, who had been told by economists that some inflation was the price of low unemployment (The Phillips Curve, named for English economist W. A. Phillips, had established this widely accepted myth), were suddenly finding that it was possible to have both rising inflation and rising unemployment. Unemployment climbed to 5.6% of the work force in 1974 from 4.9% in 1973 and kept on rising to the 8.5% rate of 1975.

Mr. Ford, groping for a policy to meet the worsening economic situation, assembled some of the nation's leading economists for a grand seminar of advice in the fall of 1974, shortly after having been thrust so unexpectedly into the Presidency. The consensus—one that reflected badly on the value of economic advice—was in favor of a tax increase, which, in light of the movement toward recession, might have proved disastrous. Tax burdens were rising rapidly enough without help from an increase in tax rates. A tax boost would have been an excellent way to plunge the country into a deep recession. Fortunately, the President's immediate advisers (chiefly Alan Greenspan, whom Mr. Ford had appointed head of his Council of Economic Advisers, and Treasury Secretary William Simon) were wiser than the consensus and the President was himself wise enough to listen to their counsel. By the beginning of 1975 they had reversed the policy line and were proposing a tax cut to Congress, or more precisely, a tax rebate. As economic medicine it wasn't much, but it was better than a tax increase.

Quite fortunately, the powerful American economy has a lot of natural resiliency. The Federal Reserve Board, having learned a few things from the results of its money-creation binge in 1972, held to a relatively conservative monetary policy in the face of uninformed complaints from Congress that such restraint would have an adverse effect on the economy by raising interest rates. (Long-term interest rates, which are the ones that might have such an effect, rise primarily on the anticipation of inflation as lenders seek to protect themselves against being paid back in cheaper dollars. Conservative monetary policy is more likely to lower such rates than raise them.)

The economy slowly began to recover in 1975; inflation subsided under conservative money management and renewed growth in industrial production. Jerry Ford's chances of winning election to the Presidency in his own right started to improve as the morale of the country began to be restored.

As we know, he almost made it. He missed by only a percentage point of the popular vote and would have won with the swing his way of one or two large states. But the traumas of the first half of the 1970s—certainly blamable in part on a Democratic Congress, but all occurring with a Republican in the White House—were a heavy burden for a Republican seeking the Presidency, particularly one who himself had been closely identified with Washington for 25 years. Despite the recovery, government still was held in relatively low esteem. A major reason, as the Watts and Free survey shows, was the inroads of inflation. The economy, while recovering, still had some soft spots—housing, for example. Some prices, for hospital care, for instance, still were rising rapidly. Businessmen were still afflicted with gnawing doubts about the strength of the recovery and were not rushing to invest and create new jobs and opportunities.

Despite all this, Mr. Ford had made a good record, well based in classical economic theory and far better than many of the elected Presidents of the past. Money had become sounder. He had sought to remove the vestiges of the Nixon controls—although some bad political advice had caused him to muff a chance to remove crude-oil controls in late 1975, and some bad political management had lost him a close vote in the House that would have removed the natural-gas price controls first imposed in 1954. Had he decontrolled energy, we would be hearing far less, and probably nothing at all, about an "energy crisis" today.

Thus, despite these missteps, Mr. Ford was gradually laying the basis for a return to stable economic growth. And he would probably have kept his hold on the White House, but for one of those peculiar twists of fate that rule the universe. At a time when Mr. Ford was rapidly chipping away at Mr. Carter's lead in the opinion polls in August 1976, the economy began to slow. The Industrial Production Index, seasonally adjusted, slipped by half a percentage point in September from August, and unemployment blipped up slightly. The Ford forces described it, although not articulately enough, as a "pause." The Democrats described it, with "I told you so" vigor, as a relapse, which they had been predicting would result from Mr. Ford's conservative budgetary policies and the Fed's downhold on money growth. The President, they said, was aborting the recovery.

Mr. Carter, who had taken some excursions into liberal social philosophy that had apparently cost him ground in the polls, returned to the economic theme, charging that the President had insufficient concern for the jobless and for stimulating economic growth. It was noted, among other things, that the government had even fallen $12.5 billion short of spending the money Congress had appropriated for the 1976 fiscal year.

We know now that the economy was, in fact, in a pause brought about by a temporary work-off of inventories after the rapid expansion in the early part of 1976, industrial production resumed its growth in November. But the pause, coupled with Mr. Ford's clumsy and puzzling comment in the second televised debate that Eastern Europe was not under Soviet domination, may well have tipped the balance to Mr. Carter.

The lack of public confidence had taken its toll of a President who was universally respected for his personal qualities, even by his political opponents, and who had compiled a record in two years that historians may some day treat very kindly. The public had registered its wishes by calling up a new, younger man. It now was to be seen whether he could deal with the problems of unemployment, inflation, and economic growth that had been so instrumental in winning him the election.

CHAPTER THREE
ORIGINS AND OPTIONS

I think he was a pretty good governor. He knew how to stretch the money.—A young black taxi driver in Atlanta, December 1976.

He's tight as a tick.–Presidential Press Secretary Jody Powell.

DURING THE NATIONAL CRISES OF 1971 THROUGH 1974, JIMMY Carter had indeed been trying to stretch the budget of Georgia, which is not the poorest but by no means the richest of states. In fact, it ranked 37th in per capita personal income in 1975, a slight decline from 1970, when it ranked 35th. Mr. Carter's reputation as a conservative spender, both in his personal habits and in his management of state government, was no doubt one of the qualities that made him appealing to an American electorate that was, in 1976, concerned over rising public debt, government profligacy, and chronic inflation. This was evident in Mr. Carter's slippage in the popularity polls during the 1976 campaign when he shifted his emphasis for a time from fiscal conservatism to appeals for the votes of economic liberals.

His reputation, as with many things about Mr. Carter, was based partly on rhetoric and style rather than objective reality. Although he certainly was not a wild spender as Georgia's governor, he was not particularly conservative either. The Georgia state budget for fiscal 1974 was $512 on a per capita basis, an increase of 54% from fiscal 1970, when Mr. Carter was elected governor. By comparison, the per capita average for all state budgets in the United States in 1974 was $569, a rise of only 48% from 1970. Georgia had, however, moved from 15th ranking in the nation in state per capita expenditures down to 16th. Given these two offsetting measurements, it would have to be said that Mr. Carter's record on stretching the money was somewhere close to the national average.

Mr. Carter had been an activist governor, however, which no doubt accounts for the higher-than-average rise in expenditures. He had reorganized state government, primarily through creation of a comprehensive Human Resources Department in 1972 to take over most of the state's social welfare programs, a major part of state government with about one-third of all state employes. He had set up a system of zero-base budgeting designed to require government departments to justify their budget requests and objectives each year. He had lopped off some 100 staff jobs in the human resources area. He had reduced the number of state agencies to 22 from 300.

Although Mr. Carter made much of his record as an administrator during the campaign, none of the results of his reorganization were particularly dramatic. During the remainder of his term after the reorganization he never fully managed to establish the new department's authority over the once separate agencies, the directors of which were jealous of their prerogatives. The number of families receiving Aid to Families with Dependent Children (the state-local-federal program that most people mean when they say "welfare," although welfare is somewhat more comprehensive in that it encompasses several other programs as well) rose under his administration to 111,517 from 90,514. Overpayments and payments to ineligibles also rose, in contrast to states, such as California, that were achieving better records of AFDC administration.

In Mr. Carter's view the expansion of the welfare rolls was a mark of success. He felt that he was extending welfare to more families at less administrative cost. He was not cutting state spending, but he was "stretching" it. There can be differences of opinion about this, depending on personal perspectives, whether Mr. Carter was too easy or too tough on the state bureaucracy, whether there was any significant improvement in the quality and efficiency of state government, whether a 24% rise in state employes, a 54% expansion in the state's per capita budget, and a 66% rise in the aggregate budget, at a time when the federal budget aggregate was rising only 37%—should be counted as an achievement.

But there can be little doubt that Mr. Carter's successful campaign for President can be attributed heavily to his claim—which no one could clearly refute—that he embodied two attractive qualities, managerial skill and human compassion. (It might be more accurate to say that his opponent in the 1976 election did not try very hard to refute the claim with the kind of factual data that would impress voters, which suggests that President Ford was not blessed with superior campaign staff.) Mr. Carter persuaded the voters that he could take those two qualities to Washington and make some sense out of a huge, confused, unresponsive bureaucracy with overlapping and tangled lines of responsibility and authority and an enormous capacity to waste taxpayer money and retard legitimate, productive human endeavor. He proposed a 90% reduction in the number of federal agencies, from some 1900 to 200.

The 50.1% of American voters who voted for Mr. Carter obviously believed that he could deliver, or at least were willing to give him a try in the absence of a more attractive looking offer. Some percentage of that group of supporters no doubt found it appealing that Mr. Carter was promising a compassionate government; others, more appealing that he was promising well-managed government. It may not have occurred to either that managerial efficiency and human compassion (at least as they have come to be defined in the adminis-tration of government programs) can at times be at odds with each other. That contradiction was to become more evident as Jimmy Carter moved deeper into his administration of the Presidency.

Mr. Carter's ambivalence on this point—an ambivalence that both his primary opponents and Jerry Ford attempted to exploit, but without fatal consequences—was of course the kind of prerogative that most politicians exercise. But it also had natural origins, and its genuine qualities probably were perceived by the voters.

During the campaign year, Mr. Carter was heard to say that "those who understand the South would understand a major portion of me." Indeed, some understanding of Jimmy Carter's origins in Plains, Georgia, seems essential to anyone who would understand the themes that elected him and the decisions he has made as President. It has often been said that he is the first President from the Deep South since the Civil War, but to make that claim you have to exclude Andrew Johnson, who was born in Raleigh, North Carolina; Woodrow Wilson of Virginia, and Lyndon B. Johnson, from Texas. Rather than argue the point, it suffices to say that Mr. Carter, as a Georgian, carried with him a special set of regional attitudes and a cultural background not always well understood by non-Georgians.

Georgia, to a greater degree than most Deep South states, with the possible exception of South Carolina and Virginia, has a patrician heritage—perhaps best evoked in *Gone With the Wind,* novel and film. Its capital city, Atlanta, is in essence the capital of the South: long a center of culture, a nexus for transportation and commerce, and a place of relatively moderate attitudes on race, alcohol, and gover-nance. This heritage has lent a certain grace and charm to the conduct of public affairs in the state—although Georgia certainly has also had its share of political corruption—not always present elsewhere in Dixie.

The human qualities of Georgian leadership were best evident in the 1960s, when the smoothness with which Atlanta accommodated to the Supreme Court's desegregation decisions was in sharp contrast to the bad temper and violence, much of it inspired by state and local political leaders, of Birmingham, another Deep South city with much shallower cultural traditions with which Atlanta is often con-trasted. Combined with this sense of history and heritage in Georgia and the unique role of its capital city in the South is a certain self-confidence and regional pride. It may not be of Texan dimensions, but it is existent nonetheless. Combined with these qualities, is a certain resentment of both the money men and liberal intellectuals of the North, or anyone else who fails to take Georgia seriously.

The best elements of the Georgian leadership style, a combination of graceful self-confidence and hard-headedness, are very much embodied in Mr. Carter. In a state where family is important, he can even claim a measure of patrician background; his family tree traces one of its roots to colonial Virginia. One government official has been quoted as saying, "He is a naturally assured and authoritative man. There is a difference between assurance and arrogance. Assurance listens to other people. Arrogance doesn't."[1]

Added another close associate: "Mr. Carter is so confident and self-assured because, growing up and working in a small town, he got used to being the smartest man around. The good thing is that it leads to a kind of intellectual confidence Nixon and Johnson never had. The bad thing about it is that when you know you're so brilliant, you feel you don't need much help. The President has assembled a mediocre staff and Cabinet."[2]

Be that as it may, it is a matter of highest importance that black voters found Mr. Carter's qualities appealing; he would not have been elected had he not polled a phenomenal 90% of the black vote. In his 1971 inaugural address as the newly elected governor of Georgia, Mr. Carter had attracted national publicity with his forthright denunciation of racial discrimination: "I say to you quite frankly that the time for racial discrimination is over. . . . No poor, rural, weak or black person should ever have to bear the additional burden of being deprived of the opportunity of an education, a job or simple justice." But that only partly explains his following among blacks and their role in electing him. The explanation has to go deeper.

There was always some considerable truth to the claim of white Southerners that their relationship with black Southerners was misunderstood, even under policies of official segregation. Northern liberals and desegregationists were usually furious at this complaint, saying that what the Southern segregationists wanted to perpetuate was a master-slave relationship.

There was some truth to that charge, too, but Southerners could legitimately claim that in the South blacks and whites at least had direct personal contacts—on the job, in the small, rural towns, and through the role of black servants and nursemaids in the more affluent Southern households. In the North, they insisted, the two races were more isolated from each other, with blacks usually concentrated in urban ghettoes. In the South and more often than Northerners were usually willing to concede, they would add, the individual relationships between blacks and whites were warm ones. To whatever extent that is true, there was and is a black-white relationship in the South, and it is important to the psyches of both Southern whites and blacks. White Southerners have derived part of their sense of identity, as well as their social guilts and wellsprings of compassion, from having blacks living among them as inferiors. The blacks, for all their fears and misery, have gained a sense of orientation from placing some trust in the best of the whites, the ones they felt they could trust.

In his book, *Promises to Keep,* Robert Shogan writes that Eleanor Holmes Norton, New York City's black Commissioner for Human Rights, told him during the New York Democratic primary campaign in 1976: "There is no good man like a good white Southerner. You can talk about a born-again Christian, but a man who's been born again to civil rights, who speaks with a Southern accent and is good on civil rights issues, is the best form of civil rights advocate."[3]

There was also a certain bond of shared suffering. Even today, many Southern whites feel themselves to be victims of the economic manipulations of the Yankees who have traditionally controlled the big industries, the big banks, and the federal government. It has always been felt, with justification, that the North rigged rail-freight rates in the late nineteenth and early twentieth centuries to hobble Southern economic development.

This resentment is one of the sources of Southern populism, which represents a strong streak in President Carter's make-up. He has frequently described himself as a populist. His leadership style—the decision to walk, rather than ride, with his family from the inauguration ceremonies back to the White House, his disdain for government limousines and "three-martini" lunches, his intemperate attack on the big oil companies in the heat of the energy debate—reflect populist attitudes, which are more clearly definable in such terms than as a distinct political philosophy.

Dennis Farney, the *Wall Street Journal*'s White House correspondent, commented to us early in 1977, after close observations of Jimmy Carter on the campaign trail, that he seemed almost to be a libertarian, with a distrust of all bigness—big corporations, big government, big labor unions, and so on.

Southern blacks, to a greater degree than most Northerners imagine, very often share these populist resentments and suspicions. A Southern black civil-rights worker confided to us in Atlanta in 1961 that "there's no one more arrogant (in his approach to civil rights in the South) than a third-generation black Yankee!"

Thus many blacks in the South, and a good many blacks in the North not far removed from their Southern origins, felt a certain kinship with Jimmy Carter—a white man from the South who knew what the South was all about, a man whose mother, Lillian Carter, had nursed the poor black folks of Plains and nearby Archery, where Jimmy Carter was born. Miss Lillian was the kind of strong country woman who could reach out to help the weak and poor. As Jimmy Carter has said many times, she was also a strong source of inspiration to her son. Blacks felt they saw human warmth and a Southern soul in Jimmy Carter.

There are other Georgia origins in Mr. Carter's obvious appeal to blacks and others traditionally regarded as have-nots. Anyone who traveled through Georgia in the 1930s and 1940s, the formative years for Mr. Carter, knows that it was indeed a poor land. Stretching dollars was a habit of survival. Life and work in the red dust of Georgia farms was hard and the rewards often slim. Though the Carter family was by no means poor, Mr. Carter absorbed the ambience of poverty. He knew personally the kind of people he referred to in his speech accepting the Democratic nomination in New York's Madison Square Garden in July 1976:

"Now our party was built out of the sweatshops of the old Lower East Side, the dark mills of New Hampshire, the blazing hearths of Illinois, the coal mines of Pennsylvania, the hardscrabble farms of the Southern coastal plains and the unlimited frontiers of America.

"Ours is a party that welcomed generations of immigrants—the Jews, the Irish, the Italians, the Poles and all the others—enlisted them in its ranks, and fought the political battles that helped bring them into the American mainstream—and they have shaped the character of our party. . . .

"Too many have had to suffer at the hands of a political and economic elite who have shaped decisions and never had to account for mistakes nor to suffer from injustice. When unemployment prevails, they never stand in line looking for a job. When deprivation results from a confused and bewildering welfare system, they never do without food or clothing or a place to sleep. . . .

"Too often, unholy, self-perpetuating alliances have been formed between money and politics, and the average citizen has been held at arm's length."

And later, in his inaugural address: "Our government must at the same time be both competent and compassionate."

It is tempting to take all political rhetoric as mere posturing. And certainly Jimmy Carter is a skillful politician, capable of pushing the right rhetorical buttons to draw support from the particular audience he happens to be addressing. Both during the election campaign and in his administration of the Presidency he has been accused of being all things to all people. There is some justice in that complaint.

But it should be remembered that the essence of political leadership is to represent the diverse elements of a political constituency, to mediate between the warring elements of a society. And it should also be remembered that it would be very difficult for a national leader to be constantly exposed to public scrutiny for the space of time Mr. Carter has held that role without exposing some genuine inner motivations.

What does all this have to do with the President's economic policies? The short answer is "everything." A political economy is not an ordered plan of wise men with computers. In reality, it is a complex amalgam of the attitudes and motivations of individuals: their willingness to work, their self-confidence, their belief in the future, their willingness to save and invest, their ability to cooperate with each other in joint enterprises, their creative impulses that produce technological and managerial innovation. The presence or absence of these qualities in political leadership, and thus the extent to which they are encouraged among the people, is the true essence of economic policymaking.

It also goes without saying that the leadership supplied by the American President is important to the continued economic growth and development of the nation and the world. The quality of that leadership depends on many things—the wisdom of his advisers, his ability to perceive the most critical economic problems that he must attempt to solve, his ability to mobilize the government itself toward solutions of problems, and the creation of an environment that encourages human productivity. It also depends importantly on the culture that shaped him.

Mr. Carter emerged from the culture of Plains as a man with a strong sense of self-assurance, who, as he himself has often said, is not afflicted with timidity when it comes to overhauling a government department or program, who sees himself as a man who can apply his engineering training to the tasks of public policy, as an executive who is not afraid of 16-hour workdays, as a stickler for detail, as a source of moral leadership. His culture had taught him to be careful with money and compassionate toward his fellow man.

All these qualities are admirable ones, and this certainly accounts for the high degree of public support Mr. Carter attracted in the early months of his Presidency. But some would be sources of misjudgments as his economic policies evolved.

His self-assurance would bring him into conflict with Congress, which had developed a strong sense of independence from the White House in the years when Republicans ran the executive branch. His populism would stir fears among businessmen that they were faced with an enemy in the White House. His immersion in detail and the tendency to make decisions without consulting the Treasury or some other government branch with a direct stake in the implementation of policy would stir doubts within his own administration.

Mr. Carter's sense of compassion for the jobless would quickly stir him to expand the Ford budget's allotment for Housing and Urban Development by $15.4 billion. But that measure was in conflict with his promises of fiscal responsibility and a balanced budget.

The high expectations he raised among blacks would erupt in July of 1977 into a dispute with Vernon E. Jordan, Jr., Executive Director of the National Urban League, who complained that the President was not fulfilling his campaign promises to blacks. Mr. Carter replied that he had no apologies to make for his approach to the problems of the poor minorities and appeared to be accusing Mr. Jordan of ingratitude for steps the President already had taken on their behalf. *Pravda*, the official Soviet Communist Party newspaper, chose to enter this particular argument, no doubt in part because the President had made an issue of human rights within the Soviet Union. Even before Mr. Jordan launched his attack, *Pravda* accused the President of having reneged on his promises to blacks. Said writer Georgi Ratiani: "Having secured—thanks to his demagogic promises—90% of the Negro votes and won the Presidency, J. Carter has geared his economic strategy to meeting the interests of the biggest monopolies, which are well represented in his administration."[4]

Mr. Carter's focus on "moral" leadership, a product of his upbringing as a Southern Baptist, contributed to his political troubles. His economic programs reflected, to a greater degree than those of past

Presidents, a seeming belief that mere rectitude could correct mistaken policies. His energy program was based on the principle of conservation, and you could almost hear the old injunction, "waste not, want not" in his defense of it. (In the summer of 1977 the *Wall Street Journal* likened his complaints that Americans were not responding well enough to his call for energy conservation to the famous Jonathan Edwards sermon, "Sinners in the hands of a Just God.") The Carter welfare program in August 1977 also reflected a notion that moral weakness was somehow responsible for the failure of the welfare state. In short, his economic messages often had the ring of that admonition which Southern Baptists and members of most other religious denominations hear on Sunday mornings: "Repent."

While moral and ethical leadership has a place in government and an argument could be made that Americans have not always had as much of it from Presidents as would be helpful to the common good, there is a fundamental conflict between moralism and the market system. A fundamental theme of religious ethics is that men should put aside the needs of the flesh and their base desires for private gain in order to find spiritual peace and redemption. Market economics, as articulated by Adam Smith and his disciples, argues that the desire for private gain is a normal human impulse, not something that can be, or should be, suppressed. Rather it should be free of unnecessary restraint so that it can be employed toward the creation of economic wealth for the common good. It demands not that men forsake private gain and worldly comforts, but that they seek these things so that an economy can generate capital and move all its members to a higher standard of living.

The Adam Smith market economy and the Judeo-Christian ethic have coexisted nicely, by and large, in the Western democracies and have, in fact, generated a sort of dynamic balance between the flesh and the soul that has supplied satisfactions to both. The church-goer has typically paid his due to religious ethics on the Sabbath or through the broad charitable works of the church or temple and saluted the gods of the marketplace on weekdays. The friction between the two pursuits has often been constructive, the religious ethic encouraging the exploiter of the market place toward good behavior and generosity toward those less fortunate than he. In return he receives the psychic benefits granted by the church for exercises in self-abnegation.

The religious ethic in many ways bears a closer resemblance to Marxism, with the vital exception that in the United States it is practiced out of free will and independently of state power. Like Marxism, it is suspicious of human motivations left unchecked by higher authority. While market capitalism assures the individual that there is no basic inconsistency between the needs of the community and his wish to profit from his brains and industry—that, in fact, the two are complementary—religion, and Christianity in particular, often suggests, along with Marxism, that there is something morally repellent about acquiring extensive individual material wealth. In Marxist thought, "careerism" and its focus on the self is a high sin. In the Judeo-Christian litany, the imprecations against gluttony, adultery, covetousness, and other sins have not only practical applications but also attack the general sin of self-indulgence.

Jimmy Carter, of course, is not a Marxist. He would be shocked at any such suggestion. As a Christian businessman he fully embodies that happy marriage of Judeo-Christianity and capitalism which has served the United States and other Western democracies so well—that delicately balanced compromise between the individual and authority.

But it is probably no accident that the men Mr. Carter has been most attracted to as personal advisers include some with notions of moral authority that closely parallel his own. Lawrence Klein, the principal economic adviser to Mr. Carter during his campaign, flirted with Marxism in his youth, as did many other intellectuals of his era. James Schlesinger, who was in charge of developing the Carter energy program, has been heard to use the Biblical word "prodigal" in his arguments that the United States is wasteful of energy.

This kind of economic moralism is, of course, fully within the bounds of American tradition and thought. The fact that it bears a resemblance to Marxist philosophy—which remains anathema to most Americans—does not rule it out as a tool of persuasion.

But its overuse, particularly when it is translated too liberally into public policy, can make it the enemy of economic growth. In the absence of economic growth, the only way there can be more comforts for America's have-nots, for whom Mr. Carter feels a deep compassion, is through wealth redistribution. That implies a strong role for the state and the risk that the economy will not only cease to grow but will start regressing to the extent that everyone, the haves and have-nots alike, will have less.

This crucial problem was reflected in the widespread criticism of President Carter's energy program. In its stress on conservation, it contained few incentives for production. It displayed, in fact, a profound mistrust of energy producers, those "giant oil companies" of so much political legend. It also displayed an unfounded trust in the capacity of government to exercise a superior moral authority, to see to it that Americans use just as much energy as they need, and no more.

Fortunately, the American political process, with all its pluralism and contention, recognized this fundamental flaw in the energy program. By attempting to express moral authority, the President paradoxically weakened his political credibility. The distressing thing, it is generally recognized, is that some of the new President's fundamental instincts, born out of his experience and background, had led him astray. Being a good man in the Christian sense is admirable, but the evidence of the early stages of the Carter administration suggests that this quality gained too much ascendency over the other side of his character, the analytical approach of the engineer. It remained to be seen whether the two qualities would come back into better balance.

CHAPTER FOUR
CONTENDING THEORIES

. . . the ideas of economists and philosophers . . . are more powerful than is commonly understood. Indeed the world is ruled by little else.—John Maynard Keynes, 1936.[1]

I was the only non-Keynesian there.—John Maynard Keynes, 1944.[2]

WHAT LORD KEYNES, THE GREAT ENGLISH ECONOMIC theorist, had to say in 1936 and then later in 1944 demonstrates, respectively, the power and the weakness of economic theories. The first, written at the end of his classic *General Theory*, attests to the power of ideas to rule men's lives through their influence on the policies of the state. The second, a comment made to friends after a meeting with American "Keynesians" in Washington, is a rueful reference to the tendency of policymakers to select only the ideas of great philosophers that have political appeal and, very often, to reinterpret those ideas to suit their own political needs.

This, of course, has been the fate of great philosophers through the centuries. It does not suggest that the philosophers are always right and the politicians always wrong. It is merely a reminder that public policy is constructed not from single ideas, however powerful and persuasive they might be, but from many, melded together to represent a consensus of the times, with theory, expediency, and the practical considerations of politics all well represented.

There are times when the public policies formed out of this consensus respond to the real economic problems of the world, serve the public well, and thus generate confidence in economic philosophy and government. The early 1960s was such a period in United States history. The country was enjoying vigorous economic growth; unemployment was low; prices were relatively stable. The "New Economics" of demand management through adjustment of fiscal policies, as espoused by Walter Heller and other influential economists of the time, seemed to offer the promise of smoothing out business cycles and permitting long-term, well-managed growth. The famous Kennedy tax cut, proposed by the President before his death and put into effect a few months afterward, produced an economic stimulus that seemed to confirm the wisdom of the New Economics.

There are other times when confidence in both government and its economic advisers ebbs. Real-world problems, such as inflation and chronic unemployment, suggest that macroeconomics—the application of economic analysis to broad national or global problems—has gone astray, that the government policies growing out of such analysis are not working. Then, the conflicts and contradictions of competing economic theories are more evident than points of agreement. The political process reflects a public yearning for more certainty and order. The middle years of the 1970s have been such a period for the United States and the market economies of the world.

As a reflection of the times, the Harvard social critic and icono-clast, John Kenneth Galbraith, offered an acerbic attack on his fellow economists in the May 1977 issue of *Esquire*: ". . . in recent elections economists have far outpaced even the generals and the cold warriors as the architects of domestic political disaster. In elections lost, we are well ahead of the Pentagon and those who saw the unfolding of the American dream in Saigon. . . . Had Nixon listened to his economists and had McGovern ignored his economists, of whom I was one (I strongly favored the guaranteed income and though I had doubts about the $1,000-to-all design and its recovery, I registered no audible objec-tion), the election would certainly have been closer than it was."

Professor Galbraith attributes his profession's failings to, among other things, a deep instinct that what worked before will always work again—a tendency to measure policies by the applause they evoke from the affluent and a failure to see that what inspires business confi-dence does not necessarily make the economy work well.

Professor Galbraith's uncharacteristic lapse into self-abjuration about his role in the McGovern campaign did not disguise the fact that the *Esquire* article was mainly an assault on market economic theories. David Kelley, writing in *Barron's* (August 1, 1977), offered a more full-bodied abjuration of Galbraithean economics in an attack on "The Age of Uncertainty," a public television series prepared by Professor Galbraith in 1977 to instruct the nation in economic history.

Calling much of it "crude and obvious propaganda," Mr. Kelley said that "the series is skewed by Galbraith's ideology. In order to invent a negative history for capitalism and a positive one for socialism, he concentrates on minor facts, manufactures others and ignores almost everything of significance." He described Professor Galbraith's statist notions—the advocacy of wage and price controls, for example—as a throwback to the medieval doctrine of altruism. "Altruism holds that man has no right to live for himself; that he belongs to others—whether to God, or to the state—whose interests he must serve. . . . The Age of Reason rejected the principle, enunciating the right of the individual to his own life, to the pursuit of happiness."

As this pointed attack on Professor Galbraith reflects, an underly-ing theme of the great economic debate of the 1970s, and the uncer-tainties it generated, was the conflict between socialism and capitalism. This struggle has been underway at least since the publica-tion of the *Communist Manifesto* by Karl Marx in Paris in 1848. If it is redefined in its modern manifestations as a struggle between private enterprise and the state, it has been underway through most of recorded history. Part of the underlying disquiet in the United States in the early 1970s, particularly the weakened confidence of business, stemmed from a fear that socialism, despite its defects, might indeed be the wave of the future, given the political dynamics at work in the world. The United States defeat in Vietnam, the rise of Eurocommunism, and the expansion of government power in this country fed this fear.

Although it might seem that the loss of confidence in economic theories and in government policy would cut in exactly the opposite direction since socialism is founded on the belief that a wise government, peopled with double-domed economists, can make better decisions than the free market on the allocation of economic resources, there is another side to the coin. Government economic intervention seems to generate yet broader intervention, rather than less, when it fails to achieve the hoped-for results. Politicians feel compelled to come up with new "solutions" rather than simply dismantle the old solutions and let the market think for itself. In the 1970s there was a sense among market economists that they were winning many little battles, by demonstrating the failures resulting from government market interventions and the costs and inefficiencies that resulted, but that they were losing the war simply because of the dynamics of the political process.

Most of the actual economic debate, however, was on a far less cosmic level, dealing with the narrower problems of economic analysis. And here, no less than on the cosmic level, there was a loss of public confidence in the ability of economists to come up with the right answers. There is far more to the debate than just a war between socialism and capitalism. Economic processes in a society as rich and complex as the United States are too complicated to be reduced to such simple terms. Economic management is an amalgam of state power, the decisions of large, broadly owned public corporations that bear little resemblance to nineteenth century capitalism, and of private entrepreneurship.

Operating this complex of economic organization is the richest and best educated national society in all history. Ben J. Wattenberg, in *The Real America*,[3] defined the middle class as "people who own their own homes, live in the suburbs, don't have large families, send their children to nursery school and kindergarten, don't let their teen-agers drop out of high school, send their kids to college, have good jobs, retire, take vacations, own washers, dryers, air conditioners, television sets, dishwashers, cars and second cars, have good incomes, play tennis and get divorced.

"Not so long ago—a decade ago, surely two decades ago—most of such middle-class attributes characterized only a minority of Americans. In the last dozen or so years, say, since the 1960 census, each of these attributes expanded in America, most of them enormously, many to a point where they are now commonly shared not only by a majority of Americans, but by three fifths, two thirds, three quarters or four fifths of the population—massive majorities of middle-class folk (except tennis and maybe divorce).

"These changes have made America the first Massive Majority Middle Class society in history."

(For all the authors of this book know, Mr. Wattenberg may already be out of date on his exceptions, judging from the recent popularity of both tennis and divorce.)

The difficulties of analyzing the performance of such a rich and diversified economy and making forecasts about what it will do are reflected in remarks by Guy E. Noyes, Senior Vice President and Economist for Morgan Guaranty Trust Company, to a conference for investors at New York City's New School for Social Research in January 1977. He noted that economic forecasts made in 1975 had 1976 ending in everything from an inflationary boom to a recession. "The fact that the consensus, and our own projection for that matter, called for year-over-year growth in real GNP (Gross National Product) at something like the 6% that actually emerged gives me no comfort at all. I have examined a couple of dozen projections that I tossed in a cabinet behind my desk. Not one, again including our own, in either the quarterly pattern of projected output and price changes, or in the accompanying discussion, describes a year that even remotely resembles the kind of one we've been through."

Even more rueful about the perils of economic forecasting were President Ford's economic advisers, who had failed to foresee the economic pause that began to show up in the economic statistics in September 1976 and to warn the President that he might be vulnerable to political attack because the slowdown could be associated (although not very fairly) with a so-called shortfall in government spending below the figure that had been budgeted for the 1976 fiscal year. The shortfall had been revealed by Mr. Ford's Office of Management and Budget as $12.5 billion.

Mr. Ford's opponents were able to attribute the slowdown in

real-GNP growth in the third quarter of 1976—to a 4% annual rate from 4.5% in the second quarter and 9.2% in the first—to this uncommon phenomenon. In fact, as events later demonstrated and as some economists were able to discern at the time, the slowdown had a simple and ordinary cause. It resulted not from a slowdown in demand but from a slowing of inventory building after a rapid rate of growth in the first half of the year. Retail sales continued to rise briskly during the "slowdown," and by December the GNP was surging upward again. The mysterious shortfalls continued right on into the Carter administration, where Office of Management and Budget director Bert Lance attributed them mainly to government inertia matched against the sheer physical difficulties of disposing of $450 billion in a single year.

Paul MacAvoy, a member of Mr. Ford's Council of Economic Advisers, confided to friends after the election that the failure of Mr. Ford's advisers to foresee the slowdown might have cost him the election. Whether that is true, Mr. MacAvoy, CEA Chief Alan Greenspan, and the third CEA member, Burton G. Malkiel, need not be ridden with guilt. The management of economic policy under Mr. Ford, who relied heavily on the advice of Mr. Greenspan and the council, could boast some noteworthy and fundamental achievements. The Ford administration had not done anything, and through liberal use of the veto had prevented Congress from doing anything, to abort the natural forces of economic recovery. It encouraged conservative monetary management by the Fed that helped pull the nation back from a dangerous level of inflation and that probably contributed most of all to the strength of the 1976 recovery.

It could also be said with some assurance that, given the obloquy of Watergate and the Nixon pardon, Mr. Ford might have lost by an even larger margin had it not been for the economic recovery that occurred during the two years he was in office. But the misgivings of the Ford economic team are but another evidence of the loss of self-assurance among economists in the 1970s. Nowhere is that doubt better manifested than in revised attitudes toward the science of econometrics.

Econometrics applies a system of equations to attempt to construct a model of the economy, taking into account the various factors of money growth, unemployment, unused industrial capacity, and a great mix of other economic statistics. All this is fed into a computer, which is programmed to juggle the variables and predict the effect of some changed variable—a cut in tax rates, for example—on general economic outcomes, such as the rate of GNP growth. No doubt in part because of the public fascination with computers, there were high hopes for computerized econometrics when the models were being built in the 1960s. The principal practitioners of this arcane art form today are Data Resources, Inc. of Lexington, Massachusetts, Wharton Econometric Forecasting Associates at the University of Pennsylvania, in Philadelphia, Chase Econometric Associates of Bala Cynwyd, Pennsylvania (a subsidiary of the Chase Manhattan Bank), and Merrill Lynch Economics, an affiliate of the brokerage firm.

But as with any computerized study, the results are only as good as the equations themselves and the data that go into the equations. The model builders are finding it tougher to model a complex economy than they had thought. One mistaken assumption can blow the whole game.

The result is that econometric forecasts, though popular with business and government economists alike, appear to be no more accurate than conventional forecasts. This finding is based on comparisons made by the American Statistical Association and the National Bureau of Economic Research since 1968 and reported by two NBER economists, Vincent and Josephine Su, in 1975 in the NBER publication *Explorations in Economic Research*.

As quoted by Lindley H. Clark, Jr., in the *Wall Street Journal*, August 2, 1977, F. Gerard Adams, treasurer of Wharton Econometric, says: "The unfortunate thing about forecasting is that the future remains the future. What we do is half magic, half science. Science is concerned with the past. When you get into the future, it's part magic."

Indeed, Gunnar Myrdal, who shared a Noble prize in economics with Friedrich A. Hayek in 1974, wrote to the Stockholm newspaper *Dagens Nyheter* in 1977 that economics did not deserve a Nobel prize because it was a "soft science" in which social and political events disturb attempts at scientific precision.

But despite all the doubts, economic theories still contend—the free-marketers represented by Milton Friedman and Friedrich Hayek, the neo-Keynesians or interventionists by Walter Heller and Paul Samuelson, the monetarists by Professor Friedman and Karl Brunner of Rochester and Berne, the state planners by Wassily Leontiev of NYU. There are also other, less-well-known theorists such as the supply-side fiscalists, who believe that tax cuts to stimulate production are the economy's number one need.

Amid all the contention, there was in 1977 hardly a single

economic shibboleth not under attack. The Phillips Curve, which as we have mentioned bears the name of British economist W. A. Phillips, had been a victim of the "slumpflation" of 1974. Professor Phillips had held that there was a trade-off between unemployment and inflation: if you want low unemployment you have to accept higher inflation, and vice versa. But in 1974 the rate of both unemployment and inflation rose in the United States and much of the Western world. Milton Friedman and other economists with a dim view of the Phillips Curve took some pains to point out that the concept and events were at odds, but that did not prevent a good many policymakers, including some of Mr. Carter's closest economic advisers, from continuing to discuss political economics in Phillips Curve terms as a struggle between economists who want low unemployment and those who want low inflation.

Neo-Keynesian notions of demand management by government also were under heavy attack. The attack was launched by a bright young Oxford professor, Walter Eltis, who observed that Lord Keynes' theories calling for public-sector spending to stimulate aggregate demand had been appropriate for the conditions of 1936 when there was a general depression, but had been misused by modern political leaders as a rationale for expanding the public sector even at the risk of inflation and damage to the private economy. This was followed up by an editorial in the *Wall Street Journal* titled "Keynes is Dead" in January 1977. It quoted a study by Hudson Research Europe, Ltd., associating a high level of government spending in nations with a low rate of economic growth.

Walter Eltis had pointed out that through most of Lord Keynes' life, the British pound had a gold value exactly equal to the value Sir Isaac Newton had set for it in the eighteenth century, the *Journal* said: "If we had Lord Keynes today, surely he would have something instructive to say about an age of inflation. Unhappily, Lord Keynes is dead.

"We are left with his disciples, who apply his theories so mechanically they even write them into computers. Staring into the computers trying to divine the future, the disciples lose touch with both the real world around them and the original mysteries of their craft. They do not notice that in fact deficits fail to stimulate and have forgotten why they were ever supposed to. . . ."[4]

Even economic statistics were under attack. Lindley Clark noted in the "Outlook" column of the *Wall Street Journal* on August 1, 1977 that revisions in GNP statistics by the Department of Commerce suggested that the first half of 1976 was not as strong as the GNP growth numbers then indicated and that the second half was not as weak. He wrote: "In view of the closeness of last November's election, it's possible that Jimmy Carter may be our first seasonally adjusted President."

Whatever doubts there may be today about economic theories in general, there can be little doubt that the economy prospered for a time when the neo-Keynesian New Economics was in its heyday. Real GNP climbed 25% from 1960 to 1965, more than it had before in any postwar half-decade and more than it has since.

That is not to say that the country had no problems. The threat from Russia seemed more direct and real than it does today. The country was only then awakening to the evils of racial discrimination. The United States was moving toward the Vietnam trap. Of course, the trauma of President Kennedy's assassination had struck the nation and the world a severe blow. But the United States economy was working fine.

Maybe too fine. As with all ideas that succeed spectacularly, the New Economics had created a false sense of power and knowledge. President Johnson, a man of great dreams and an unwillingness to submit to economic realities, came to feel that the United States economy was rich enough and powerful enough to bear almost any burden. Mr. Galbraith had contributed to this notion with his best-selling book of 1958, *The Affluent Society,* which had as its primary thesis the idea that as the American economy grew richer, more and more of the tasks that needed doing and that would contribute most to the quality of life in the United States would be those traditionally undertaken by the "public" rather than the "private" sector. It was a prophetic vision, beautiful in its clarity and simplicity. The United States in the 1960s conducted an enormous expansion of its schools, tripling total school expenditures. It built a large part of the vast interstate highway system. It built acres of public housing. It dotted the country with large new terminals to accommodate air travel's rapid expansion. It launched a space effort that was to send a man to the moon. It undertook to finance medical care for the poor and and aged. And it fought a costly war in Asia.

At the same time, the nation's great private production machine was humming at home and expanding throughout the world. General Motors increased its sales from $11.4 billion in 1961 to $28.3 billion in 1971. DuPont approximately doubled its sales.

The intellectual thrust and self-confidence of the New Economics could take some credit for bringing about that dramatic expansion of the United States economy in the 1960s.

But the assumption that government was to be held responsible for "creating" economic growth caught on too well. It attracted a large public following that came to look to government as the source of prosperity. With the large expansion of jobs in the public sector, for many it was. But alas, by the late 1960s, it was becoming evident that if there was ever a government power to create prosperity it was diminishing. Some of its projects were proving to be less than overwhelming successes. Public housing was an example. The Pruitt-Igoe public-housing project in St. Louis finally was razed to the ground in 1972, less than 20 years after it had been built at a cost of $36 million (unmanageable problems with crime and vandalism were blamed). In addition, Medicaid and Medicare had created a sharp increase in the demand for medical care, with the result that costs of medical services were climbing at a rate higher than the overall inflation rate. General inflation was making itself felt. The federal budget was being stretched to the limit as the combination of continued increases in spending and a slowing rate of revenue growth due to a slower rate of economic expansion made itself felt. Increasingly, Social Security recipients felt the pressure of inflation.

More and more of the budget was going into income-transfer programs—taking money from the productive population and giving it to the nonproductive—that contributed nothing to real economic growth. The percentage of the national income accounted for by transfers—Social Security benefits, unemployment compensation, welfare, and the like—is currently about 14%, double the level in 1960. The total amount of such income exceeds $200 billion. The recipients of income transfers are a significant political constituency.

Budget deficits resulting from rising expenditures and a slowing rate of revenue growth began to put a damper on the creation of new government-spending programs in about 1970. But the federal bureaucracy and the Congress were not long in finding an answer to this inhibition. They began devising ways to transfer more of the costs of government initiatives to the private sector by simply passing laws mandating business expenditures for social purposes. A whole series of federal acts followed—the Clean Air Act Amendments of 1970, which mandated stricter air pollution controls for cars, electric power plants, and other pollution sources; the Noise Control Act of 1972, which required that products meet noise emission standards; the Occupational Safety and Health Act (OSHA), which required industry to meet health and safety standards set by the Department of Labor; The Employee Retirement Income Security Act of 1974 (ERISA), which set minimum standards for private pension plans; and a variety of other programs.

Although the objectives of these programs were in many cases desirable and worthy of the public support they received, they generated serious problems. The writers of the federal standards initially felt little pressure to consider cost-benefit relationships, with the result that some standards represented costly "overkill" or were in some cases just plain silly. The costs of the programs were hidden, borne by the consumer in the prices of products rather than through his tax bill, which meant that business was forced not only to meet the standards but also to face the ire of consumers over higher prices. Many felt that government was hitching a free ride, and this began to poison the relationship between business and government.

Moreover, the programs, along with the wage and price controls imposed by President Nixon and Congress in August 1971, represented an unprecedented intervention by the federal government into the market economy. The propagandizing, mainly against business, launched by government in support of this intervention began in the early 1970s to have a polarizing effect on United States politics. Businessmen and the market economists attempted to launch a counterattack, and with some success in terms of public sentiments—there began to be a perception among the general public, as reflected in polls, that government had become too powerful and pervasive, and this perception no doubt had something to do with the election of an "outsider," Jimmy Carter, to the Presidency, in 1976.

But the interventionists had by then attracted a broad-based support from beneficiaries of income transfers, from environmentalists, from a free-floating set of "public interest" lobbyists who sometimes overlapped with the environmentalists and whose role model was Ralph Nader, from an influential segment of organized labor, from an expanded population of public workers whose jobs depended on the expanded role of the public sector, from a rising number of young lawyers pouring out of the law schools who were fascinated by the possibility of doing good works in the public-interest field or who could see a bright economic future for themselves in either government or business in dealing with the expanding body of law and regulation, and finally, from a small but newly emboldened group of advocates who were now freely admitting something that they would not have dared to admit 20 years before—that they were, in fact, Marxists in favor of the state going all the way with its intervention.

The New Economics had come a long way from 1961, and it had picked up a lot of baggage in the form of government intervention and private frustration that made it difficult for even the most ardent fine-tuner to think of manipulating the economy as Walter Heller and John F. Kennedy had done, or at least as everyone thought they had done, in the early 1960s. The economic discussion had moved increasingly from the dry academic formulas of the monetarists versus the Keynesians to a head-on conflict between capitalists and socialists.

In this milieu, it was not too surprising to see the venerable and much-loved Senator Hubert Humphrey cosponsoring a bill, the so-called Humphrey–Hawkins bill, that seemed to its critics like a big step down the road toward a centrally planned economy. Or to read in a new book by two elderly New Dealers, Harry Magdoff and Paul M. Sweezy,[5] that because of the failures of Keynesianism and the rising burdens of public and private debt, "radical" change was necessary to "A society in which product for profit is replaced by production for use, and money and finance are reduced to their proper role as modest accessories to rational planning." Or to read Socialist Michael Harrington, in the September 1977 *Harper's,* attacking Jimmy Carter for not spending enough at a time when the President had just finished launching a whole series of tax and spending programs.

While the calls for "rational planning" were seen by business as part of a march toward socialism, the would-be planners were operating under some handicap, mainly an inability to explain clearly how one would go about planning an economy that had reached the size, complexity, and advancement the United States economy has reached. Herbert Stein, former chief economic adviser to President Nixon, exposed this weakness in a paper published by the American Enterprise Institute in 1975.

He quoted Myron E. Sharpe, a member of the Initiative Committee for National Economic Planning which, after studying planning abroad, had an important role in writing the Senate version of Humphrey–Hawkins: ". . . A planning commission that makes forecasts to which nobody pays attention is not what we have in mind. Nor do we have in mind a tug-of-war between planning technocrats, the Finance Minister, and the Prime Minister. Nor yet a summary of the investment intentions of all the businesses in the country. Nor a planning system that is boycotted by unions because they are aligned with opposition parties. Least of all do we have in mind a pro forma planning procedure that is rubber-stamped by parliament and actually negotiated by chairmen of the boards of the largest corporations. . . ."

Mr. Stein's response: "So the present surge of enthusiasm for planning in the United States arises not because of the success of foreign planning but despite its failure. American planning is to be unlike any planning known anywhere up to now. This leaves open, of course, the question what it is to be like. . . . Its opponents sometimes talk as if it means converting the United States into the Gulag Archipelago. Its supporters sometimes seem to mean that the American economy should be run like a progressive kindergarten, in which the pupils reach a consensus each morning on what they will do that day—who will pour the lemonade and who will serve the cookies. But the first interpretation is not inevitable and the second is not possible."[6]

The Nobel-laureate economist Friedrich Hayek, in The Road to Serfdom, had this to say about the planning movement: "Planning owes its popularity largely to the fact that everybody desires, of course, that we should handle our common problems as rationally as possible and that, in so doing, we should use as much foresight as we can command. In this sense everybody who is not a complete fatalist is a planner, every political act is (or ought to be) an act of planning, and there can be differences only between good and bad, between wise and foresighted and foolish and shortsighted planning. An economist, whose whole task is the study of how men actually do and how they might plan their affairs, is the last person who could object to planning in this general sense. But it is not in this sense that our enthusiasts for a planned society now employ this term, nor merely in this sense that we must plan if we want the distribution of income or wealth to conform to some particular standard. According to the modern planners . . . it is not sufficient to design the most rational permanent framework within which the various activities would be conducted by different persons according to their individual plans. This liberal plan [Professor Hayek used the word liberal in the classical English, not the modern American, sense], according to them, is no plan—and it is, indeed, not a plan designed to satisfy particular views about who should have what. What our planners demand is central direction of all economic activity according to a single plan, laying down how the resources of society should be 'consciously directed' to serve particular ends in a definite way.

"The dispute between the modern planners and their opponents is, therefore, *not* a dispute on whether we ought to choose intelligently between the various possible organizations of society; it is not a dispute on whether we ought to employ foresight and systematic thinking in planning our common affairs. It is a dispute about what is the best way of so doing. The question is whether for this purpose it is better that the holder of coercive power should confine himself in general to creating conditions under which the knowledge and initiative of individuals are given the best scope so that *they* can plan most successfully; or whether a rational utilization of our resources requires *central* direction and organization of all our activities according to some consciously constructed 'blueprint'. The socialists of all parties have appropriated the term 'planning' for planning of the latter type, and it is now generally accepted in this sense. But though this is meant to suggest that this is the only rational way of handling our affairs, it does not, of course, prove this. It remains the point on which the planners and liberals disagree.'"[7]

In repeating this section of his classic book in an article in the Morgan Guaranty Survey in January 1976, Professor Hayek recalled that the great economist J. A. Shumpeter accused him of "politeness to a fault" because he "hardly ever attributed to opponents anything beyond intellectual error." In the 1976 article he was not quite so generous toward modern American advocates of planning. He noted that both Senator Humphrey and Senator Javits insisted that the Balanced Growth and Economic Planning Act of 1975 was not intended to expand government control over the economy.

Wrote Professor Hayek: "It is difficult for an outsider to understand how, after introducing so ill-considered and irresponsible a piece of legislation—which promises merely an empty machinery with no stated purpose, which will perhaps give us input-output tables for a few hundred commodities that will be of no conceivable use to anybody except some future economic historian, but which may incidentally be used to enforce the disclosure of various sorts of information that would be exceedingly useful to a future authoritarian government—Senator Humphrey should be able to boast that it is his 'single most important piece of legislation.' Somebody as innocent of American politics as this writer might suspect that the Senator from Minnesota is the unwitting tool of some other, presumably collectivist, wire pullers who want to use the machinery thus created for aims they prefer not to disclose. But when one rereads the accounts of how the campaign for national planning has evolved in the articles of the magazine *Challenge,* whose hand one seems to recognize also in several other statements supporting the plan, one feels reassured that nothing more sinister than sheer intellectual muddle is at work."

Congress was not ready for anything so abstruse as the Humphrey–Javits bill, which when twinned with its counterpart in the House became the Humphrey–Hawkins bill. But the concept did not die. President Carter last year indicated support for a modified Humphrey–Hawkins bill that would set general economic goals, such as a lowering of unemployment to 4% of the work force by 1983.

The flirtation with collectivism in Congress and the White House was only that, a flirtation, but there can be no doubt that this had something to do with the phenomenon that was observed in the early stages of the Carter administration: a lack of business confidence. It was reflected most obviously in the weak recovery of capital spending and in the declining stock market. Throughout the period 1970 through 1977, chief executives of corporations were asking themselves and whomever else they could buttonhole why business was so much under attack.

Paul Johnson, former editor of the English weekly *New Statesman,* wrote in his recent book, *The Enemies of Society,*[8] that the phenomenon was not so new and that, in fact, capitalism had been under attack from its very beginnings. The book was reviewed in the *Wall Street Journal* of September 16, 1977, by Robert Nisbet, Albert Schweitzer Professor in the Humanities at Columbia University. Professor Nisbet wrote that the question raised by Mr. Johnson was why capitalism, with its unique record in the production of goods and services and its vital role in making possible the liberal democracies of the West, should face so much attack. He noted that economist Shumpeter had raised the same question 50 years ago and that both he and Mr. Johnson had provided a similar answer. The attack, they said, comes from the intellectual class.

Wrote Professor Nisbet: "It is hard to dispute Schumpeter. There are exceptions—Adam Smith preeminent—but from Hobbes through Rousseau, even Burke and Tocqueville, down to the present, the prevailing attitude of intellectuals toward businessmen and what they do has been negative. It has ranged from contempt and caricature to outright hostility and attack. With today's big and growing government effectively in the hands of intellectuals who dominate congressional, judicial and presidential staffs, we may expect this attitude to become more rather than less evident.

"Mr. Johnson gives us 13 chapters of examples in which the enemies of capitalist, middle class society are identified, often brilliantly and always clearly and pertinently. These enemies include ecological fanatics, philosophers, social scientists, artists, novelists and dramatists, college professors, teachers in the schools and those at home and out in the Third World who have been inspired by minds such as those of Herbert Marcuse and Franz Fanon. . . .

". . . I am sorry Mr. Johnson didn't see fit to include those New Prohibitionists who, with hands not on the Old Testament but the latest FDA report, jump gleefully to the task of preventing the great majority of us from having our smoking, drinking, driving, dressing and eating pleasures—not, God knows in the interests of saving, but of making wretched, our lives and, of course, smiting the business class. Not since I was five years old, in the presence of the Biblebelters, have I heard cigarets and liquor spoken of as they are today in just about any Berkeley or Hampton household."

Michael Novak, a Catholic lay theologian, writer, and professor of religion at Syracuse University, picked up a similar theme in the *Christian Century* of February 23, 1977: ". . . Socialism—to play on the Volvo slogan—is the thinking man's economics. They go together, socialism and intellectual life. Capitalism is abandoned to practical men and women of affairs. Democratic capitalism as we experience it in the U.S. has no 'manifesto,' and pitifully scant theoretical interests. There are many fundamentalist preachers of the creed—in Rotary clubs, at the AMA—but there is no serious theology accessible to the ordinary reader. All the fashionable theoreticians—John Kenneth Galbraith, Robert Lekachman, Michael Harrington and a scattering of others—are socialists and review each other's books."

Nobel laureate Milton Friedman invoked Adam Smith, the patron saint of market economists, in a symposium in late 1976 at Dartmouth College, celebrating the American Bicentennial, the bicentennial of Adam Smith's *An Inquiry into the Nature and Causes of the Wealth of Nations,* and the 75th anniversary of Dartmouth's Amos Tuck School of Business Administration. Said Professor Friedman: "The error of modern, well-intentioned liberals, central planners of the Humphrey–Hawkins type, the error of those who seek to attack major social problems by the political mechanism, is brought out, I think, extremely well in my favorite quotation from Smith, again from *The Theory of Moral Sentiments.* Smith had a name for the kind of man you all are familiar with, who believes that society should be run by central direction, who believes that able smart men should design a system for the rest of us, who believes that these men should sit in a central location with tentacles spread throughout the society, deciding social priorities and who should do what. He called such people 'men of system,' and this is what he had to say about them:

" 'The man of system seems to imagine that he can arrange the different members of a great society with as much ease as the hand arranges the different pieces upon a chessboard; he does not consider that the pieces upon the chessboard have no other principle of motion besides that which the hand impresses upon them; but that, in the great chessboard of human society, every single piece has a principle of motion of its own, altogether different from that which the legislature might choose to impress upon it. If these two principles coincide and act in the same direction, the game of human society will go on easily and harmoniously, and is very likely to be happy and successful. If they are opposite or different, the game will go on miserably, and the society must be at all times in the highest degree of disorder.' "

To this Professor Friedman added: "Now that last sentence is not a bad description of the present. 'Society must be at all times in the highest degree of disorder.' Why? Because a man of system has tried to treat the individual citizen of a country as if he were a piece on a chessboard, instead of an autonomous human being with his own motives, his own urges, his own values. The failure to understand this central insight of Adam Smith is the reason why I believe that there is an invisible hand in politics as there is in economics, but one that works in the opposite direction. Adam Smith pointed out that in the economic market, the man who intends only his own good will tends to promote the good of society better than the man who intends to promote the good of society. In the practical world, the invisible hand operates in the other way. The well-meaning reformer who intends solely to promote the interest of society is led by an invisible hand to promote private interest that it was no part of his intention to promote. And he and his fellows produce in the process that 'highest degree of disorder.' That is above all, the lesson Adam Smith had to teach."

Yet another attack on socialism was offered in a 1976 paper by Alan A. Walters, Sir Ernest Cassel Professor of Economics at the London School of Economics, an institution better known as a haven for Fabian socialists than for free-market philosophers. Wrote Professor Walters: "In socialist theory government is the epitome of disinterested wisdom. A socialist government would consist of selfless politicians seeking only the public good, aided by benevolent public servants devoted to the highest ideals. Reality is different. Under a democratic regime, even the purist politician has to get himself elected. Out of office he is a mere cypher. He must respond to the pressures of his constituents to capture the all-important marginal or swing vote. In order to induce the marginal voter to deliver him into office, the candidate must in turn deliver a quid pro quo.

"In practice this means that the candidate must *buy* the vote. The currency in which the vote is bought is not the coin of the realm (at least I believe that there is no convincing evidence that money changes hands), but the promises of support for certain policies that will benefit the groups of interest to which the marginal vote adheres. In principle the voter *sells* his vote for policies that will benefit him either materially or emotionally, and the incipient member or councillor trades off one group against another in his attempt to obtain office. . . ."[9]

The professor ended his essay on a pessimistic note: "The simple democratic process which has served as a model, if not a reality, for so long in the West is now producing what many philosophers have long feared—a new kind of tyranny. I can see no reason why the technological progress which we saw in many other human endeavors should not extend to the democratic and political process. The many constraints that at present limit the exercise of political power will be much diminished over time. More and more economic decisions will be taken into the public fold. Our freedoms, born in the 18th Century and blossoming in the 19th, already seem quaint and will one day appear almost antediluvian.

"As a secondary, but still quite important, matter we are likely to see a decline in the useful output of the economy. Of course, it is not beyond the wit of governments to design measures of output that will show phenomomenal rates of growth—as one can readily see in almost any socialist country. But as a matter of fact few of us really enjoy the services of an army of bureaucrats engaged in telling us what we may not do, although, in the calculations of statisticians, the high-priced 'output' of bureaucratic services is religiously represented as part of the national output."

Still more testimony from the beleagured free marketers comes in a 1977 paper by Michael C. Jensen and William H. Meckling, both of the Graduate School of Management at the University of Rochester. Titled *Can the Corporation Survive?*,[10] it carries an introduction by Armen A. Alchian, Professor of Economics at the University of California, Los Angeles. Wrote Professor Alchian: "Man has a history of strong political restriction and direction over his economic striving. Those who have experienced the American nation's development are among the few in history who have lived in societies organized as private property systems. But normality is being restored. Overwhelming political power over property rights is again superceding personal freedoms, which depend on private rights to the use of property."

Professors Jensen and Meckling wrote: "Given the incentives of government officials to undermine the private rights system, and given the way representative government functions, we see little reason to believe that the trend toward more and more government will be arrested. In particular, the process cannot be checked by electing the 'right' people to office. Only a radical change of some sort in the basic structure of our political institutions could at this point alter the course of events, and it is hard to imagine how such a radical change could ever be brought about.

"The private corporation has been an enormously productive social invention, but it is on the way to being destroyed. Large corporations will become more like Conrail, Amtrak and the Post Office. One likely scenario begins with the creation of a crisis by the politicians and the media. In some cases, the crisis will be blamed on the 'bad' things corporations do or might do. The remedy will be more and more controls on corporations (something like what has been happening in the transportation and oil industries). When the controls endanger the financial structure of the corporations, they will be subsidized by the public sector at the cost of more controls. When the controls bring the industry to the brink of collapse, the government will take over. The details of the scenario will no doubt vary. Moreover, some firms will simply be driven out of business because of regulatory costs and the inability to raise capital.

"There will be more 'public' directors on the boards of large corporations. There will be increasing involvement of labor in the control and management of corporations. In West Germany, corporations are now required to have labor union representatives on their boards of directors.

"Although we believe that the probability our forecasts will be realized is high, it is not a certainty. Indeed, we hope that bringing the problem to the attention of the public will generate a solution. Moreover, even if our predictions are realized, it won't happen tomorrow, and it won't mean the end of humanity. It will mean only that we will be much poorer and less free.

"Humanity has survived in various states of tyranny for thousands of years—one might say this is the natural state of affairs for man. Future historians may look back and see the period 1776 to 1976, when real freedoms existed, as a brief 200-year accident."

Finally, William E. Simon, Secretary of the Treasury under President Ford, had this to say in a speech delivered at the Hillsdale College Freedom Fund's "Weekend for Freedom": [there is] "an unhealthy aspect in much of the cynicism and negativism that we find in America today. I believe this more ugly mood is the result of the demonstrated failure of collectivist big-government approaches to national problems that promised so much but delivered so little. In the process, a mood of dependence on government has increased which feeds upon itself, creating still more demands for benefits without recognizing that the bills must be paid—either directly in current taxes or indirectly through accelerating inflation and economic disruption.

"The accumulation of economic distortions must now be faced. The longer we delay the hard adjustment decisions the more difficult and costly the needed solutions will become. And if we delay too long the opportunities to restore stable economic progress may be lost."

We have quoted at length here from the writings of free-market libertarians because their pessimistic warnings of a trend toward collectivism are a persistent undercurrent of the total economic debate. They may be entirely too pessimistic. The United States is a pluralistic society with many voices saying many things and a political process that makes adjustments between all the competing claims and philosophies. Its ability to make such adjustments is its greatest strength. If the country is indeed heading toward collectivism, who is to say that this is not part of an inevitable historical process that serves the imperatives of long-range economic and social development?

That, however, is an admittedly fatalistic view. If Professor Walters is correct and democracy must eventually destroy human freedoms and make us poorer, it is hardly a prospect to look upon with equanimity, even if it is historically inevitable.

It is impossible to disassociate the election of Jimmy Carter from this debate. In the Democratic primaries he won out over a collection of candidates who had been associated with strong central government. Oklahoma Senator Fred Harris, the most extreme of this group, was quickly rejected. So was Senator Birch Bayh of Indiana. And so ultimately were Morris Udall, an environmentalist and advocate of land-use planning, and Henry Jackson, bête noire to the oil companies.

A former businessman and farmer, Mr. Carter, with his attacks on Washington and big government, stirred hopes among the libertarians that he might become their Trojan Horse inside Washington and the Democratic party. Those hopes may have helped elect him over Gerald Ford, who had strong libertarian credentials of his own and had assembled a libertarian administration, but who had worked within the Washington system for 25 years. It is, of course, equally true that Mr. Carter was at the same time appealing to other groups with an interest in income redistribution and other enticements of big government. Organized labor and disadvantaged minorities assembled behind his banner.

However, it has become obvious since the election that Jimmy Carter is a political mediator, not an espouser of a distinct political theology. His energy and Social Security programs (both with sharp increases in taxes), his responses to demands for more subsidies and protections from various interest groups, all of which expand the federal budget, and his intemperate attack on the oil companies, have given scant comfort to the libertarians. The philosophical battle between the collectivists and the libertarians rages all around him as he occupies himself with the business of designing government programs and trying to gain acceptance for them in Congress. His critics from both sides have come to wonder whether he fully understands the fundamentals of the political struggle that is shaking the world.

CHAPTER FIVE

THE ECONOMIC TEAM

. . . . *men in large organizations rely on their staffs, and on the quality of the people they choose to work for them. When issues get confused on the way to the top, the chance for wise decisions is less than it might have been at lower levels. I have to remember that I am very dependent on the people below me.*—Michael Blumenthal, as quoted in *Fortune*, January 1973.

IN THE FALL OF 1977, PRESIDENT CARTER, LIKE MANAGER BILLY Martin of the New York Yankees, was shuffling his economic team. Some star players had faded, others had been relegated to the bench, and some minor leaguers were being called up. Bert Lance, the President's close friend and most influential adviser, had left his post as director of the Office of Management and Budget and gone home to Georgia after a stormy investigation into his personal finances. Charles Schultze, head of the President's Council of Economic Advisors, was having trouble getting the President's ear long enough to advise him. And Michael Blumenthal, the liberal businessman at the Treasury, was getting mixed reviews both from the White House and from businessmen.

It also appeared that Mr. Carter's economic goals were in jeopardy. Those goals, as laid down by Mr. Schultze in May of 1977, were a cut in the unemployment rate to 4¾% from 7%, a cut in the rate of inflation to 4% from a current trend rate of 6%, a cut in the share of federal spending in the GNP to 21% from 23%, and a balanced federal budget.

In fact, his economic policies in the first year of his administration had been shaped by Cabinet members and subcabinet officials with very little dedication to such goals. Energy Secretary James Schlesinger had designed a complex energy program that involved a sharp boost in taxes and a massive intervention by government in directing private industry in what forms of energy would be used and in conservation schemes; Housing and Urban Development Secretary Patricia Harris had lobbied through a sharp increase in the HUD budget; Labor Secretary Ray Marshall had been instrumental in helping organized labor gain an increase in the minimum wage, which most economists felt would raise teenage unemployment and thus negate whatever employment benefits there might be in the expanded HUD spending; Agriculture Secretary Robert Bergland had lobbied for higher price supports for farmers, an idea that Congress had multiplied into a massive Treasury raid; environmentalist Cecil Andrus, Secretary of the Interior, had stalled offshore oil exploration and proposed government redistribution of western farm lands irrigated with federal water; and Health, Education and Welfare Secretary Joseph Califano had proposed increased Social Security taxes, falling mainly on employers, and a large dip into Treasury general funds to bail out the ailing program.

After the departure of Mr. Lance, the President had turned to a young White House aide from Atlanta, Stuart E. Eizenstat, as a principal economic adviser. Considering the fact that Mr. Eisenstat is a lawyer, not an economist, this was a perplexing move for a President who had more Cabinet members with PhDs in economics than any past President.

To add to the confusion, the Carter administration had accumulated a large cadre of second-echelon officials with liberal, interventionist views. In an article in the October 1977 *Fortune*, entitled "Nader's Invaders Are Inside the Gates," Juan Cameron counted 59 such officials drawn from the ranks of consumerists, public-interest lawyers, civil-rights workers, and environmentalists.

In essence the President was running two administrations, one conservative and the other liberal, reflecting the fundamental dichotomy of the Democratic Party, a diverse and pluralistic organization that the President had somehow managed to pull together in winning the 1976 election. The results were not altogether pleasing to either conservatives or liberals.

Alan Abelson, writing in *Barron's* of August 1, 1977 about the dim view of the administration reflected in a steady decline of stock prices, had this to say: "The stock market hates certainty. Yes, we know the conventional wisdom has it the other way round, but the conventional wisdom also warns not to quarrel with the tape. And one big reason why the market took that fabulous dive on Wednesday was certainty. What Wall Street is now certain of is the quality of the administration's financial honchoes. So long as there was some room for doubt, there was cause for hope. . . ."

Mr. Abelson was specifically referring to two of the more conservative members of the administration, Mr. Blumenthal and Mr. Lance. Mr. Blumenthal had just made some ill-chosen remarks that seemed to say that the U.S. Treasury didn't mind seeing the dollar depreciate, which had contributed to a further sell-off of dollars in the world's money markets. Mr. Lance was in the process of seeing his personal financial difficulties exposed to public view.

From the left, the Carter economic team's main members were similarly under attack, even though it could hardly be said that they had succeeded well in shaping substantive policies. Writing in *Harper's* of September 1977, socialist Michael Harrington complained that "Schultze, . . . Blumenthal, and . . . Lance have been designing all programs to 'win the confidence' of business. The political idealism of the last generation is being sacrificed to 'existing institutional structures.' "

As these attacks indicate, Mr. Carter's economic policies were somewhere close to the center, how close or on which side depending on individual views. There can be little doubt that his economic attitudes had been drawn from many sources and could hardly be said to represent a specific philosophy. This contributed to the considerable confusion about where the President actually stood, which had become evident during the election campaign and became more so during his first year in office.

The elements of conservatism in his make-up had been shaped by his background as a Georgia farmer, businessman, and legislator. An element of classic liberalism, in the Adam Smith sense, had been injected by Southern populism and its distrust of concentrated power, although that illusive philosophy, populism, also contains an important measure of modern liberalism and its distrust for Wall Street, bankers, and big business. The People's (Populist) Party, a relatively powerful third party in the election of 1892, had advocated, among other things, government ownership of transportation and communications facilities.[1]

Another influence on Mr. Carter's thinking was probably his association in the 1970s with two groups of thinkers and scholars—the Trilateral Commission in New York City, which focuses on international relations, and the Brookings Institution in Washington, a policy think tank that has often been regarded as primarily a haven for Democrats temporarily out of power.

During the campaign, Mr. Carter had still another source of economic advice in Professor Lawrence Klein, an econometric whiz from the University of Pennsylvania, who was the candidate's chief economic adviser. Professor Klein is essentially a Keynesian economist. Although he turned down a major post in the administration, he has served as a consultant to the President's Council of Economic Advisers.

Professor Klein, who is the university's Benjamin Franklin Professor of Economics and Finance as well as chairman of Wharton Econometric Forecasting Associates, Inc., at the university, delivered a paper as part of the University of Pennsylvania's President's Lecture series in March 1977 that revealed some of his then-current economic views. The new problems that economic policy must face up to, he said, are materials shortages cum speculative waves (especially like those of 1973–1974), OPEC pricing and energy "shortfalls," environmental deterioration and "quality of life," existence of large-scale structural unemployment and grain failures, and population growth. ". . . In one way or another, they all lead to substantial inflationary pressure because they cost money or resources to overcome, although they are genuine problems apart from the inflationary aspect. . . . Having adequate effective demand is probably a necessary ingredient in their treatment, but it is surely not sufficient. The New New Economics must extend the broad macro considerations of Keynesian policy prescriptions to deal with issues like these.

"It is my opinion that the market mechanism, if left to its own free play, will not deal appropriately with these issues. They will not be handled in a fair and just way in terms of social equity, and they will not be handled in a stable way if left to market forces, either totally or primarily."

The professor's recommendations: "Buffer stocks to deal with material shortages; policies of conservation, extended use of coal, research into synthetic fuels, fuel stockpiling and use of price incentives to improve the supply/demand balance in energy; recognition of economic costs of protecting the environment and slowing of growth as conventionally measured; the initiation of extensive programs in manpower training and reform of labor market conditions to deal more effectively with structural unemployment; the stimulation of larger food supplies through use of acreage allocations and improved practices to increase yields."

Professor Klein's remarks (which, incidentally, included a challenge to the *Wall Street Journal*'s "Keynes is Dead" editorial discussed in Chapter Four of this book) are noteworthy because of the resemblance between his prescriptions and the programs President Carter actually proposed in his first few months in office. The President's controversial energy program, in particular, stressed conservation, extended use of coal, synthetic fuel research, and so forth, although it was short on price incentives. His farm policy stressed price stabilization through acreage allocations. And in none of his policies so far has he shown much inclination to give free rein to market mechanisms.

Some of Professor Klein's proposals are confusing. It is not clear, for example, how acreage allocations would contribute toward expanding the world food supply. But on at least one point he departs from neo-Keynesianism in a potentially fruitful direction, suggesting that it is in the direction of "supply side policies that economic thinking must turn." His tack for getting there suggests yet more neo-Keynesian market intervention, but the President might be well advised to embrace the basic idea of encouraging producers, if not the prescription for doing so.

The role of economists in presidential campaigning and in the making of government policy has come a long way from their lowly status in FDR's 1932 campaign, if a story told by Paul Samuelson in *Newsweek*[2] can be believed. According to economist Samuelson, Leon Henderson, the first big-name economist to work on a campaign team, was being interviewed by Charles Michelson, one of FDR's political lieutenants. "See these buttons on my coat sleeve?" Mr. Michelson is said to have asked. "They're not worth a damn, but everyone says I have to have them. Well, that, Leon, is how I feel about an economist on the campaign staff."

Which economists other than Professor Klein impressed Jimmy Carter the most is his own secret, but he didn't stint on consulting a broad range of advisers. Among them were Martin Feldstein of Harvard, sometimes called Carter's "house conservative"; Carolyn Shaw Bell, known for her forceful advocacy of female equality in the job market; Lester Thurow of the Massachusetts Institute of Technology, possibly the most liberal member of the team and more likely to wring his hands over the inequality of wealth than over inflation; Michael Wachter of the University of Pennsylvania, more conservative in his views, particularly with regard to the link between economic stimulus and inflation; Albert T. Sommers of the Conference Board, in Professor Samuelson's view an excellent forecaster; and Richard N. Cooper of Yale, a well-respected international economics specialist. Professor Cooper, one of the few campaign economic advisers actually to take a job in the Carter administration, was appointed Undersecretary of State in charge of economic affairs.

Despite this talented brain trust, Mr. Carter made some serious slip-ups during the campaign. A glaring example was his naive statement about how he would achieve a balanced budget, made during the first televised debate with President Ford. Since his first economic pronouncements in April 1976, Mr. Carter had begun to espouse more and more federal spending programs while continuing to promise a balanced budget. One of the panel of reporters questioning the candidates at the debate, *New Yorker* writer Elizabeth Drew, began to press him on the contradictions inherent in his promises. Here is an excerpt from the debate transcript:

MISS DREW: *Governor Carter, you have proposed a number of new or enlarged programs, including jobs, health, welfare reform, child care, aid to education, aid to cities, changes in Social Security, and housing subsidies. You have also said that you want to balance the* budget by the end of your first term. Now, you haven't put a price tag on these programs, but even if we priced them conservatively, and we account for full employment by the end of your first term, and we account for the economic growth that would occur during that period, there still isn't enough money to pay for those programs and balance the budget by any estimates that I have been able to see. So in that case, what would give?

MR. CARTER: Well, as a matter of fact, there is. If we assume a rate of growth of our economy equivalent to what it was during President Johnson, President Kennedy—even before the Vietnamese War; and if we assume that at the end of the four-year period we can cut our unemployment rate down to 4% to 4½%, under those circumstances, even assuming no elimination of unnecessary programs, and assuming an increase in the allotment of money to finance programs, increasing as the inflation rate does, my economic projections—confirmed by the House and the Senate Committees—have been with a $60-billion extra amount of money that can be spent in fiscal year '81, which would be the last year of this next term, within that $60-billion increase, they would befit the programs that I promise the American people.

I might say, too, that if we see that these goals cannot be reached, and I believe that they are reasonable goals, that I would cut back on the rate of implementation of new programs in order to accommodate a balanced budget by fiscal year '81, which is the last year of the next term. I believe we ought to have a balanced budget during normal economic circumstances, and these projections have been very carefully made. I stand behind them, and if they should be in error, slightly on the down side, then I will phase in the programs that we have so advocated more slowly.

MISS DREW: Governor, according to the budget committees of the Congress that you referred to, if we get the full employment, they project a 4% unemployment, and as you say, even allowing for the inflation in the programs, there would not be anything more than a surplus of $5 billion by 1981, and conservative estimates of your programs would be that they would be about $85- to $100-billion. So how do you say that you are going to be able to do these things and balance the budget?

MR. CARTER: Well, the assumption that you have described as different is in the rate of growth of our economy.

MISS DREW: *No, but we took that into account in those figures.*

MR. CARTER: *I believe that it is accurate to say that the commit-tees to whom you refer, the employment rate that you state and with the 5 to 5½% growth rate in our economy, that the projections would be a $60-billion increase in the amount of money that we have to spend in 1981, compared to now, and with that framework would befit any improvements in the program.*

Now this does not include extra control over unnecessary spend-ing, the weeding out of obsolete or obsolescent programs. We will have a safety version built in, with complete reorganization of the Executive Branch of government, which I have pledged to do. The present bureaucratic structure of the federal government is a mess. And if I am elected President, that is going to be a top priority of mine: to completely revise the structure of the federal government to make it economical, efficient, purposeful and manageable for a change. And also, I am going to institute zero-base budgeting, which I used four years in Georgia, which assesses every program every year, and elimi-nates those programs that are obsolete or obsolescent.

With these projections, we will have a balanced budget by fiscal year 1981, if I am elected President. I keep my promises to the Ameri-can people and it is just predicated on very modest, but, I think, accurate projections of employment increase and a growth in our national economy equal to what was experienced under Kennedy— Johnson before the Vietnam War.

After this display of confusion, Mr. Carter was widely conceded by the press to have "lost" the first debate. But he did better in the second debate, which focused on foreign policy and thus required less specificity about troublesome subjects like money.

Mr. Carter's confusions about how to spend more money and still achieve a balanced budget may have simply reflected an overexposure to intricate economic theorizing. Some may have been absorbed in the tranquil, scholarly atmosphere of the Brookings Institution in Washington, where he began attending briefings in mid-1975.

Brookings is an avowedly nonpartisan, nonprofit center where scholars study and write position papers on the problems and functions of government. Located just eight blocks north of the White House, it has been a source of high-level manpower for Presidents since 1946, when Harry Truman was the first Chief Executive to turn to it for recruitment, picking Brookings Vice President Edwin Nourse as the first chairman of the first President's Council of Economic Advisers. John Kennedy and Lyndon Johnson also drew heavily from Brookings when choosing staff; many of those selected returned to the institution when their White House service ended, giving the place a reputation among Republicans as a Democrat shadow government.

One of the pet theories of Democrat economists at Brookings that Mr. Carter may have adopted, at least for a time, is that of a "full-employment budget," which purports to be a guide to how large a federal budget deficit is acceptable. In brief, it holds that any deficit is acceptable—in fact, desirable for purposes of economic stimulus—so long as expenditures are such that the budget would theoretically balance at full employment (meaning 4% unemployment) because of the additional revenue that would flow in at that employment level. The concept is controversial, seen by its opponents as merely a means to rationalize deficit spending by government and as another manifestation of the neo-Keynesian notion that it is possible for a government to spend a nation into perpetual prosperity.

At any rate, his remarks during the debate about increased spending and a balanced budget (by this time the target date had been moved back from 1978 to 1981) suggested to many viewers that Mr. Carter did not have a very good grasp of federal budget problems and raised suspicions that he was, contrary to his campaign claims, but one more member of the "money-doesn't-matter" school of politics.

He made another serious slip during the debate that was probably not obvious to most viewers but would have been noticed by economists, particularly those of the monetarist school. *Wall Street Journal* reporter James P. Gannon asked about Mr. Carter's views of the Federal Reserve Board, whether or not they were compatible with those of Fed Chairman Arthur Burns, and whether or not he would seek Burns' resignation.

Mr. Carter replied, "What I have said is that the President ought to have a chance to appoint a chairman of the Federal Reserve Board to have a co-terminous term: in other words, both of them serve the same four years. *The Congress can modify the supply of money by modifying the income tax laws.* The President can modify the economic structure of our country by public statements and general attitudes on the budget that he proposes. The Federal Reserve has an independent status that ought to be preserved. I think that Mr. Burns did take a typical erroneous Republican attitude in the 1973 year when inflation was so high.

They assume that the inflation rate was because of excessive demand, and therefore put into effect tight constraint on the economy, very high interest rates, which is typical also of a Republican administration, tried to increase the tax payments by individuals, cut the tax payments by corporations.

"I would have done the opposite. I think the problem should have been addressed by increasing productivity, by putting people back to work so they could purchase more goods; lower income taxes on individuals, perhaps raise them if necessary on corporations in comparison. But Mr. Burns, in that respect, made a very serious mistake.

"I would not want to destroy the independence of the Federal Reserve Board, but I do think that we ought to have a cohesive economic policy with at least a chairman of the Federal Reserve Board and the President's terms being the same, and then the Congress, of course being the third entity with independence, subject only to the President's veto."

The flaw in Mr. Carter's bold remarks about the Fed during the debate was the comment that "The Congress can modify the supply of money by modifying the tax laws." The money supply is, of course, controlled by the Fed, which regulates the supply mainly by selling Treasury securities to private banks to reduce the money supply or buying them to increase it. Monetarist economists, such as Milton Friedman, feel that prudent money-supply regulation is central to the avoidance of inflation. Money supply is definitely not controlled by adjusting taxes. The indication here that Mr. Carter had only a fuzzy notion of the central bank's role, destroyed some of the credibility of his attack on Chairman Burns. Later, during his administration, he would take a friendlier attitude toward Chairman Burns, holding frequent discussions with him at the White House, presumably to learn more about how the money supply is regulated.

After the election, when the new President actually went shopping for his official economic team, he drew Bert Lance from his coterie of Georgia friends, Charles Schultze from Brookings, and Michael Blumenthal from the Trilateral Commission and the Bendix Corporation, where he was chairman and chief executive officer.

Of that trio, Mr. Schultze had by far the most government experience, having spent nearly 25 of his 52 years in and around the councils that set government economic policy. Gregarious and unpretentious, he was born and raised in Arlington, Virginia, almost in the shadow of the White House, was content to enter the army during World War II as a private, serve in Europe, and then leave, still a private, to obtain his undergraduate and master's degrees in economics from Georgetown University.

Mr. Schultze taught economics briefly in Minnesota and Indiana, but soon returned to home base in the Washington area where he served, during the Eisenhower administration, on the staff of the council he now heads. He got his PhD from the University of Maryland, often teaching there subsequently, and in 1961 joined the Kennedy administration in the Bureau of the Budget. In 1965, at the age of 40 and at the invitation of Lyndon B. Johnson, he became the youngest man ever to head that bureau, which is now the Office of Management and Budget.

During the Johnson administration, Mr. Schultze was in a position to implement and promote the government spending and intervention in the economy that reached historic (some say hysteric) highs and became known as the Great Society splurge.

But several years of sober reflection as a senior fellow at Brookings seem to have tempered Mr. Schultze's views of the role and capability of government in economic affairs. Just before he accepted his current assignment, Mr. Schultze said in a lecture at Harvard that he was increasingly doubtful about federal intervention in the marketplace. Government is "imposing command and control solutions over an ever widening sphere of social and economic activity," he warned, adding that the problems that the government tries to correct are too complex for quick remedies.

The other two members of the CEA were also middle-of-the-road economists. They were Lyle E. Gramley, plucked from his job as senior Federal Reserve Board economist, and William D. Nordhaus of Yale, a 35-year-old specialist in the causes of inflation. Mr. Gramley, a highly regarded economic forecaster, had been at Maryland with Mr. Schultze, and the two were long-time friends. He would take responsibility for macroeconomic analysis and forecasting on the council. According to an article by Clyde H. Farnsworth in the New York Times,[3] Mr. Gramley supports an independent role for the Fed, saying at his confirmation hearing, in response to a question from Senator Proxmire, that "we should not want to strongarm the Fed."

Mr. Nordhaus was given responsibility for microeconomic policy—in other words, specific problems, such as energy shortages. Mr. Farnsworth quoted him as raising the question whether the United States should continue to subsidize energy consumption, as some economists feel it has done through government energy policies. "Both are economists in the role of a pragmatic President," wrote Mr. Farnsworth. "Neither is very political or ideological. They are Keynesian in the sense that they believe the government has a major economic role to play."

Mr. Carter drew Mr. Blumenthal and 15 other top appointees to his administration from members of the Trilaterial Commission, a collection of some 200 prominent people from the world's three leading non-Communist industrial areas: the United States, Western Europe, and Japan. The commission was founded in 1973, under the aegis of Chase Manhattan Bank Chairman David Rockefeller, to debate and seek solutions to the political, economic, and security problems common to the three areas. Jimmy Carter, who was invited to join as a leading Southern political figure, later wrote in his book *Why Not the Best?* that the commission was a "splendid learning opportunity" in foreign affairs for him.

It was also a splendid employment agency. Indeed, Mr. Carter's choice of so many commission members for his administration brought an accusation from Christopher Lydon in the July 1977 *Atlantic* that the President had been revealed as a "Rockefeller Republican." It is a bit surprising that a liberal critic would have been concerned about that, since Rockefeller Republicans often have been more liberal than Southern Democrats. Indeed, the Trilateral Commission and its professional staff are not only internationalist-minded but tolerant of a wide spectrum of economic and political philosophies.

The Treasury Secretary Mr. Carter drew from this milieu, "Mike" Blumenthal, is every inch the internationalist, liberal, intellectual type of businessman who fits naturally into Trilateral Commission deliberations. He was described in the *Wall Street Journal* as a "profit-conscious but socially aware executive with extensive government experience in international economics [who] will give the Carter economic team a slight liberal cast."[4]

Traditionally, the top Treasury job has gone to bankers. But it was obvious at the Atlanta press conference where Mr. Carter announced the Blumenthal appointment that Mr. Carter had been impressed both by Mr. Blumenthal's liberal credentials and his impressive business record. Bendix had just been named by *Dun's Review*[5] as one of the five best-managed corporations in America, and though Mr. Carter was a bit tangled up about this honor in his introduction of Mr. Blumenthal, it seemed obvious that he had heard of it from one of his talent scouts.

Also, Mr. Blumenthal's background had provided him with insights into international economic problems, although not necessarily with the same degree of caution that most bankers would apply to monetary questions. He was born of Jewish parents in Nazi Germany. When he was 13 the family fled to Shanghai, where they were interned by the Japanese until the end of World War II. Mr. Blumenthal came to the United States in 1947 with $60 in his pocket and began a brilliant academic career, graduating Phi Beta Kappa from the University of California at Berkeley with a degree in international economics. He then earned a master's degree in both economics and public affairs and a PhD in economics, after which he taught at Princeton for four years.

After several years in business Mr. Blumenthal joined the Kennedy administration, serving two years as Deputy Assistant Secretary of State for Economic Affairs and four more years as chairman of the United States delegation to the Kennedy Round of trade negotiations that in 1967 lowered tariffs by one-third (see page 00). Later he joined the Bendix Corporation as head of international operations, became its chief executive officer (a job earning nearly $500,000 a year), and initiated policies that nearly doubled the company's sales. At the same time, he devoted much time to public affairs and tried unsuccessfully to establish a group that would set up an ethical code for American businessmen.

The third member of the troika, Bert Lance, was regarded as a first among equals because of his close personal relationship with the President. Mr. Lance is a friendly, voluble man who, like Mr. Carter, was raised in a small Georgia town, built a small business (the Calhoun First National Bank) into a large one, and ran for governor. His bid, in 1974, was unsuccessful. Before that he had worked in Mr. Carter's unsuccessful first bid for the Georgia governorship, and later, after Mr. Carter was elected governor, had served as Georgia highway director.

In an admiring piece in the *National Journal*,[6] titled "Good ol' Boy Bert," Dom Bonafede described Mr. Lance as "a friendly bear of a guy with the charm of an old song-and-dance man and the irrepressible guile of a safecracker. . . . He brings a sense of humanity to one of the most vital jobs in government."

Too human, as it turned out. Even though Mr. Lance had some of the qualities that a President seeks in a budget director—in his case a sort of down-home gift for argument useful to a man whose primary job is to say no to requests for higher budget allotments—Mr. Lance soon proved to be an incredibly bad choice. This began to be evident as stories sifted out about the troubles Mr. Lance had had with representatives of the Comptroller of the Currency over his habits of granting large overdraft privileges at his Calhoun bank to his family, friends, and campaign committee. The plot thickened when it was revealed that he had used the same collateral to obtain two large loans, one from the Manufacturers Hanover Trust Company in New York and the other from the First National Bank of Chicago.

"Lancegate," as it came to be known, dominated the headlines in the spring and summer of 1977, embarrassing the President and distracting him from other affairs of state. It soon became apparent that Mr. Lance had lost much of his usefulness as the man in charge of the budget. "How can a man who has trouble managing his own finances be expected to run a $450 billion federal budget?" was the question being asked all around the country. Finally, Mr. Carter asked Mr. Lance to make a decision on whether he should resign, which was the same as asking him to resign. And on September 21, the President went before the television cameras, sadly and with barely restrained emotion, to read a letter of resignation from his old friend and closest advisor. Mr. Lance, still able to smile, went home to Georgia.

The other two members of the troika, Mr. Schultze and Mr. Blumenthal, had nothing so shattering to contend with, but they, too, suffered embarrassments in the first months of the new administration. Their problem was not with the press or the bank examiners but with the President himself.

The President, it turned out, had a habit of making decisions on major questions of economic policy without consulting either his chief economic advisor or the man responsible for maintaining the solvency of the United States Treasury. Mr. Schultze, acting the good soldier, was still stumping for the $50 tax rebate, which Mr. Carter had proposed to Congress early in his administration as an economic stimulus, when the President reversed himself and publicly renounced it. The CEA chairman commented wryly to his staff: "If I seem to be limping, it's because someone dropped a rebate on my foot."[7]

An account in the June 1977 *Fortune* by Juan Cameron describes still another incident: "One afternoon last March . . . Secretary of the Treasury Michael Blumenthal was working in his large and elegant corner office when the light on his telephone console blinked. It was an excited Charles Schultze on the line. 'Mike,' said the chairman of the CEA, 'did you hear what the President just said at his press conference?' 'No,' said the Secretary, he had been working, not listening. 'He said we will deliver a very strong anti-inflation program to Congress in two weeks!' Blumenthal, who only a few days earlier had told reporters that the anti-inflation program wasn't even on the agenda at the EPG (economic policy group) says that as he put down the phone he thought of that beneficial effect of a deadline first remarked upon by Dr. Johnson: 'Depend upon it, Sir, when a man knows he is to be hanged in a fortnight, it concentrates the mind wonderfully.' "

And finally, the energy package, which in reality was an enormous tax program, was not discussed with the economic advisers until Mr. Blumenthal and Mr. Schultze wrote a stiff note of protest. Just two weeks before the package was sent to Congress, the two were invited to sit down with the President and in a four-hour session, managed to rein a few of the excesses of Energy Adviser Schlesinger's staff.

According to Mr. Cameron, the President had said to Vice President-elect Fritz Mondale shortly after the election: "I know the problems and I may get beaten, but I intend to do it my way." That is a noble spirit of self-confidence, and indeed a chief executive does have to make final decisions. Harry Truman's legendary desk motto, "The Buck Stops Here," is well understood by anyone who has responsibility for an enterprise large or small. But Mr. Carter was obviously not making full use of the broad spectrum of advice an executive staff is supposed to provide.

That soon began to cast doubts on his talents as an administrator, something that he had always regarded as one of his strong points. It was also no doubt in part responsible for the troubles he would encounter later with Congress, the press, and the public as he began proposing complex, sweeping, and expensive programs, only to see them cut to pieces by a host of critics almost before the ink was dry.

The machinery to explore economic problems in full and perhaps avoid such miscalculations, however, was at hand right from the beginning of the Carter administration. Every week, usually on Monday afternoons at about two, the Economic Policy Group gathers around the big oak table in the Roosevelt Room at the White House to talk about any economic problem that has arisen. In regular attendance in the months before Mr. Lance's eviction were Mr. Lance, Mr. Schultze, and Mr. Blumenthal; Mr. Cooper of State; the Secretaries of Labor, Commerce, and HUD; and occasionally other department heads.

Fortune's Mr. Cameron wrote that "never before have so many PhDs in economics held such high positions in government." On the

EPG there are five—Blumenthal, Schultze, Cooper, Juanita Kreps of Commerce, and Labor Secretary Ray Marshall.

Of that group, Mrs. Kreps deserves special mention. The position of Commerce Secretary has not traditionally been a source of economic wisdom, although the department is responsible for a good many economic statistics the government collects. It publishes, for example, the authoritative Survey of Current Business, which gives a monthly statistical picture of the economy. And it houses a good many of the 4000 or so professional economists employed by the government.

Mrs. Kreps, who was described by the Wall Street Journal[8] at mid-year 1977 as "the strong man of the Carter administration" because of her forthright statements on Social Security and other government problems, was not one to play a passive role. She was the first economist as well as the first woman to head the sprawling Commerce Department, which employs 35,000 people. A coal miner's daughter from Kentucky, she earned her way through Berea College and Duke University graduate school, eventually working her way up to become vice president of Duke, acquiring membership on a long list of corporate and foundation boards along the way.

She had a reputation for organizational skills and intended to use them, both to make Commerce more efficient and to strengthen the department's role in making national economic policy. Shortly after her appointment she told a New York Times reporter that as she saw it, one of her functions was to "make sure that the Government knows precisely what the business community thinks about particular issues. I think it would be very short-sighted of any Government to draw up economic or business-related policies without consultation."[9] The soft-spoken Mrs. Kreps added that she felt the administration ought to stress strengthening business investment rather than concentrating so heavily on trying to stimulate consumer demand and consumption. Her proposal apparently had some impact with the President, because one of the theoretical goals of the tax program he was to introduce in 1978 was to stimulate capital formation and investment.

Later, Mrs. Kreps was quoted by the Washington Post[10] as saying "in strictly economic matters, in the policy group, I've had as much impact as any Cabinet officer. The President is a very accessible President. He is eager to hear what any Cabinet officer thinks about any issue."

Accessible, perhaps, but not always responsive. Another member of the EPG, Labor Secretary Ray Marshall, also has a tendency to speak his own mind. The Secretary, 48 at the time of his appointment and drawn from the economics department of the University of Texas, was selected in part because of his longtime support for the goals or organized labor. But he had not yet received Senate confirmation when he publicly criticized President-elect Carter's jobs program as being too limited. George Meany, head of the AFL–CIO, was voicing similar criticisms.

Later Mr. Marshall endorsed an increase in the minimum wage to $2.65 from $2.30 an hour, even though he seemed to have some misgivings about the risk of expanding unemployment when the minimum wage is set too high. Mr. Carter actually proposed an increase to only $2.50 an hour, signaling that he had not been persuaded by his Labor Secretary. But Congress proved to be more generous, giving organized labor something closer to its demands, a subject we discuss in a later chapter.

Another member of the Economic Policy Group was Patricia Roberts Harris, Secretary of HUD, who filled the dual role of providing Mr. Carter with a second woman and a second black in a Cabinet-level job, fulfilling his promise to put more women and blacks in top jobs. Like Mrs. Kreps, Mrs. Harris had humble beginnings. Her father was a railroad waiter. She left her Illinois cornbelt home to finish first in her class at Howard University and at George Washington University Law School. Age 52 at the time of her appointment, she had been a member of a Washington law firm, former ambassador to Luxembourg under President Johnson, and holder of 30 honorary degrees and seats on the boards of IBM, Scott Paper, and the Chase Manhattan Bank.

Although not regarded as a powerful advocate in Cabinet meetings, Mrs. Harris played some role in persuading the President to boost the 1977 HUD budget authorization allotted by Mr. Ford by $15.4 billion and the fiscal 1978 authorization by $9.5 billion, in both cases to help create jobs. Since that initial success she has been less effective in getting Presidential approval for programs designed at HUD, a department that has suffered more than its share of difficulties and embarrassments over the last decade.

In the final week of 1977 the President announced two long-awaited appointments, one to his administration, the other to the chairmanship of the Federal Reserve Board. James McIntyre, Jr., who had filled in as acting OMB director after the departure of Mr. Lance, was picked to head the agency; and G. William Miller, chairman and chief executive of Textron Corp, was named to replace Mr. Burns, whose term was expiring.

Mr. McIntyre, who is also from Georgia, was not expected to have the political clout of his predecessor, and he would probably serve as an administrator while leaving economic policy decisions to other members of the team.

The headline of the *Wall Street Journal* article of December 29 announcing Mr. Miller's appointment was "William Who?", an indication of the general surprise that greeted the elevation of an outsider unknown to most Washingtonians to one of the major economic posts in the country. Mr. Miller was quoted as saying that he intended to continue the policies of Mr. Burns in fighting inflation and strengthening business confidence, but little was known as the year ended about his own views on economic policy.

In summary, Mr. Carter's first team on economic policy has not had an impressive record in influencing government policy. Advisers normally regarded as outside the economic policy area have played a more significant role. In some cases, these were not first-line executives. We deal with some of their policies, and the problems created for Mr. Carter, in later chapters.

CHAPTER SIX

EARLY CONFUSIONS

. . . I took office a couple of weeks ago in the middle of the worst economic slowdown of the last 40 years.—Jimmy Carter, in his first presidential report to the nation, February 2, 1977.

WHEN MR. CARTER MADE THE CHAPTER-OPENING STATEMENT IN his first televised "fireside chat" from the White House, looking relaxed and casual in a cardigan sweater, the reaction of many economists was that he was a bit *too* relaxed and casual. The economy, far from being in a slowdown of any kind, had been in a state of recovery for 22 months, as adjudged by the National Bureau of Economic Research, which charts business cycles.

After the much-discussed economic "pause" in the third quarter of 1976, which, as we have said before, may have been crucial in the defeat of President Ford in the November election, the economy resumed a strong upward climb. New car sales in December rose 15% from a year earlier; retail sales jumped 4.2% on a seasonally adjusted basis from November, the sharpest increase in four years; some 2 million more people were employed than at the 1974 prerecession peak; the Federal Reserve's industrial production index, seasonally adjusted, closed the year on a strong upswing, with the result that the average for the year was up 12 points from 1975, despite the September–October pause. Housing starts in December were a phenomenal 51% above a year earlier, a time when housing was still a depressed industry. That was the highest rate in three and a half years.

Indeed, the economy was rolling so well that the 1976 recovery would remain strong through the first six months of 1977, prompting Alfred L. Malabre, Jr. to write in the *Wall Street Journal*'s "Outlook" column on July 18 that Mr. Carter should have said, "I took office during the strongest business recovery in 40 years."

Mr. Malabre cited data compiled by the St. Louis Federal Reserve Bank that compared the first 26 months of five economic recovery periods—from October 1949 to December 1951, August 1954 to October 1956, February 1961 to April 1963, November 1970 to January 1973, and March 1975 to May 1977.

Wrote Mr. Malabre: "The St. Louis Fed's data clearly show that the current expansion has no peer in the most important area of job generation. Civilian employment in the 1975–77 period rose at an average annual rate of 3.3%. This compares with annual job growth of 2.6% in the 1949–51 period, 3.1% in 1954–56, 1.4% in 1961–63 and 2.4% in 1970–73. Growth in industrial production during the 1975–77 period was exceeded only by the 1949–51 period, when production was expanding rapidly to meet the military needs of the Korean War. Retail sales in the latest period, adjusted for inflation, ranked second only to the growth in 1970–73 when the combination of price controls and rapid expansion of the money supply created an artificial boom."

The only serious weak spot in the recovery—one that we discuss in greater detail in a later chapter because it was indeed a serious weak spot—was in business-capital expansion. But by the spring of 1977, prospects were looking up here, too.

Indeed, the economy was recovering so strongly in December of 1976 that the most serious risk seemed to be another outbreak of inflation. The OPEC countries that month were able to raise prices of crude oil an average of about 8% despite a split in their ranks when Saudi Arabia and the Arab emirates along the Arabian or Persian Gulf refused to go along with the other OPEC nations on a 10% increase. The Saudi group went up only 5%.

The Associated Press market-basket survey of food prices also showed an upward blip in December. By mid-January 1977, when the Consumer Price Index for December appeared, it had become evident that prices were once again climbing. This phenomenon was also being reflected in more sophisticated ways. The stock market, which had been strong in December, began slipping in January. The price of the dollar relative to other important currencies also began falling. Both circumstances, on the basis of past performance, could easily be associated with a rising rate of inflation.

Why, then, did Mr. Carter think the country was in a depression when he took office? Whatever answer is given to this question, it does not reflect well on the President.

There were critics who ascribed the "worst economic slow-down" statement to a cynical political calculation. It was an attempt, they said, to plant the idea in the public mind that the outgoing administration had been a miserable failure. It would have the double benefit of protecting the President if the economy should turn sour early in his administration. He could merely say that he had inherited a mess and was having difficulty straightening it out.

An equally damning theory was that the President had become the victim of his own campaign rhetoric. He had been saying that the economy was in trouble so often during the campaign that he had come to believe in that myth. In short, he was living in a fantasy world of his own making.

But the explanation need not be so harsh, even though it is not at all uncommon for politicians either to be shrewdly calculating or to imagine themselves in the role of white knights arriving just in the nick of time to save the world from some dire catastrophe. Probably the best answer is that Mr. Carter was simply listening to the wrong people. There was no shortage of people to tell him that he had arrived just in the nick of time and that, if he adopted their particular programs, the Republic would indeed be saved.

The President was, in fact, under broad-scale pressure from organized labor, liberal economists, liberal Congressmen, and the liberal press to shape an economic policy that would address the unemployment statistic, which was still high despite the sharp rise in employment. (The employment rise, incidentally, went largely unnoticed by these groups, as did the renewed threat of inflation.)

Walter W. Heller, the father of the New Economics as adviser to Presidents Kennedy and Johnson and now professor of economics at the University of Minnesota and a member of the *Wall Street Journal*'s Board of Contributers (which was formed to present a broad spectrum of opinion on the editorial page), wrote in the *Journal* on January 7, 1977 that the "long economic lull" in the fall of 1976 demonstrated the "flabbiness" of the economic recovery.

Professor Heller said, for example, that "Industrial production, after finally climbing back in mid-1976 to the levels first reached in 1973, had been stuck at those levels for about six months." That was a rather remarkable statement, considering the fact that the Fed's industrial production index had climbed three points between June and December, despite the September–October pause.

Professor Heller recommended a remedy similar to the one the President himself was able to announce: a tax rebate and expanded federal spending.

Alice M. Rivlin, who had been plucked out of Brookings by the Democratic majority in Congress in 1975 to be the first head of the Congressional Budget Office, offered a similar analysis. In releasing a series of CBO reports on the economy, economist Rivlin described the recovery as "disappointing," saying that in spite of the recent economic improvements there now seemed almost no chance of meeting the output and unemployment goals envisioned by Congress in the fall, *"under current budget policy."* This was on January 11, when, of course, current budget policy meant the policy of Mr. Ford. The CBO press release quoting Dr. Rivlin's remarks carried the customary disclaimer that "in keeping with the mandate of the Congressional Budget Office, the report contains no recommendations," an addendum that had become amusing in light of the strong hints in almost every CBO report about what might be the most desirable government policy.

A *Wall Street Journal* editorial on December 13 had urged the President to follow his own instincts rather than quick-fix entreaties, noting the then-evident inflation signals and arguing that the unemployment rate would respond better to anti-inflationary measures than to economic stimulus. The premise was that the unemployment figure represented, in addition to demographic factors, a sharp rise in the number of additional members of households (mainly wives) seeking jobs to cope with the impact of inflation on household budgets.

The President-elect, however, was more attuned to the Walter Heller side of the *Journal* editorial page than to the advice of the *Journal*'s editorial writers. On January 5 and 6 he held a meeting with his economic team and the leaders of Congress at Plains to thresh out a stimulus package. The program was announced on January 7, which was 13 days before Mr. Carter's inauguration.

Budget Director Bert Lance was later to say that the President-elect instructed his new economic team that he wanted only enough stimulus to do the job, and no more. Although he felt a stimulus was needed, he was concerned about the danger of inflation if it were too great. In addition, according to Mr. Lance, Mr. Carter is naturally conservative on matters of fiscal policy. He had, after all, promised a balanced budget by 1981.

When it was announced the next day, the stimulus package proved to be a grab bag, as might be expected of a program worked out with so many pressures and in such a short time. It called for $31.2 billion in federal stimulus over two years, which was a compromise between advocates of no stimulus at all and those forces that wanted an immediate injection of some $20 billion or more. In some ways it was more conservative than the simple $12.5 billion in permanent individual- and business-tax cuts being proposed by outgoing President Ford, in that it relied more heavily on temporary tax benefits. That, however, was not viewed by many conservative economists as a plus, a subject we discuss in greater detail later.

The main feature of the stimulus package was a "rebate" (more precisely, a grant) of $50 for each taxpayer and his or her dependents plus $50 to nontaxpayers who were retired, earning too little to pay taxes, or receiving supplemental security income from the government. Treasury Secretary Blumenthal estimated that the rebates would pump some $11.4 billion into the economy in the spring if Congress acted promptly, giving a boost to consumer demand.

In addition, there was a permanent tax cut for individuals, mainly aimed at low-income workers, achieved through raising the standard deduction for taxpayers who did not itemize deductions. This was valued at $1.5 billion. Then there was a cut for business estimated at $900 million for fiscal 1977. Businesses could choose to take an income-tax credit equal to 4% of the half-share they contributed to employes' Social Security wage taxes. Or they could opt instead for an increase in the tax credit they received on new investments in plant equipment, to 12% from 10% of the cost of the investment. The idea here was to equalize the incentive to business to hire additional workers as compared to spending money on more efficient plants.

The lion's share of the fiscal 1977 stimulus, estimated at a total of $15.7 billion, would thus consist of the rebate and small permanent tax cuts. The other half of the stimulus, mainly aimed at fiscal 1978, was the jobs program. It called for increased revenue-sharing to the states, increased spending on public-works jobs, and an expansion of spending under the Comprehensive Employment and Training Act (CETA) for public-service jobs and to equip unemployed workers for new jobs.

The stimulus package would later be incorporated into the Carter revisions of President Ford's fiscal 1977 and 1978 budgets. (The outgoing administration prepares the budget to be submitted to Congress for the approaching fiscal year, which begins on October 1.) The budget revisions, announced by Mr. Carter on February 22, raised Mr. Ford's projected outlays for fiscal 1977 by $6.2 billion and lowered his projected receipts by $4.7 billion. This raised the estimated fiscal 1977 federal deficit to $68 billion from $57.2 billion. For fiscal 1978 Mr. Ford's estimated outlays were boosted $19.4 billion to $459.4 billion and his estimated receipts by $8.6 billion, lifting the projected deficit by about the same amount as the projected fiscal 1977 deficit, $10.8 billion. Thus Mr. Carter projected a fiscal 1978 deficit of a little over $57.7 billion compared with a little under $47 billion for Mr. Ford.

Although this bit of deficit boosting cast considerable doubt on Mr. Carter's promise to balance the federal budget by fiscal 1981, the stimulus package pleased almost no one. George Meany of the AFL–CIO had wanted an immediate jobs program of at least $30 billion, compared with the $13 billion he got if you count all the business incentives as a jobs stimulus.

The "rebate" came under heavy fire, too, mainly from conservative critics. President Ford, before leaving office, had proposed a simple tax-cut program amounting to $12.5 billion. It involved $10 billion in personal-income-tax cuts, mainly by raising the personal exemption to $1000 from $750, and $2.5 billion for corporations, through cutting the corporate-income-tax rate to 46% from 48%.

Although it involved about the same amount of money as the tax-rebate proposal of Mr. Carter's team, Mr. Ford's proposal had the support of many conservative economists, whereas Mr. Carter's did not. It was felt that Mr. Ford's permanent, across-the-board reductions would be noninflationary because they would stimulate production by improving incentives for businessmen and wage earners as well as expanding consumer demand. The rebate, it was felt, would only stimulate demand, since it offered no promise of improved future after-tax earnings.

Nobel laureate Milton Friedman, interviewed in the March 7 issue of *U.S. News & World Report,* said he believed that the Carter program, on the whole, would do more harm than good.

"I'm in favor of tax reduction under any and all circumstances as the only effective way to put a lid on total government spending," Professor Friedman said. "But the particular form of tax reduction that is proposed in this program is undesirable. It proposes to give rebates on a basis that has no relation to current activity. If we're going to reduce taxes, we should at least reduce them in a way that will give people an incentive to save more and work harder, not simply drop checks out of airplanes. We ought to make it a permanent reduction in taxes."

Professor Friedman argued that the new President was actually proposing to increase, rather than reduce, taxes: "The real tax burden on the American people is the amount the government spends, not the amount that is labeled 'taxes.' If the federal government spends 460 billion dollars in fiscal year 1978, which is roughly what the President proposes, and takes in something like 400 billion in taxes, who do you suppose pays the other 60 billion? The tooth fairy? Or the Arab sheiks? The American people pay it. It's paid in the form of the hidden tax of inflation, or, if it's financed by borrowing from the public, then in the form of higher taxes that will be needed in the future to pay the interest and the principal. That means that it lowers the value of all property today to the extent that property will be subject to higher future tax burdens."

Albert H. Cox, Jr., chief economist for Merrill Lynch & Company, parent company of the nation's largest securities firm, testified before the Senate Finance Committee on March 9, with similar reservations. He noted that the economy was making strong gains and that there was a serious risk that the stimulus would prove to be mainly a stimulus to inflation.

Mr. Cox also felt that both the unemployment rate and the estimates of the extent to which the nation's productive plant was being utilized might be misleading:

"The so-called 'hardship unemployment rate' (those unemployed 15 weeks or more) was 2.4% (seasonally adjusted) in January and that for adults out of work five weeks or more, according to our estimates, was only 4.1%. These and other breakdowns of the unemployment statistics are far less reassuring, in terms of the availability of productive labor, than total unemployment and the total unemployment rate.

". . . Similar reservations apply to the aggregate statistics for plant and equipment utilization. The Federal Reserve's new monthly series on capacity utilization of materials industries shows a utilization rate of 80% for last December, seemingly a noninflationary level. Yet the figure for one of the major components of the total, paper materials, was at nearly 90%, not so reassuring in this sector. Potential bottlenecks are hidden in the aggregate."

Fed Chairman Arthur Burns warned the Joint Economic Committee of Congress on March 11 that "the increase in the federal budget causes fear of inflation that creates a self-fulfilling prophecy." By this he no doubt meant that inflation expectations themselves generate inflation as people hurry to spend their money, rather than save it, before it depreciates in value.

Even before the general attack on the rebate, a *Wall Street Journal* editorial had warned on February 16 that the Carter package was a perfect inflationary one-two punch. "First a left to the financial sector, with a sharp federal borrowing upsurge [to finance the rebate] neatly timed to catch the upswing in private borrowing. Followed by a right to the real sector, with public jobs and public works neatly timed to come in at the peak of the [business] cycle." The flak from liberals was almost equally strong. Many labor leaders and liberal Congressmen felt that the rebate was merely "giving money away" that could be used for their favorite programs. In an uncommon spirit of agreement with Milton Friedman, Senator Floyd Haskell of Colorado, a liberal Democrat, adopted Professor Friedman's simile and said, "It's like shoveling money out of an airplane." Although he voted for the rebate in the Finance Committee, he vowed that he would vote against it when it reached the floor.

Some Congressmen, particularly those from Western and Southern states, were annoyed because the President, in his budget revisions, had unilaterally decided to economize by chopping 18 water-resource projects out of the fiscal 1978 budget at a cost saving estimated at $300 million. Congressional Democrats, upset because they hadn't been warned in advance, decided that killing the rebate would be a good way to retaliate. Philip Burton of California, leader of the liberal Democrats in the House, told the President that there was a theory in Congress that the President was seeking a confrontation, a theory which the President denied.

The AFL-CIO claimed that the two-year package was "too small, takes too long and is too ill-advised to give the economy the stimulus it needs. We consider this a retreat from the goals which we understood President-elect Carter to have set during last year's campaign."

But amid all the grousing, the President's economic team set about to sell the stimulus package. Labor Secretary Marshall fell into step with his boss and argued that if Congress failed to approve the rebate it could undermine consumer confidence and frustrate efforts to reduce unemployment. Charles Schultze lobbied hard for it. So did Secretary Blumenthal, although he may not have done the program, or himself, much good when he jokingly suggested at a breakfast meeting with a group of senators, "hold your nose and vote for it."

President Carter himself sent a letter to Senate Democrats just before the Eastern congressional recess arguing that the rebate would create 250,000 jobs and add $15 billion to the GNP by the end of the year, but all to no avail. Just six days later, on April 13, the President announced that he was withdrawing his tax-rebate proposal, along with the two optional tax credits for business.

On April 30, at the annual dinner of the White House Correspondents Association, the President could joke about his defeat. He noted that the $50 rebate had been a firm commitment but that "my economists, though, discovered that so many people spent the $50 before they got it, that we didn't have to give it to them."

He also joked that "I've had a lot of setbacks and a lot of troubles, as you know, and you've been kind enough to make those clear to the American people, which is legitimate and expected, and I don't have any reason to think that objecting to it would help."

Despite all the critics of the rebate, however, withdrawal also attracted criticism. Senator Edmund S. Muskie of Maine, chairman of the Senate Budget Committee, said that the administration's sudden change of signals had created a "crisis of confidence" in the budget process. "If economic conditions in April justify this abandonment of the course we set two months ago, Congress has a right to know why those conditions were misjudged in February when the program was proposed," said the Senator at a Budget Committee hearing called to demand an explanation of the rebate withdrawal from the President's economic aides. The answer from Messrs. Blumenthal, Lance, and Schultze, was that the economy was recovering faster than had been expected.

An editorial in the *New York Times* theorized that the President had dumped the rebate to preserve his precious political capital in Congress for the forthcoming energy-package debate. But it concluded that such calculation "will be of little comfort to millions of people now looking for jobs."

In the end Congress wrote a stimulus package of its own by appropriating an additional $21 billion for various jobs programs, including $4 billion for local public-works projects, nearly $5 billion for revenue-sharing, nearly $8 billion for public-service jobs, and $1.4 billion for job training. It also passed, and the President signed, a bill advertised as a $30 billion tax reduction over 28 months. In fact, about half the "reduction" was merely an extension of tax cuts already made and due to expire over the period. But there was a $5 billion cut, through an increase in the standard deduction along the lines proposed by the President, for some 47 million low- and middle-income taxpayers. And most interesting of all, there was a novel tax incentive designed to encourage employers to hire additional workers.

This "employment credit," designed by Al Ullman, Democratic chairman of the House Ways and Means Committee, and by Senator Lloyd Bentsen of Texas, was billed as a $3 billion incentive for business over two years. But a good many businessmen were puzzled by the complexities of the provision, and some economists questioned whether it would provide the 600,000 additional jobs its sponsors hoped to generate. Mr. Carter's economic advisers, in particular, were not especially keen about the credit. Secretary Blumenthal noted that because the credit was mainly designed to help small business, it would exclude nearly two-thirds of the labor market from any benefits.

In essence the program would provide a tax credit of up to $1,092 for each new worker hired by an employer after his payroll has grown 2% from the year before. The maximum credit for any one employer would be $100,000, which means that big companies or companies growing rapidly would not particularly notice the incentive's benefits.

Of course, the provision should lower the marginal cost to employers of hiring an additional worker, and on that basis it might yield some benefits. At least it is a direct form of employment subsidy, which is more than can be said of some of the other federal jobs programs. The $8 billion public-service program, for example, often seems to end up as more of a subsidy to local governments rather than a generator of additional employment. Of that, more in a later chapter.

It is debatable whether the economic stimulus program that Congress finally provided was an improvement over the one that Mr. Carter proposed. But the tax rebate defeat was a signal to the President that he would have a great deal of trouble reconciling the fundamental forces of American politics, those calling for reduced federal spending and taxation and those demanding more federal programs and not particularly worried about the federal deficit or other potentially depressive and inflationary effects of expanding government.

However, it is also clear that the new President's power to lead would have been improved by a firmer grasp of real economic conditions in the nation. His own economic instincts appeared to be largely conservative when he took office, but his false claim that he took office during a terrible economic slowdown played into the hands of the big spenders of Congress and government and weakened the confidence of conservative economists and businessmen who might otherwise have been inclined to support him from the right.

The tax rebate was a simple neo-Keynesian prescription, and though the *Wall Street Journal* may have overstated the case through its use of poetic license in saying that "Keynes is dead," there can be little doubt that neo-Keynesianism is no longer high intellectual fashion. The President's advisers were on shaky ground on some other points, relying too heavily on the unemployment and industrial capacity utilization statistics as a basis for policy. As Alfred L. Malabre, Jr., noted in the *Wall Street Journal* on March 11, 1977, the capacity utilization figure is a particularly slippery statistic in the view of a good many economists of widely differing persuasions. The unemployment statistic has problems as well. Again, the emphasis by Mr. Carter himself on these two statistics in tilting toward stimulus rather than further reductions in inflationary pressures helped put him at the mercy of the left.

And finally, the early days of the Carter presidency were marked by some other concessions that sharply weakened confidence in his promise to bring the cost of government to the American public under better control. His Agriculture Secretary, Robert Bergland, responded quickly to the pressures of farmers by boosting price supports to dairy farmers by 9%, which it was estimated would cost $370 million a year in taxes and six cents a gallon of milk at the grocery store. The Agriculture Secretary also proposed higher support levels for other agricultural commodities, wheat in particular, which set Congress off and running to pass an agriculture bill far larger than even the President wanted.

In fulfillment of a campaign promise to the free-spending maritime lobby, the President proposed a "Cargo Preference Act" that would have required 9.5% of United States oil imports to be carried in United States flag tankers by 1985. Since United States–flag tankers have sharply higher operating costs than foreign flag ships, the bill would have raised the price of oil by 1.1 cents a gallon according to a General Accounting Office estimate. Several independent estimates went as high as 2.4 cents a gallon. The GAO estimate, while lower than the independent estimates, was about five times that made by the administration itself. The proposed cargo preference bill, as with the tax rebate, drew sharp criticism from both the right and left and, as with the tax rebate, for all practical purposes it too died in Congress.

There were also some not particularly important but patently silly proposals put out by White House underlings during the early months that also didn't help the administration's image. Greg Schneiders, White House projects director, proposed that the government recruit an army of high-school students to visit homes to compare the householder's energy conservation efforts against a government checklist. Mr. Schneiders said that "the thing I want to avoid obviously is the implication that an army of little uniformed inspectors are going out and checking people." He didn't manage to avoid that impression, however, when the proposal was publicized.

Then there was a proposal that there be a two-tier postage rate, one for business and the other for "citizens." The citizen's mail was to be identifiable by being written in longhand.

There was another kind of embarrassment when it was discovered that HEW Secretary Joseph A. Califano, Jr., in charge of government programs to help the poor, was maintaining his own private chef on a government salary of $12,763 a year and that the chef's role had been disguised under the job title "personal assistant to the Secretary, special activities." Then, of course, there was the big embarrassment over Bert Lance.

Such embarrassments are inevitable in a President's administration, and almost every President has had them in one form or another. Since Watergate, editors and reporters have perhaps been more likely to give greater attention to slip-ups, even fairly minor ones, than they had in the past.

But the shaky economic grasp of the new administration was a more serious problem. It was to result not only in the stimulus package debacle but also in the introduction of an energy package with enormous tax implications, not to mention the other economic implications, which we discuss later.

The shakiness of that grasp was confided by a money expert who happened to be present at one of the President's early economic-policy meetings. He said that he was shocked when the President asked the assemblage of economic advisers whether a weak currency was a good thing or a bad thing.

"But I was even more shocked at the variety of answers the President got," he said. "It seems that some of the President's top economic advisors thought that depreciation of a nation's currency—in other words, inflation—might be a good thing. No wonder the President seems to be confused about money sometimes."

Given the early confusions of the administration, there was some sense of relief in the country when Mr. Carter said at a press conference on October 28 that there might not be many more major programs in his administration, since he had deliberately chosen to put most of his most important proposals on the table during the first year. The stock market, which had been falling during the first 10 months of the Carter administration, bounced up for a time on that news.

But although doing something can create problems, doing nothing can as well. The economy does have real structural problems, despite the recovery from 1975. And it can be hoped that the President is learning from his early mistakes.

CHAPTER SEVEN

MR. CARTER AND CONGRESS

. . . there may be nothing about the White House less generally understood than the ease with which a Congress can drive a President quite out of his mind and up the wall. . . . —Bryce N. Harlow, White House Director of Liaison with Congress in the Eisenhower administration and the first two years of President Nixon's first term.[1]

. . . I've learned how to work much more harmoniously with the Congress. . . . —President Carter, at a news conference, July 29, 1977.

THE WALK THAT JIMMY CARTER TOOK, HAND IN HAND WITH his wife Rosalyn, from Capitol Hill to his new address on Pennsylvania Avenue on Inauguration Day may have been only one and a half miles. But at certain periods in the nation's history the man sitting in lonely splendor in the executive mansion has surely imagined that the distance between him and the domed Capitol should be measured in light years rather than a paltry mile or so.

From the first Presidency onward, these two branches of government—executive and legislative—have been wary of drawing too close to each other. George Washington, feeling his way in setting American constitutional government in motion, sat with the Senate through two days of debate to obtain "advice and consent" for a treaty with the Creek Indians. When the Senate, perhaps intimidated by his presence, voted to refer the matter to a select committee, Washington stamped out, slamming the door and vowing that he would "be damned if he ever went there again."

As historian Emmet John Hughes notes, President Washington slammed the door against any future President's ever personally coming to share in a Senate debate.[2]

Every President has had his ups and downs in dealing with the Congress, and the more forceful the man in the White House, the more forceful his comments about relations with legislators. Abraham Lincoln fumed that he would show them at the other end of the avenue whether he was President or not.[3] Theodore Roosevelt ruminated on how he would manage things if he could only be President and Congress too for just 10 minutes.[4] And Harry S. Truman, with typical combativeness, declared, "I've always said that the President who didn't have a fight with the Congress wasn't any good anyhow."[5]

Indeed, a good case could be made that the Republic is safer when Congress and the President are at odds with each other than when they are not. The era of good feeling between President Johnson and a Democratic Congress after he was elected in his own right in 1964 produced a spate of spending legislation that was later to play a major role in generating serious inflationary pressures. President Ford, on the other hand, exercised the veto liberally (20 times in 1976 alone) and helped keep Congressional spending, and thus inflation, under some semblance of control.

President Carter did not engage in any head-on confrontations with Congress in the first year of his administration. He cast only one significant veto, when Congress went against his wishes and authorized $80 million for continued preliminary development work on the nuclear breeder reactor on the Clinch River, near Oak Ridge, Tennessee. But the President and Congress were hardly on harmonious terms on his major legislative initiatives. At one point, when the Senate Finance Committee was cutting up his energy program, he conducted, at a televised press conference, something very close to an attack by suggesting that Congress was falling prey to the "special interests" of the energy industry.

In short, the widely predicted honeymoon between the Democratic President and the Democratic Congress, after eight years in which Congress and the White House were controlled by separate parties, never quite came to pass. And while the ongoing struggle had no clear victor, Mr. Carter was left with every reason to feel the same frustrations that past Presidents had felt. Considering the haste with which some of his programs were prepared and the minimal consideration given to their potential economic impact, that was just as well, although it would be hard to say that Congress improved much on their quality.

The President's first defeat involved his economic stimulus bill. Congress didn't like the main feature of the program, the $50 tax rebate, and forced him to drop it. But it soon became obvious that the objections were not so much over the rebate's unsoundness in economic terms as over the reluctance of Congress to yield up money that it had other plans for. For the two-year, $31 billion Carter "stimulus" program, Congress substituted a one-year, $21 billion stimulus program. Featuring public works, public-service employment, and countercyclical aid to states and cities, it was billed as a "jobs" program. As we explain later, it was, in reality, a massive federal subsidy to hard-pressed cities. Mr. Carter signed it happily, even though he had initially instructed his economic team to design a stimulus program that would be no larger than absolutely necessary.

After that, Congress overhauled the President's program for pulling Social Security back from the brink of insolvency, although it hardly improved on his formula. It turned up its nose at his welfare program, postponing any action for another day. And finally, after a reasonably easy time in the House, his energy program was vivisected in the Senate to the accompaniment of loud complaints from the President about the importance of the program as an answer to the nation's energy troubles. In short, all the President's major initiatives in his first year fell victim, in one way or another, to congressional independence. We discuss the flaws of those programs, along with the flaws of the Congressional alterations, in later chapters.

Mr. Carter's experience was but one more vivid sign that Congress was reasserting its more customary role in American government and operating with a relatively high degree of independence from the executive branch. Indeed, contrary to the partisan rhetoric in the early 1970s about an "Imperial Presidency" (an expression coined by former Kennedy adviser Arthur Schlesinger, Jr.), this process had been going on for some time. President Nixon was hardly a master of Congress, as attested to by the fact that he was finally forced out of office. President Ford achieved some mastery only by his sweeping use of the veto power, no doubt in part because he could do that and still retain many of his old friendships in the legislature he had been a part of for so long. But his was only a sort of negative mastery, restraining Congress but not controlling it.

And President Carter, interviewed by Saul Pett for the Associated Press in the tenth month of his Presidency, "nodded his head instantly, almost like an 'amen,' " when asked if he had found the powers of his office more limited than he expected. He was particularly surprised, he said, over the power Congress exercises over foreign policy, which was once an area where Presidents had a great deal more authority and independence of action than now.

It is probably true that the reemergence of Congress as the dominant force in shaping federal policy is one of the great undiscovered facts in American politics. A friend of ours, fellow journalist Edmund K. Faltermayer of *Fortune,* created something of a stir at a party by asserting that the Presidency was the most overrated job in the country in terms of its importance and power. Certainly, a good case can be made that the enormous attention focused on the President every day is out of proportion to his actual powers vis-a-vis Congress.

On the other hand, it should be remembered that the great expansion of the federal government's overall power in the last two decades is in part responsible for the attention the President receives. The President may not be as much a force as most people think, but the federal government certainly has a potent and pervasive influence on the lives of all Americans, and this awareness focuses attention on the man who stands at the head of government.

The new independence of Congress is a return to a role that was customary in the nineteenth century. In 1946 Lawrence H. Chamberlin, in an article in the *Political Science Quarterly,* said that "It was only when Theodore Roosevelt came into office that the philosophy of the Executive dominant in legislation received conscious application."[6] He went on to cite Woodrow Wilson and Franklin D. Roosevelt as Presidents whom many regarded as "chief legislators."

And then he said, "During the periods when the chief executive assumes the lead, the partnership between the executive and the Congress usually operates more efficiently. This does not mean that Congress has become less important. The legislative process is not like a seesaw where as one end goes down the other must automatically go up. It is, rather, like a gasoline engine which operates most efficiently when all of its cylinders are functioning. When the President becomes unusually active, there is a tendency to assume that the Congressional cylinder has ceased to function. Such is not necessarily the case."[7]

As it turned out, Mr. Chamberlain need not have worried about the gasoline engine not functioning on all cylinders. It has been roaring at an ever-increasing pitch through most of the 30 years since he wrote his article, cranking out more and more legislation, spending more and more money, and becoming a more and more dominant factor in the American political economy.

The role of Congress in this process is something akin to a marketplace. In fact, there are those economists who believe that as government grows larger, the political marketplace, as represented primarily by Congress, is supplanting the economic marketplace. Broad market forces once set prices and allocated resources to those areas where demands existed. Increasingly, they believe, that role is being taken over by political bartering. A vast army of professional lobbyists, upward of 5,000 in number, plus an even larger number of nonprofessionals, attempts daily to bring influence to bear on 535 Representatives and Senators and on the President and his executive-branch bureaucracy. They represent everything from antiabortion forces to racing-horse breeders to General Motors. Washington has become a boom town with sharply increased housing costs, soaring restaurant prices, rapid office-building expansion and dozens of other signs of the magetizing force of federal power in bringing individuals to the national capital to try to strike deals that will either work in their favor or keep them from being hurt.

The Congress is the focus for this activity because Congressmen are in the closest daily contact with these representatives of thousands of "special interests." As a result of being the focus, the legislative branch has been the fastest growing branch of government in terms of people employed and money spent. It also occupies some of the most impressive edifices in Washington—the supercostly Rayburn office building, for example.

In 1976, the Tax Foundation, Inc. published a study titled *The Legislative Branch: The Next Billion Dollar Bureaucracy,* noting that the budget just for running Congress is approaching that awesome sum, a threefold increase just since 1970. The legislative budget includes such new congressional offshoots as the Congressional Budget Office and the Office of Technology Assessment, which is supposed to provide advice on scientific and technological matters Congressmen would not be expected to understand. It also includes some old functions, such as the Government Printing Office, the Library of Congress, and the General Accounting Office, which snoops around trying to find places where the executive branch is wasting money or not doing what Congress meant for it do do when it passed authorizing legislation.

But the most impressive growth has been in the legislative staff. Employes of Congressmen in their offices and on the various congressional committees expanded 44% from 1970 to 1975 to 17,039 workers. Although a sizable proportion of this staff is involved in fairly routine constitutency work—answering phone calls or letters or trying to help someone in Dubuque find out how he is supposed to deal with the latest OSHA regulation—there is also a large cadre of well-educated, well-paid staffers who are very much involved in the bartering process that eventually ends up as legislation. It is not at all uncommon these days for a chief staff member of an important congressional committee to be invited to speak before some business or professional group on the assumption that he or she will be better able than a Congressman to explain some tricky piece of legislation. That may be because he or she wrote it. Nor is it at all uncommon for key staff aides to do some bartering themselves, either with each other or with outside lobbyists, to try to adjust differences of opinion.

The *New York Times* took note of this influential group in an article on September 15, 1977, appropriately titled "Aides to Congress, the Shadow Government." Written by Martin Tolchin, a *Times* congressional correspondent, the article quoted Norman D. Dicks, who had just been elected as a Representative from the state of Washington after eight years as an aide to Senator Warren G. Magnuson. Only half joking, Congressman Dicks said: "People asked me how I felt being elected to Congress, and I told them I never thought I'd give up that much power voluntarily."

Wrote Mr. Tolchin: "Congressional aides may be seen on the floor of the House and Senate, whispering advice and handing documents to those they serve. At hearings and markup sessions, they occupy the high-backed chairs around the conference tables, questioning witnesses and making deals on behalf of their principals. Their functions include selecting issues for discussion, conducting hearings, drafting legislation and even mobilizing public opinion."

The Public Interest, an influential quarterly coedited by Irving Kristol, took note of staff power in its Spring 1977 issue with two articles paired under the title, "Our Unelected Representatives."

In one article, Michael Andrew Scully described why the aides have so much influence on decisions: "A Senator today . . . must stay abreast of legislation on the floor. As a member of several committees and numerous subcommittees, he must attend a half dozen or more meetings per week, where he must display detailed knowledge of committee legislation and the activities of executive agencies. He must listen to representatives from interest groups concerning issues as diverse as abortion and rebuilding locks on the Mississippi River. At the same time, he must harry the bureaucracy to release job funds for a city in his home state, and search for Mrs. Jones' lost Social Security check. He receives 50,000 or more letters a year from constituents—and all of them must be answered, for he is, after all, a politician. And he must make numerous speeches in his home state every year."[8]

Mr. Scully also quoted a statement made by freshman Senator Robert Morgan of North Carolina on the Senate floor in 1976: "This country is basically run by the legislative staff of the members of the Senate and members of the House of Representatives. We ought to have the best staffs available . . . because they are the ones who give us advice as to how to vote, and then we vote on their recommendations."[9]

In the other half of the two-part discussion, "Congressional Committee Staffs: Who's in Charge Here?", Michael J. Malbin cited the way staffs are able to substantively affect every step in the legislative process: ". . . their ability to run committee investigations, the results of which they can skillfully leak to the media, gives them influence over the items Members choose to put on the legislative agenda. Once something is on the agenda, the staff works to assemble a coalition supporting a specific piece of legislation. As it sets up committee hearings, the staff will reach as broadly as possible without sacrificing the goals the chairman, often at their urging, has adopted. Then, when a bill is "marked up" (amended and passed in committee), the staff will be expected to reconcile competing interest-group demands. When conflicts cannot be resolved, the Members may then learn enough about the details to weigh the political costs of compromise. But if the major differences raised by the normally vocal interest groups can be settled otherwise, most Members will be content to leave the details to the staff, as well—details that can frequently mean everything to whole industries or groups of people."[10]

One wonders how often this burgeoning army of congressional aides and committee staffers, scurrying around looking for something to do, is responsible for creating issues, fomenting debate, and designing legislation that really is not needed. Is this restless retinue responsible even in part for the "legislative explosion" that has occurred in the last two decades?

Or are Senators and Representatives themselves, seeking "good publicity" and perhaps a line or two in history books, initiating questionable investigations and laws? Mr. Malbin has suggested this possibility: "If there is a problem throw a law at it; if the law fails to achieve the desired end, it can be fixed up later. A chairman needs some legislation before the next election, to show his 'deep concern.' "

Business Week did not mince words when it took issue editorially with Senator Lee Metcalf (D., Mont.) and his Government Operations Subcommittee in 1977 for what looked to many like an unnecessary and slipshod investigation. The report released by the Metcalf committee on what it saw as unethical practices by the accounting profession was, according to the editorial, ". . . incompetently researched and grossly biased. Metcalf and his staff have tried to solve a complex problem by pounding it with a sledgehammer, and the result is pure junk. Unfortunately some people—including some Congressmen—will take the report seriously. If they succeed in writing its recommendations into law, they will strap U.S. business and U.S. securities markets into a meaningless, stultifying straightjacket of government-dictated accounting rules."[12]

However much power you might want to ascribe to congressional staffs, there can be little doubt that legislative-branch bartering and dealing in billions and billions of dollars of tax money and borrowings far dwarfs the ancient courts of kings and emperors where feudal leaders came to ask favors or redress. Today's supplicants are corporation presidents, trade association executives, mayors and governors, building contractors, and thousands of others seeking to trade votes and homage, (and sometimes, it seems, even money) for a few kind words written into a multibillion-dollar appropriations bill.

The fact that President Carter's bold initiatives did not fare very well in Congress did not apparently reflect personal animosity toward the President or any conscious sense of direction in Congress that was at variance with that in which the President was attempting to move. Rather, his bills simply went onto the bartering table to be argued over, debated in the press and over expensive lobbyist luncheons, and finally amended and marked up in some way representing the dominant forces in a complex market process.

It might be said that the President was justified in deploring the role of "special interests" in the carving his energy bill received. But we have some doubts about that. It is true, of course, that the legislative marketplace is far from being a satisfactory way of allocating economic resources. It is, first of all, highly inefficient in the time it takes and the uncertainties it creates for all the millions of people in the economy who are trying to make guesses about legislative and regulatory outcomes. We discuss later the impact of this in creating a very serious problem of capital formation in the United States, a problem very closely related to the chronic inflation the country has been suffering for the last decade.

But imperfect as it is, political bartering is probably preferable to having vast economy-shaking programs dreamed up in a White House room by a group of presidential advisors and then rubber-stamped by a compliant Congress. At least the legislative process receives thousands of inputs from people who are operating in the real world and who know something about the complex market processes economic legislation attempts to influence. Presidential aides, particularly those who have a high opinion of their own intelligence and the delusion that the American economy can be operated like a computer console, seldom receive such broad inputs or bother to use the ones they have. The energy program, cooked up in a few weeks by such a group in so much of a hurry that some members of the team couldn't even explain how they arrived at decisions involving billions of dollars, is a perfect case in point. Had it become law as originally conceived, potentially adding something like an $80 billion additional tax burden to the economy, it would be hard to imagine the dire consequences.

The open question about Congress, however, has to do with how much the economic processes it manages correspond to the wishes and needs of the country. Congress has always had a role in the economic life of the country, not only using the government's sovereign powers to regulate commerce but also building roads and dams, parceling out federal lands, and involving itself in all sorts of transactions with private entrepreneurs. As critics of businessmen's "free enterprise" rhetoric say quite correctly, there never has been any such thing as truly "free" enterprise in the United States; the concept is only relative. And there has been a constant struggle from the very beginning of the Republic between those forces that seek to reduce the economic role of government and those that seek to increase it.

It can be argued that the democratic process protects the country from excesses in either direction. However, that argument may be too complacent. It is also true that great societies fall as well as rise, that excessive government and taxation are usually a factor, and that the only ones who will know when the decline of a society began are those who will look back on it 50 years later and say, "it probably was about then."

But it is difficult to write confidently about trends in Congress and their role in American economic life because the processes of Congress are complex and, when all the trades are made, the effects of its laws sometimes aren't even well understood by the Congressmen themselves. Mr. Carter had his work cut out for him in trying to deal with this body.

Of course, the Democratic party (also a highly pluralistic and puzzling organization) had practically taken root in Congress when Mr. Carter arrived on the scene. It had dominated that body since 1955. The actual percentage of its majority rose and fell during those 22 years, but the Democrats were always in firm control. In 1977 they held 67% of the seats in the House and 62% in the Senate.

After eight years of feuding with Republican Presidents, there was optimism tinged with caution among seasoned Democrats when Mr. Carter took office. House Chief Deputy Whip Dan Rostenkowski, quoted in the *Wall Street Journal,* said of Mr. Carter: "I am convinced he wants a marriage that will last." But then he added darkly, "On a lot of issues Congress is going to be a hell of a lot more liberal than Carter, and I don't know how he'll react. I just hope we won't go back to vetoes and vetoes."[13]

The *Journal* article, by Albert R. Hunt, noted that congressional leaders were aware of Mr. Carter's often hostile attitude toward the

Georgia legislature when he was governor and were worried about rumors that top Carter aides viewed Congress with disdain. A Senate aide commented: "I can just see the *Time* magazine cover story about the third week of February—'Whatever Happened to the Honeymoon Between Carter and Congress?' "

Actually, the aide's timing was just about on the button. In late February, stories issuing from Capital Hill were filled with mutterings about such things as the "Washington's Birthday Ambush," when Mr. Carter ordered a review of pet Congressional water projects without prior notification; about appointments being made without consulting this leader or that chairman; about phone calls from Congressmen to the White House that were not returned. *Time* did not use the predicted cover story, but carried an equivocal story on March 7 with the headline "Skating Deftly, but on Thin Ice" in reporting the President's performance.

Despite the sniping, there was a flurry of legislation passed during the first four months, moving the Democratic whip in the House, John Brademas of Indiana, to exult, "No President in memory has seen so many major laws enacted into permanent law in so short a time except Franklin Roosevelt."[14]

Mr. Brademas, in support of his claim, cited legislation that actually had been heavily reworked in Congress: tax cuts, public-works jobs, the Comprehensive Employment Training Act, and antirecession assistance, among others.

Were the early misunderstandings a tempest in a teapot, merely an awkward liaison between an inexperienced new White House staff and Congress? Or were they the tip of an iceberg of discord? The assessments varied when we were in Washington in late June 1977 to hear Senators, Representatives, and Cabinet members discuss the goals of Congress and the Administration before the Financial Analysts Federation and to talk with individual Congressmen. During the three-day Analysts conference, a subject that cropped up again and again, both from the speaker's platform and in private conversations, was the strained relations between Mr. Carter and Congress. Senator Alan B. Cranston, the Senate Majority Whip, told the audience that "Relations are not as bad between Congress and President Carter as you might think from reading the papers. We were on the way to one-man rule during the New Deal and Watergate years. Congress is now reclaiming its role."

Congresswoman Millicent Fenwick, the Republican from New

Jersey, was amused. She said at a party, "It's fun to sit on the sidelines and watch. The Democrats in Congress used to enjoy baiting the Republican administration. It was like a bullfight, with Congress always waving its cape, baiting the bull. I think they got to enjoy it so much that they don't want to quit. They still like to bait the President, even though he's in their own party."

A young sophomore Democratic Representative from Indiana, David W. Evans, in another conversation put his finger on perhaps the most striking characteristic of the current Congress when he talked of its independence. Noting that there is no commitment to any party line in the Indiana delegation to the house (eight Democrats and three Republicans), he said, "We vote the way we think."

Congressman Evans theorized that there is probably a realignment of philosophy and principle in the Democratic party as a whole. "My Democrat constituents, for instance, are much more conservative than, say, the liberals in New York, and that's the way I vote."

The Deep South has returned to the political and social mainstream of the nation. With the civil-rights battles of the 1950s and 1960s ended, there is no longer a passionate issue binding it together. This change was reflected in the 1976 elections. Not only was Mr. Carter, with his progressive attitudes on race relations, wholeheartedly supported by the South but many Southern moderates and some liberals of both races were elected to Congress.

Although many Southerners in Congress still have a conservative bent, especially in fiscal matters, they no longer have as much clout. Returning its own members year after year to Washington, the Southern bloc once used the seniority system to build up a formidable control of committees. Only five years ago, 6 of the 12 major committees in the House and 7 of 11 in the Senate were headed by Southerners. But under rules adopted by the Democratic Caucus in the House in 1973, committee chairmen no longer inherit their jobs and keep them indefinitely; rather, they are generally required to submit to a secret ballot of the Caucus every two years. Other changes have given new members much greater opportunity to serve on the committee of their choice. In 1977 there was only one Southern chairman in the House.

The growing independence of Congress stems from the same national mood that elected Jimmy Carter. That mood first asserted itself in the elections of 1974 when the electorate, weary of the whole Washington establishment in the aftermath of Watergate, elected what

Sanford J. Ungar, in an article in *The Atlantic* about the House of Representatives, called a "large band of young rebels and doubters." Describing these new politicians as a "cultural shock to their elders," he added: "They went home to their districts at least every other weekend, like most members, but when they got there, they tended to climb into vans they called 'mobile district offices.' As they toured the countryside, they took their constituents' blood pressure and asked their advice. At the same time, the 'Class of '74' acted and talked as if they were themselves largely responsible for the spirit of reform in the House. . . . They seemed to feel as if they had an exclusive mandate to help the House find its new destiny."[15]

There has been some grumbling among Washington observers that this new independence is less concerned with legislators' shaping national policy than with their simply being errand boys for constituents, that they ignore public policy unless it directly affects their own district. During the summer of 1977, Alan L. Otten wrote of this trend in the "Politics and People" column of the *Wall Street Journal*,[16] observing that in this day of public alienation from government the ombudsman role—acting as a buffer between the frustrated citizen and the frustrating bureaucrat—may actually be a Congressman's most important job.

In another column, Mr. Otten commented on a trend in the electorate that he saw affecting the actions of the new breed of legislators. He reported that a "great majority of voters including young people, union members, and many others who provided much of the thrust for earlier 'liberal' legislation—has turned inward, away from politics and government and towards their own affairs."[17] He also cited Carter adviser Pat Caddell's comment that "When the general public is not concerned with large issues, the small constituency issues, those where small numbers of people feel intensely, become much more prominent."

Thus according to this view the explanation of the attitude of Congressmen of the 1970s is not so much independence of their national party leaders as it is dependence on the whims of the vocal individuals or groups among their constituents.

Such groups have helped to rearrange the old coalitions that used to influence congressional actions so much. Replacing party and regional loyalties, there are now the Black Caucus, the Hispanic Caucus, a Rural Caucus, a Blue Collar Caucus, and a Northwest–Midwest Economic Advancement Coalition in the House. There is also the occasional rural–urban coalition that will, for example, trade votes on farm subsidies for votes on urban-renewal projects. And replacing Yankee–Dixie animosities is the Sunbelt–Snowbelt feud over distributing federal funds. Then, of course, there are Naderites, environmentalists, central planners, etc., etc.

If President Carter had a troika composed of Messrs. Blumenthal, Schultze, and Lance to direct the charting of White House economic policy at the beginning of his term, the Capitol Hill counterpart would surely be Messrs. O'Neill, Byrd, and Long. The first two were the leaders of, respectively, the House and Senate. The third, Senator Russell B. Long of Louisiana, was the chairman of the Senate Finance Committee and perhaps the most influential legislator in the 95th Congress.

Thomas P. "Tip" O'Neill, Jr., the affable Irishman who rose from the machine politics of Boston to become Speaker of the House, was generally expected to be the strongest, most activist leader to hold that powerful post since the days of Sam Rayburn. And he was not long in fulfilling that expectation in the eyes of his admirers. Within months of the beginning of the new administration he had whipped his congressional troops into shape, exercising a subtle combination of Irish charm and arm-twisting to extract from a reluctant House membership a stringent new code of ethics. The vote, representing an unspoken realization that committee assignments and all sorts of political favors were at stake, was 344 to 79.

Mr. O'Neill regards party loyalty as paramount, and that includes all the perquisites of patronage he deems due to the party in power. With such views, he was for a time at odds with the new President on the decision to review 18 major water-development projects as well as on dozens of minor complaints from House members who felt that they were being ignored by the White House.

Soon, however, Mr. Carter and Mr. O'Neill got their act together and the Speaker was steamrolling the energy package through the House with a dispatch that left viewers gasping. Setting a tight timetable, he sidestepped some potentially foot-dragging committees by creating a hand-picked ad hoc committee and ordering it to mesh all the complicated issues by mid-July for floor action. When one member voiced objections to the rush, Mr. O'Neill is said to have told him, "John, you know when I was speaker of the Massachusetts House and told a committee chairman to report out a bill by a certain date, if he didn't I'd have a new chairman the next day. That's the power of persuasion." He added, with a smile, "Of course, I don't have that power here."[18]

At another point, when President Carter was annoyed by some threatened changes in the energy package, he told Mr. O'Neill that he would go on television to protest; the Speaker persuaded the President that that would be a mistake.

By the first week in August Mr. O'Neill's reputation for forcefulness was fulfilled, at least for the moment, when the House passed a major chunk of the energy package, including the large tax on the wellhead price of crude oil, a tax on business use of oil and gas, a "gas guzzler" tax on cars, broadened federal controls on natural-gas prices, and 30 or so other complex provisions. It did not go along with Mr. Carter's proposal that gasoline taxes be raised 5 cents annually to a maximum of 50 cents a gallon, a proposal that had attracted some of the heaviest flak from the public. But Mr. O'Neill and Mr. Carter had every reason to be pleased with their success in putting so much complex and far-reaching legislation through the House so rapidly.

As the year waned, however, and the House-passed energy package began to draw increasing fire from both the Senate and the public, Mr. O'Neill's tactics were increasingly resisted by Congressmen who wondered whether they had made themselves look ridiculous by voting for so much complex economic intervention so quickly and with so little study of the potential damage. Mr. O'Neill began to suffer defeats in committees and on the House floor, prompting a *Wall Street Journal* editorial to say that Czar O'Neill had been demoted to the Russian diminuitive of czar, "czardine."[19]

Indeed, it was something of a surprise in the first place that all those supposedly "independent" Young Turks in the House went along so docilely with the leadership on the energy bill. The explanation might be that the Young Turks (more than half of the Democratic majority had only six or fewer years of House experience) were philosophically disposed toward economic intervention and were not overly concerned about the details. They simply followed the leadership when it was going in that general direction. A less complimentary judgment would be that they were simply too inexperienced to understand the enormous implications of the energy bills they were approving.

But the situation was a great deal different when the energy package got to the Senate. There the membership was older and more experienced and the leadership less disposed than Mr. O'Neill and company to treat a major economic initiative as merely an exercise in delivering votes to a Democratic President in return for presidential favor.

The Senate Majority Leader was Robert C. Byrd of West Virginia, who had won his role through dedicated and efficient application to the tasks of the Senate. He was regarded as an expert legislative technician and a tireless worker. Originally a Southern-style conservative, he had moved toward the center of the Democratic party and had cultivated, in his leadership role, a reputation for fairness and for holding the arm-twisting type of leadership to a minimum.

Senator Byrd maintained a low profile in relations with the White House through much of the year, tending to business in the Senate and leaving to others vocal criticism of Mr. Carter's occasional blunders in dealing with Congress. While Tip O'Neill several times publicly criticized Mr. Carter and the White House staff for real or fancied errors, Senator Byrd's harshest open reproof occurred when he accused the President of "overreacting" to early setbacks in the passage of the energy package in the House.

But the Senator demonstrated that he was anything but a cream puff in the fall of 1977 when the Senate came into direct conflict with the President and the House on gas deregulation. The House had voted for continued regulation of the wellhead price of gas and for expanding controls to intrastate sales; the Senate had before it a bill that would end price regulation at the wellhead. Senators Metzenbaum of Ohio and Abourezk of South Dakota, representing the party's far left, attempted to block the bill with a filibuster. In a complex bit of maneuvering the Majority Leader managed to enlist the help of Vice President Mondale, himself a former member of the Senate's liberal wing and now the Senate's presiding officer. The filibuster was choked off, evoking outrage from Senators Metzenbaum and Abourezk, and gas deregulation passed the Senate. The confrontation cost Mr. Byrd some Senate support, but it also confirmed that he was a leader to be reckoned with by any Senator or President.

The other dominant figure in the 95th Congress was Russell B. Long of Louisiana, chairman of the Senate Finance Committee. The Finance Committee screens every piece of legislation that involves taxation, which means most of the important pieces of legislation the Senate considers. Reams of newspaper copy have been written about Senator Long's political skills, which have been assessed as a product of quick intelligence and charisma. He is much admired and well liked in Congress, despite his formidable ability to manipulate legislation to suit his own tastes and those of his constituencies. As with any other group of professionals, politicians admire the true pro, and Mr. Long comes as close to that description as any of the great names of the past, including such luminaries as Lyndon Baines Johnson, Arthur H. Vandenberg, and the redoubtable Sam Rayburn of Texas.

Senator Long, as with most successful politicians, is a master of the kind of subtle and even humorous repartee that says one thing and means the opposite. He once told a group of reporters at a cocktail party, "Call me anything you want to, boys, but don't call me powerful." Of course, Senator Long and all the reporters knew that he was powerful, and in the dozen years he has chaired the Finance Committee, that is the adjective that has most often been used to describe him.

Mr. Long's counterpart in the House is the chairman of the Ways and Means Committee, which since the retirement of Wilbur Mills has been headed by Al Ullman of Oregon. Mr. Mills, also usually described as "powerful" during his tenure, was a frequent match for Mr. Long in those situations in which the House and Senate were at odds over a tax bill and it was up to the two committees to work out a compromise. Mr. Ullman is no pushover, but he lacks the experience and expertise of Mr. Long.

Time magazine of November 7, 1977 said that Mr. Long has raised the art of political horse-trading to the highest level in living congressional memory, leaving his imprint on every piece of tax legislation since 1966. One of his favorite ploys is to load bills with amendments and then to bargain away those he doesn't really want in return for support for those he wants to keep. He once had said in 1971 that "My impression is that we've been successful in persuading the House to take about two-thirds of the things we initiate. And I wouldn't expect to do any better than that no matter who I was conferring with."

Mr. Long showed some early exasperation with Mr. Carter's congressional liaison team, which he seemed to feel was not sufficiently cognizant of the role Congress plays in making important national decisions. At one White House meeting early in the new administration, the Senator introduced himself with amusing irony, saying "My name is Russell Long and I am chairman of the Senate Finance Committee," as if addressing a group of dull schoolboys who might not have heard of Russell Long.

It did not take long for the administration to hear more of Russell Long in 1977, however. It soon learned that the Senator had his own ideas about all four major subjects that the administration had hoped to address in its first year: tax reform, Social Security, welfare, and energy. The administration's Social Security bill was heavily reworked in Congress, welfare was shelved, and late in the year the administration prudently decided not to put a tax-reform package on the table after hearing reactions to some of its preliminary proposals, such as an increase in capital-gains taxes.

Energy was where the big battle of 1977 was fought, and this was a subject very dear indeed to Senator Long's heart. He is, of course, from an oil- and gas-producing state and has long been regarded as a friend of oil and gas producers, particularly the independent producers who command more votes that the big oil companies. He had long favored gas deregulation and had been annoyed, along with producing-state governors, when President Carter reneged on his campaign promise to work for that end. Senator Long had won support for gas deregulation in the Senate in 1976, only to see it defeated by a narrow margin in the House, and he was instrumental in pushing it through the Senate again in 1977.

He and his committee also took a hard look at the other provisions of the energy package. Mr. Long, for example, wanted to have revenues from the wellhead tax on crude oil used in part to encourage oil and gas exploraiton. He was not much concerned with the seeming inconsistency of the government's taking money away from producers and then giving it back to them. Mr. Long's focus, as always, was on politics, not economic efficiency.

And indeed, for all of Mr. Long's vaunted skills as a politician, he can be strongly criticized for the end products of his bargains. Though he has been able to blunt some of the more wrong-headed liberal initiatives for taxing and spending vast quantities of money, it has often been at the cost of piling more and more complexities onto the already overloaded body of federal law. As we mention later, his successful efforts in promoting "workfare," whereby recipients of the various welfare benefits would be required to seek jobs, have disintegrated into something of a sham and may be seriously distorting unemployment statistics, giving policymakers the impression that unemployment is higher than it actually is.

In short, Mr. Long, for all his moderating influence, is not a long-range strategist with some clearly defined goal of drawing government back from its pervasive intervention in the nation's economic life. Rather, he is a tactician, intent upon winning battles for his constituencies and maintaining his role as one of the Senate's most effective professionals.

And indeed, the same can be said of most of the strong leaders of the Senate and House. They work more within the context of those bodies than with any broad view of where the country might or should be heading. The most successful leaders, men like Mr. O'Neill and Mr. Long, are successful because they have mastered the complex bartering process that takes place in the Congress. Mr. O'Neill, after all, was trained in one of the hardest schools of politics in the world, the Boston system. And Mr. Long comes from a political family that produced one of the most powerful politicians ever to be seen in this country, Huey Long.

Such people have abilities that allow them to rise to the top in a marketplace where votes are the currency and legislation is the product. Some politicians who have come to Washington in recent years have found themselves repelled by this process. Senator Edward Zorinsky of Nebraska, newly elected in 1976, was so sickened by all the wheeling and dealing that he talked publicly for a while of resigning and going back home to Omaha, where he had been a successful mayor. Some of the young members of the House have a reputation as antipoliticians, making a career of running against Congress back home but, very often at the same time, finally voting for new ways to expand government influence.

So far, there is very little sign of any of this aversion's translating itself into a movement to dismantle government influence and power. The political marketplace has a dynamic of its own. The billion-dollar Congress is here to stay. And Mr. Carter, even if he had had the fullest intentions of fulfilling his campaign promises and trying to arrest the momentum of Washington, would have had a very difficult time of it. As it turned out, he had a difficult time anyway, but only because his own prescriptions for expanding government complexity became a bean feast on the political bargaining table.

CHAPTER EIGHT
ENERGY AND INTERVENTION

This is a resource problem. We've shot the resource.—John O'Leary, head of the Federal Energy Administration, May 1977.

PRESIDENT CARTER'S FIRST YEAR IN OFFICE HAD ONE OVERRID-
ing theme: energy. He produced an energy plan, a scant 90 days after
he assumed office, that almost turned into a debacle. It weakened
public support for his administration, cost him the confidence of business, and was torn to pieces in Congress in much the way puppies
might rip the stuffing out of a rag doll.

Part of the problem was advice, such as the chapter-opening
quote, from people like Mr. O'Leary; the United States had not "shot"
its energy resources—it was merely, through inadvisable government
policies, destroying energy development.

Another part of the problem was the President's attempts to strike
a compromise between free-marketers and interventionists, which
ended up pleasing neither side. And further muddying the water was
Mr. Carter's insistence on interpreting every problem as a "moral"
issue, in this case his constant assertions that Americans were ex-
travagant and wasteful of energy, a proposition that betrays a fundamental misunderstanding of both human nature and economics.

All these misconceptions were factored into the most far-
reaching, complex, and costly resource program ever brought before
the American people. Had it not been waylaid by Congress it could
have been a national disaster. Some parts of it will no doubt become
law (and may have already by the time this book sees print), but other
main features are dead and buried.

One thing can be said on the President's behalf: the energy problem was not of his own making. It derived from shifts in energy-supply
patterns that had been complicated by mistaken government policies
going back more than a decade. As with so many of the problems of
the mid-1970s, it had its origins most specifically in the inflationary
pressures of the late 1960s and the economic controls in response to
those pressures in the early 1970s.

But to get a better understanding it is necessary to go back a bit
further. The starting point would be the famous Phillips decision by the
Supreme Court in 1954, which gave the Federal Power Commission
the power to apply price controls to natural-gas prices at the wellhead.
The decision settled a suit brought by the state of Wisconsin against the
Phillips Petroleum Company. The suit had charged that Phillips was
demanding too high a price for the gas it was supplying to the state.
The court never gave a particularly good reason for ruling as it did, but
it in effect established federal control of gas-producer prices and made

natural gas a much-sought-after cheap fuel. A vast pipeline network was built to supply gas to most parts of the country, supplanting such other energy sources as coal, oil, and manufactured gas. Anyone lucky enough to be hooked up to the pipeline system could count on getting a clean, convenient fuel at low prices.

This created no particular supply problems in the 1950s and early 1960s. Drillers never knew whether they would find oil or gas or both and, since there was strong demand for oil, which was not under price controls, there was plenty of drilling and plenty of both oil and gas being discovered at relatively low costs. There also was a very low rate of inflation by comparison with today, which meant that most producers could get remunerative prices for their gas even if the FPC did not make very frequent changes in the wellhead price ceilings. There was, in fact, so much fuel being produced in the United States that the government applied import quotas to protect domestic producers from excessive competition from oil brought in from abroad by the big international oil companies. And the Texas Railroad Commission used another lever against competition by controlling the "allowable" rate at which oil could be pumped in that big producing state.

The consumer suffered little from these forms of market interference. Oil products might have been even cheaper and gas more expensive had these controls not existed, and the United States might well have conserved both resources by importing more oil from abroad in those years. But in a noninflationary era the problem was of more interest to market economists than to the general public. The rapid expansion of automobile usage, and all that meant in changing and improving living styles of Americans by giving them greater mobility and more personal living space, was promoted by a plentiful supply of fuel.

In the 1960s, however, several things began to happen. The oil companies began to find it more attractive, in terms of costs, to develop crude oil resources abroad rather than in the United States. Huge fields could be developed in such places as Saudi Arabia, Kuwait, and Libya, and the cost of pumping such oil, even after local taxes, was only pennies a barrel. The international oil companies found production from these fields so profitable that they sharply expanded their refining and marketing operations around the world to provide outlets for the production. And through assiduous lobbying they managed to get the United States import quotas raised (they were finally removed altogether in the early 1970s).

Exploratory drilling for oil and gas in the United States declined, meanwhile, to roughly 7500 wells in 1970 from 12,000 in 1960. Oil and gas were becoming harder and more expensive to find in this country and were subject to higher taxes and drill-site leasing costs. And, of course, natural gas was under price controls that reduced the attractiveness of drilling in search of gas alone.

The result of this shift to foreign production is explained by Alan Greenspan, former chairman of the Council of Economic Advisers under President Ford. About 1970, he guesses, the United States margin of unutilized oil capacity, which previously could be manipulated by United States authorities to regulate the world price of oil, evaporated. The United States was no longer the marginal oil supplier to the world it had been for most of the twentieth century.[1]

Up until then, the Organization of Petroleum Exporting Countries (OPEC) had been a relatively impotent body, with its 11 members (there now are 13) spending most of their time wrangling among themselves at periodic meetings at the Vienna headquarters. But by 1970 several things were happening. Libya's King Idris, who had been relatively benign toward the oil companies, had been ousted by a revolutionary colonel, Muammar Khaddafy. Iraq had been seizing control of the oilfields in its country. The Shah of Iran had become more assertive. And suddenly, the OPEC nations became aware that the United States no longer had the power to regulate world supplies and prices.

OPEC had become the marginal supplier. And since the OPEC nations, unlike the United States, produced far more oil than they consumed, they were interested not in cheap energy but in making energy as expensive as possible. All that was necessary was for at least one of their numbers to be willing to curtail supply when necessary. Saudi Arabia, so underpopulated and insular-minded that it did not have a strong thirst for dollars and, at any rate, figured that oil in the ground was as good as dollars in a bank, proved to be the state most willing to regulate supplies.

The OPEC nations could hardly have asked for a more cooperative approach from the United States, unintentional though it was. The depreciation of the dollar from 1967 to 1971 (by some 12% in purchasing power) helped to unite the OPEC producers. They were, after all, receiving most of their revenues in dollars, which were kept on deposit in New York banks. Why should they settle for less real purchasing power when they had the power to do something about it? OPEC showed its first real power by demanding and getting joint negotiations with the major oil companies at Tehran in 1971 and there winning what at that time looked like substantial price concessions. The United States, incidentally, conveniently ignored its own antitrust laws to permit the oil companies to engage in the exercise.

But the biggest boost for OPEC was of a different type. In August of 1971, President Nixon, at the urging of Congress, put the United States economy under wage and price controls in response to inflationary pressures and a large trade deficit. Shortly thereafter, the Federal Reserve Board, with strong political urging, began to increase the United States money supply even more rapidly than before. The combination of controls and monetary stimulus created a false boom in the United States, sending consumer demand soaring while temporarily preventing the heavy demand from being translated into price increases. Because the United States consumes about one third of the world's energy, a boom in the United States has a significant impact on the world oil market. United States crude-oil and oil-product demand climbed 18% from 1970 to 1973. And because by now the low drilling activity of the 1960s was being felt, United States oil imports soared 145% in those years, supplying 21.1% of United States needs in 1973 compared with 10.2% in 1970.

Some other things were also happening in the United States economy. The Clean Air Act of 1970 was requiring electric utilities to switch from soft coal to oil or gas in their power plants to reduce air pollution. Other environmental pressures were making it increasingly difficult for oil and gas producers to find drilling and refinery sites. Nuclear power development was beginning to encounter opposition from the environmental lobbies. And, of course, price controls, now applied both to crude oil and natural gas, continued to make stateside drilling unattractive. Stateside exploratory drilling remained languid throughout the period of price controls before finally surging upward again in 1974.

We all know, of course, what happened. In October 1973, while Israel was fighting Egypt, Iraq, and Syria during the Yom Kippur war, the Arab nations slapped an embargo on crude-oil shipments to the United States, which had aided Israel. The embargo, though brief, showed the OPEC nations how much price leverage they could exercise through restricting supply. They were able to quadruple their prices. The average price of crude oil imported into the United States leaped to $11.11 a barrel in 1974 from $3.41 in 1973. The United

States for the first time in its history, suffered gasoline shortages. Lines formed at service stations, which displayed green flags when they had gasoline and red flags when they were dry.

By this time, price controls in this country had collapsed under the pressure of inflation. The United States had lost two years during which its supply industries could have been adapting to demand rather than being suppressed by price controls and environmental restrictions.

There was one obvious policy for the United States as a way of dealing with the OPEC price increases: free the United States energy industry from the price controls that remained on this most fundamental of all industries after most other controls had been dismantled, and ease up on some of the environmental rules temporarily. This would have shifted energy development back to the United States, where independent developers and even some major oil companies would have found it attractive to develop resources at the new $11.11 world price. The United States energy industry would have burgeoned under the $11 price umbrella, forcing OPEC to cut production more and more to maintain the world price. There would never be $3 oil again but oil would come back to somewhere close to its natural price, given the fact that the United States dollar in 1974 was only worth 62.5% of its 1967 level.

Instead, the United States did exactly the opposite. Mr. Nixon announced a half-baked "energy independence" policy, featuring continued price controls on domestic crude oil and natural gas and a complex bureaucracy for trying to square controlled prices in this country with uncontrolled prices in the world market. The Federal Energy Office, later to become the Federal Energy Administration (FEA) and still later to become a part of a huge new government Department of Energy, was born in the Emergency Petroleum Allocation Act (EPAA) of 1973. William E. Simon, a bright young man from Treasury who had formerly been a highly successful investment banker, was put in charge.

Through all this period hysterical estimates were coming from Congressman and government officials that if energy prices were decontrolled, gasoline would go to a dollar a gallon, there would be "obscene" profits for the oil companies, and the nation's poor would be the principal victims. Four years later, when heating oil and gasoline were in fact being set by world-market prices despite the fact that domestic crude oil and natural gas were still under price controls, gasoline could still be purchased at 60 cents a gallon in those states that had not significantly raised gasoline taxes. And in countries, such as Germany, that simply allowed domestic prices to adapt to the world level, there was none of the "shortage" hysteria that infected the United States.

The FEO–FEA started with an "allocation" program, attempting to ensure, through massive paperwork and interference with the complex oil-industry logistics, that refiners continued to serve their traditional customers. The problem with this was that consumption patterns don't remain constant. Some customers drop out and new ones come in. Before the FEA, this could be handled with a phone call, but now previously simple transactions became three-way operations involving customer, supplier, and government and enormous waste of time and expense.

Allocations were followed up by something called "entitlements." With crude-oil imports continuing to grow (they roughly doubled between 1973 and 1977 to reach nearly 40% of total United States consumption), it became evident that some refiners would be at a competitive disadvantage because of their heavier dependence on imported, more expensive crude. So refiners using a larger-than-average amount of domestic cheap crude were required, in effect, to pay an equalizing amount to refiners who were using a less-than-average amount. It should be noted here that Congress, being the kind of bargaining emporium it is, arranged to make some refiners a little more equal than others. Small refiners received slightly larger entitlements than would be necessary merely to equalize their costs. In other words, they obtained a subsidy from large refiners merely through exercise of political clout.

The economic effect of entitlements was to tax domestic production in order to subsidize imports. It should not be surprising that imports continued rising. The secondary effect was to expand the FEA bureaucracy further and to create more constituencies—the small refiners, for example—with a vested interest in a continuation of federal controls.

It should be noted here that a peculiar argument came into play in the early stages of the controls process. It was held that it would be a mistake to free prices because domestic production costs still would be higher than OPEC costs. Thus OPEC could always jerk the rug out from under domestic producers by sharply cutting prices. And imports would flow in at an even faster rate.

The strange rationale in support of this deliberate idea of keeping energy prices high and discouraging domestic production was a national security argument. If the United States became too dependent on imported crude it would be constantly vulnerable to economic blackmail from the Arab nations, for example, in the event of renewed hostilities in the Middle East. It was never explained how this country would become less vulnerable through discouraging domestic energy production than through encouraging it.

The obvious solution to the security problem was to build a crude-oil stockpile, and this was finally undertaken after much environmental hassling, making use of salt domes in Louisiana for storing crude purchased by the government. The stockpile now being built will ultimately reach a level to give the United States a six months' or larger reserve supply, which is deemed to be enough to allow the country to weather anything short of a major war, in which case the nation would have to depend on its military superiority to obtain oil supplies at any rate.

Some recognition was given to the problem of encouraging domestic supply. The United States set up a two-tier price system for domestic crude, controlling previously discovered crude at low prices and granting producers higher prices for newly discovered crude and expensive oil gained from "stripping" old wells of their remaining supplies. Thus there were now three tiers in all, counting the price of imports. And the FEA bureaucracy in charge of managing this economic horror chamber continued to grow. Even some OPEC oil ministers looked with amazement on this strange exercise in this country, wondering if it was really up to them to protect the United States from its own folly.

In late 1975 President Ford had an opportunity to bring most of this regulatory nonsense to a halt. The 1973 Emergency Act had expired and Congress had passed an extension, called the Energy Policy and Conservation Act (EPCA) of 1975. If the President had chosen to veto it, in all likelihood the FEA would have quietly passed out of existence, and the oil industry would have returned to the status of any other industry, competing in world markets and developing resources wherever costs, transportation efficiencies, taxes, availability of capital, and political risks were justified. There had already been a pickup in drilling in the United States under the higher controlled prices, and there is every reason to believe that the increase would have accelerated under decontrol.

Mr. Ford, however, acting on the advice of his ambitious young FEA administrator, Frank Zarb, chose to sign the bill. The advice from Mr. Zarb was that if Mr. Ford didn't accept the EPCA, Congress would soon come up with something worse. It was doubtful advice. Congress, too, had become weary of all the regulatory nonsense and was less susceptible than it had once been to the arguments on behalf of continued federal intervention. At the very least, a veto was a risk worth taking. Once the control system was dismantled it would be difficult to put it back together again.

The new EPCA called for the "phasing out" of price regulations on crude oil over a 40-month period, although authorizing a further extension "if necessary." The FEA was instructed to make its tiers conform to a national average price of $7.66 a barrel. It could raise the average up to 10% a year on its own authority; anything above that would have to go to Congress for a possible veto. It was never explained how this would phase out controls if the world-market price also went up at something like 10% a year. The FEA held the price of old oil at $5.25 a barrel, and set the price of "new," "stripper," and "released" oil at $11.28. ("Released" oil, by the way, was oil exempted from the "old" oil price by a formula that gave producers credit for increasing production above a 1972 base level.)

The trouble with this new formula, as would be obvious to any sixth-grade arithmetic student, was that by controlling the "average" price, Congress had arranged that the ceiling price of "old" crude could go down as producers developed more new crude. By 1977 the old crude ceiling had declined to $5.16 a barrel from $5.25. A Presidential Task Force study on Federal Energy Administration Regulation, edited by Paul W. MacAvoy, who had served on President Ford's Council of Economic Advisers, likened this to rent controls: "The crude pricing regulations are today [1977] essentially 'rent controls,' in that they are intended to prevent owners of lower cost old petroleum from gaining wealth as the market price of crude increases toward the world price of crude set by OPEC, while their own production costs remain static. At the same time, producers of new crude are permitted to receive prices approximating the world price of petroleum so that there will be an incentive to bring on line petroleum whose cost of production approaches the world selling price. This rationale is to be distinguished from the earlier purely anti-inflationary goals of the Economic Stabilization Program. Its rules were aimed at holding down prices and making businesses absorb increasing costs."[2]

In other words, the EPCA was designed to prevent "windfall" profits from accruing to oil producers, an argument to be used again by President Carter in support of his own energy program. The cost of preventing "windfall" profits was an enormous, inefficient, and far more expensive energy bureaucracy.

The task force study discovered that since the inception of the regulatory program in 1973 almost $500 million had been spent just for direct regulatory costs. The cost to refiners of meeting FEA administrative requirements were estimated at $570 million a year.

"Additionally," said the report, "businessmen must apply to the FEA for permission to engage in normal business transactions. For instance, about 2,000 to 3,000 cases per month were filed with FEA regional offices in late 1975 and early 1976."[3]

In addition to these direct costs there are hidden costs represented by reduced competition in the petroleum industry. Consumers have noticed, for example, that since the FEA came into being, gasoline pumps in various neighborhoods very often carry widely varying prices. If there were no market distortions, dealers would not be able to sustain such variations.

The task force conclusion, in short: *The FEA's costs outweigh any benefits it might yield to the consumer.*[4]

If the petroleum industry were receiving those "windfall profits" instead of their going into bureaucratic waste, it might swell reported profits of oil companies temporarily until competition brought them back into line. But most of the profits would go into capital formation, something badly needed, as we discuss in a later chapter. This would be true whether the oil companies kept them in their own coffers or paid them out to millions of stockholders, which include pension funds and college endowment funds as well as rich tycoons. Most of the money would go into investment, which is used to expand productive capacity and productive efficiency and thus provide new jobs. That sounds like a self-serving oil-industry argument, but there is no way of avoiding its truth. The real choice is between jobs for oil drillers or factory workers and jobs for federal regulators and industry accountants and lawyers. That gives some clue to why there is so much political steam in support of continued federal regulation. The bureaucratic class is better represented in Washington than blue-collar workers.

A powerful argument can also be made that decontrol would not raise prices for consumers, at least not beyond the levels that would occur anyway through general inflation. Another provision of the EPCA was to permit the government to decontrol petroleum-product prices. The Ford administration did, in fact, decontrol No. 2 fuel oil, which is used mainly for home heating. And there was very little need to decontrol gasoline prices because prices set by even distorted market competition were well below prices refiners and filling stations were permitted to charge under existing ceilings.

In short, the two major oil products used by the consumer, heating oil and gasoline, are not controlled now. According to two Rand Corporation economists, Charles E. Phelps and Rodney T. Smith, these prices are actually being set by the world market, by virtue of the fact that heating oil and gasoline imported into the United States from markets where crude oil prices are uncontrolled represent the "marginal" supply of these two products.[5] In economic lingo, prices are set on the margin, meaning that the price of a commodity will be determined by how much it costs to get the last barrelful needed to equalize supply and demand.

The Phelps–Smith argument is not universally accepted, even by oil-industry economists. The critics complain that there is not enough refined product coming in to the United States to set marginal prices. But Phelps and Smith stick to their guns and have assembled a substantial body of comparative price data for the United States and other nations to back up their contention. Of course, everyone knows that gasoline costs are considerably higher in most European countries than in the United States, but it should be remembered that prices at the gas pump in both countries include excise taxes, so it is not possible to make a comparison by mere observation.

The Phelps–Smith argument had two dramatic implications: (1) the FEA wasn't protecting consumers from anything; (2) the Carter wellhead tax, designed to increase fuel costs and thus encourage conservation, would do nothing of the sort.

Another implication, less important but interesting from a political point of view, is that decontrol would not particularly raise overall profits in the oil industry. It would merely reverse a process whereby controls transferred profits from oil production to oil refining. Again the question of vested interests raises its head when you try to determine why the oil industry itself, for example, was by no means unified in demanding an end to controls. It is partly a question of whether your major business is refining or production.

At any rate, President Ford muffed his chance to decontrol crude oil. Two months later, he also muffed a chance to deregulate natural gas. A move in the House to deregulate new natural gas—a plan that the Senate had already approved—failed because the White House did not muster a full complement of Republican Congressmen to vote for it.

The background of this vote, as with the crude-oil debacle, is intriguing. As we have mentioned earlier, wellhead regulation of natural gas had its origins with the 1954 Phillips decision. Pipeline transportation charges also are regulated, of course, as are local utilities. The Phillips case closed the one loophole in the regulatory chain, but only so far as interstate commerce was concerned. Natural gas that did not move in interstate commerce remained unregulated.

In the late 1960s this dichotomy began to have an interesting effect. Before, intrastate and controlled interstate prices had remained close together. But then the intrastate price began to rise rapidly in reflection of diminished drilling and rising demand. Since local utilities write their contracts with suppliers for up to 20 years, the spread did not have an immediate effect on supplies to utilities that buy gas interstate. But it didn't take large industrial users of natural gas long to see that if the trend continued, interstate sources would dry up. A good many chose to move their operations into gas-producing states to insure supplies.

Thus demand for intrastate gas continued to rise, and so did the prices in new supply contracts. By 1976 the price of intrastate gas in new contracts was at times exceeding $2 a thousand cubic feet (MCF) whereas the interstate price, under Federal Power Commission control, was 52 cents.

The result of this price spread was that gas producers bringing in new wells first sought a buyer in their own states, and only if they could not find one did they turn to an interstate customer. Gas consumers in the nonproducing states began to have serious worries about supply. Some Northeast utilities had to turn to expensive liquefied natural gas hauled all the way from Algeria in pressurized tankers.

A curious political turnabout began to take place. Some of these utilities, The Brooklyn Union Gas Company in New York, for example, switched from being supporters of FPC wellhead-price regulation to being opponents of such regulation. They knew that if the present situation continued they might have trouble supplying their customers. In places like Texas and Louisiana, consumers who had been lured south by the promise of plentiful supplies were opposed to interstate deregulation on the well-justified theory that this would enable the Northern consumers to compete with them for available supplies.

This interesting realignment came to a head in the House in February 1976 when a freshman Texas Congressman, Robert Krueger, introduced a deregulation amendment similar to the one for which Senators Lloyd Bentsen of Texas and James B. Pearson of Kansas had won approval in the Senate. Ths bill would deregulate new contracts for natural gas in the interstate market. Mr. Krueger, in effect, represented gas producers. And one of his principal opponents turned out to be another Texas Congressman, Bob Eckhardt, who was representing Texas consumers.

Mr. Krueger was able to marshall support from a large bloc of industrial and agricultural natural-gas users in the North who used gas for everything from grain-drying to making aluminum. They, like Brooklyn Union, were worried about their supplies. It was cheaper to pay more for gas than to buy it from Algeria or move to Texas.

Mr. Eckhardt had on his side a diverse collection of Northern utilities that hadn't caught on to the problem yet; the AFL–CIO, which was to see a number of its members thrown out of work by Northern gas shortages only a year later; Congressman Harley Staggers from West Virginia, a coal-producing state; and an ad hoc group of interventionists that called itself the Energy Action Committee. The only thing interesting about this last group was the fact that they had somehow enlisted screen actor Paul Newman to plead for their cause on the illogical grounds that higher wellhead prices somehow would be worse for Northern consumers than buying gas from Algeria.

The result was a squeaker. The House did not actually vote on the Krueger amendment. Rather, it voted on a substitute, put up by his opponents, that would have brought intrastate gas under controls along with interstate gas. This amendment, sponsored by Representative Neal Smith of Iowa, had many defects, but it was the best the Eckhardt forces could muster. And when the final vote was tallied the Smith amendment had won 205–201, with 26 absent. Most of these absentees were Republicans in favor of the Krueger amendment, or who at least had said they were. No one knows to this day whether these Congressmen simply stayed away in fear of a bad reaction back home, whether the White House was guilty of sloppy generalship, or whether the White House had sold out the gas-decontrol forces. The White House version was that its Congressional liaison men had been guilty of sloppy generalship, which is a damaging enough admission.

The Smith amendment went no further. It was not acceptable to the Senate. The vote was simply an affirmation of the status quo. However, the idea of regulating intrastate gas, despite its implications as a further erosion of the federal system, would pop up again in Mr. Carter's energy package.

One of the troubling ironies of the natural-gas deregulation vote was a seeming inability of some Northern Congressmen, such as Andrew Maguire of New Jersey and Toby Moffett of Connecticut, to understand that deregulation would have been in the best interests of their own constituents. Not only would the North have avoided gas shortages in the frigid winter to come in 1976–1977 and the economic losses in plant shutdowns and more costly substitute fuels such as propane, but there was no certain evidence that consumer costs would rise appreciably from deregulation.

The reasons for this are several. First of all, the cost to consumers represents the price of all the gas moving through the pipeline. Only a relatively small percentage of that at any time will represent new-contract gas. Most of it will be gas priced under contracts written as much as 20 years earlier, at prices that were then well below 50 cents a thousand cubic feet. So even a sharp increase in new gas prices does not raise the total wellhead cost of gas dramatically in the short run.

Second, the wellhead cost of gas is only a small part of the cost to Northern consumers. W. Philip Gramm, Professor of Economics at Texas A&M University, estimates that 81% of the residential gas bill in the Northeast goes for pipeline and distribution costs. When the interstate pipelines are running well below capacity, as they have been in recent years, it means that pipeline amortization costs, in terms of each thousand cubic feet of gas transported, must rise.

Professor Gramm cites a study by Zinder and Associates filed with the FPC estimating that if the 52-cent-per-MCF (thousand cubic feet) gas price in effect at the time of the 1976 vote had been maintained, the interstate pipelines would be 45% empty by 1980; the average wellhead price, for old and new gas, would be 37 cents; the pipeline transportation cost would be $2.03 and the point-of-use cost would be $2.40; and the unavailable gas would have to be made up with electricity, fuel oil, synthetic gas, and imported liquefied gas costing over $4.

On the other hand, with a $2 new-gas price and a full pipeline the average wellhead price would be $1.12 and the cost of pipeline transportation would be $1.27. The cost at point of consumption would be

$2.39, about the same as the estimated cost with a 52-cent new-gas cost and 55% utilization of the pipelines. Over a longer period, other estimates indicate, deregulation would actually be cheaper.

Now, the response of the regulators to this argument is that the higher price would not result in a substantial enough increase in production to fill the pipelines, so the Northern consumers would lose both ways. That is a highly dubious argument. With total energy prices rising sharply from 1972 to 1975, the price of natural gas in the unregulated intrastate market of Texas climbed to $2.20 from 75 cents. But in that same period the drilling trend of the '60s, in which the number of natural-gas producers nationwide had dropped from 18,000 in 1956 to 4000 in 1971, was reversed in Texas. Drilling rigs began to come back to the state, and in 1975 there were 2275 new wells completed in Texas compared with only 1056 in 1971. The average wellhead price in Texas fell back to $1.76.

The same effect of higher prices can be seen nationwide. After the deregulation defeat the Ford administration prevailed on the FPC to raise the interstate wellhead price to $1.42 per MCF from 52 cents, over violent objections and legal action from the Energy Action Committee and other lobbying groups. By October 1977 the *New York Times* was reporting an "unexpected" pause in the three-year decline in natural-gas production and prospects that output would begin climbing again.

The idea that we are "running out" of natural gas also got a severe jolt in the spring of 1977 from within the government itself, causing some considerable embarrassment to Mr. Carter and his energy planners, who had adopted the "sky is falling" approach in selling the President's draconian measures. In January a group of some 70 people in the Energy Research and Development Administration (ERDA), now a part of the new Department of Energy, was assembled to do a "Market Oriented Program Planning Study," later to be known as MOPPS.

The idea of this study was to predict how much natural gas would be brought forth at various price levels. In other words, the MOPPS people, drawing on estimates from all the industry and independent gas experts they could find, were trying to simulate a free market in which higher prices would bring forth new supplies and thus balance supply with demand.

The results were startling in light of all the scare talk about how natural-gas supplies had been depleted. The MOPPS study found that there were trillions of cubic feet of harder-to-produce gas reserves that could not be developed economically at $1.42 but could be brought forth at prices above that level.

The largest reserves, estimated at 20,000 to 50,000 trillion cubic feet, were "geopressured" gas, dissolved in water at depths of 15,000 feet or more both offshore and onshore. This gas is relatively expensive to obtain because it is not only deep but must also be separated from brine and the brine pumped back into the ground to prevent earth subsidence. But an ERDA pilot project in Louisiana was already demonstrating that the technical problems were not insurmountable. There were other large deposits of hard-to-get gas to be found in the Devonian shales of Appalachia and in the "tight sand" deposits in the West.

The Wall Street Journal, coming upon this study despite the fact that it was not released publicly, published an editorial titled "1,001 Years of Natural Gas"[6] that made the point that the nation's problem was not a shortage of gas but a shortage of gas at artificially controlled prices. It argued that at even a price of $2.25 some of the easier-to-get reserves would be practical to develop and there would always be those "exotic" sources, such as geopressured gas, as a more expensive backstop when the easy resources were depleted.

And considering the relative cheapness of natural gas when compared with other fuels, plus the already existing inefficiencies mentioned above that result from under-production, a $2.25 price is still a bargain. Americans currently pay about $2.05 per million BTUs for natural gas delivered to their homes, compared with $3 for fuel oil and about $10 for electricity.

Public exposure of the MOPPS study produced an interesting reaction. ERDA's management, under top administration pressure, sat down and rewrote the study in five days to make it look less optimistic, although never quite destroying the central finding that there would be more gas at higher prices. An ERDA delegation, headed by the then-acting ERDA administrator Robert Fri, called on the Wall Street Journal to explain the revisions. There was also a delegation from Exxon Corporation, which had shown a curious ambivalence toward federal regulation for complex reasons perhaps best explained by the fact that Exxon held ERDA contracts for more exotic forms of energy development such as coal gasification. The MOPPS people, who had so innocently tried to simulate a free market, found themselves in something equivalent to political Coventry for their bad political judgment.

The *Journal* followed up with an editorial entitled "ERDAgate!"[7] which concluded that the MOPPS tempest showed "how many vested interests need the energy crisis. The President needs a war to fight. Without an energy crisis the energy bureaucracies cannot grow. The energy companies are turning into a regulated industry, all of which try to dampen innovation. We now hear energy czar James Schlesinger bragging that privately most companies do not favor deregulation. This is not yet true, but in time the proposed policies certainly would reduce the oil companies to the state of the airlines."

One effect of the MOPPS episode, however, was to dampen administration rhetoric about the United States using up all its natural resources. Such a notion was not only exploded by MOPPS but by any number of other studies. A United Nations report, made available in September of 1977, concluded that published estimates of recoverable oil throughout the world cover perhaps 1% of nature-made oil in place. The other 99% can be recovered via the law of supply and demand, the report said. Dr. Joseph Barnea of Israel, a longtime UN natural-resources specialist, said in the report that "As prices expand, the natural resource base expands. As taxes and costs rise, the resource base declines." He meant of course, that governments have it within their power to apply costs that suppress resource development if they are silly enough to do so. The upshot of the UN report: the world is not going to run out of oil and gas in any future time span that needs to be of concern to present generations.[8]

And, interestingly enough, the price Americans pay for energy remains lower than it was in 1950 despite the OPEC trauma, after you take into account the depreciation of the dollar. A report by the Institute for Contemporary Studies in San Francisco shows that the average price in the United States for a gallon of gasoline in 1976, including taxes, was 59.5 cents. That compared with 63.3 cents, in terms of 1976 dollars, in 1950. On the same basis, electricity had dropped to $10.23 per million BTUs from $20 and natural gas to $1.98 from $2.01.

It should not go without mention that the big energy battles of recent years, though involving billions of dollars in special interests and all the political bargaining that goes along with that kind of money, were also fought in an ideological climate. At least one analyst, Professor Edward J. Mitchell of the University of Michigan, believes that ideology may be even more important than the bargaining.

Writing in the *Wall Street Journal* of July 7, 1977, Professor

Mitchell said, "When people (Congressmen and their constituents) do not understand an issue they fall back on ideology. By ideology I mean that general body of beliefs you consult when you have to make a judgement on something you know little or nothing about. Since the energy issue is apparently beyond the ability or inclination of most people to understand, the debate is abstract and philosophical, that is, ideological."

Rating Congressmen by the voting "score" they have been given on the issues by the liberal-minded Americans for Democratic Action (ADA) and applying that to votes on energy deregulation, Professor Mitchell concluded that a "simple prediction rule which says that if a Congressman's ADA rating is 45% or higher he will vote against deregulation and if under 45% he will vote for deregulation would be correct in 361 out of 399 cases, or better than 90% of the time."

While Professor Mitchell's findings might be open to some challenge, there can be little doubt that the record of energy deregulation votes supports his thesis. The AFL–CIO pushed for continued regulation even though its own members were going to suffer from gas shortages. "Public interest" groups such as the Energy Action Committee have been in the thick of the deregulation battles, fighting for continued government regulation on the basis of half-baked economic analysis founded on the premise that government can successfully legislate economic relationships in much the same way that it can regulate traffic signals.

Part of the ideological input is simple antipathy toward private corporations, an attitude very much evident in the attempts by Ralph Nader and his various offshoot groups to expand federal control over the inner workings of business organizations. Then there is the "limits to growth" movement, which genuinely believes the Chicken Little cry that the sky is falling and we had best stop using resources and revert to a simple primitive life. There also are the environmental radicals, who have taken a perfectly legitimate political and economic position and carried it to ridiculous extremes, again with a view toward stopping economic development entirely, not just air and water pollution.

And finally, there is the view of the world that holds that price controls, no matter how badly they work, are a protection for the poor and the weak—they will ultimately transfer resources from the rich to the poor. No amount of persuasion will convince holders of this idea that controls usually merely transfer resources from a productive middle class to a nonproductive middle class.

Such attitudes are very much a part of the magnificent jumble of intense pressures that has come to bear on the legislative process. These conflicting pressures are very often found in individuals who see themselves as striving for a brave new world that will somehow manage to yield them peace, safety, and fairness despite economic stagnation and massive government bureaucratic power. Very central to this impossible dream is the notion that the energy problems of the 1970s were in our stars, not ourselves.

That does not stand up to sophisticated analysis. And yet, it was possible for one of Mr. Carter's chief energy aides, Mr. O'Leary, still to be saying in the spring of 1977 that we've "shot the resource." Our next chapter deals with how Mr. Carter fared with this kind of energy advice.

CHAPTER NINE

THE "NATIONAL ENERGY PLAN"

The diagnosis of the U.S. energy crisis is quite simple: demand for energy is increasing, while supplies of oil and natural gas are diminishing.—Introductory sentence to President Carter's "National Energy Plan."

AS THE PRECEDING CHAPTER SHOULD HAVE MADE CLEAR, the energy "crisis" was not simple at all. Indeed, supplies of domestically produced oil and natural gas had decreased, but not because of physical limits to supply, as the President's energy plan implied throughout in fashionable "limits to growth" style. Rather, the supply-demand imbalance, evident enough in the frigid February that followed Mr. Carter's inauguration, was the result of past government regulatory and inflationary policies.

In short, the energy plan was based on a false premise, for reasons we shortly explore. Rather than dismantling the government intervention that had so badly tangled the energy market, it proposed yet more government intervention on a scale even exceeding, in some ways, President Nixon's disastrous "New Economic Plan" of 1971. It proposed enormous taxes and capital costs for the American economy, somewhere on the order of $80 billion a year or 5% of the total GNP. It proposed over 100 new federal laws. Worst of all, it applied one of the biggest tax burdens to crude-oil production, which a rational energy plan would have attempted to encourage, not discourage.

Among the plan's major potential costs:

Gasoline taxes. The 4-cent-a-gallon federal gasoline tax would be raised by up to 5 cents a gallon each year that gasoline consumption exceeded stated targets, starting in 1979. The increments could reach a maximum of 50 cents. Potential cost to the public: $50 billion a year.

The "crude oil equalization tax". It would represent the difference between the controlled domestic prices of crude and the world price. Consumers would thus become "accustomed" to paying the world price, but producers would get none of the extra money. Potential tax: $12 billion to $15 billion.

The "gas guzzler" tax. Penalty taxes ranging as high as $2488 would be applied to new cars with higher-than-standard fuel consumption. Rebates ranging as high as $493 would be made on cars with lower-than-standard fuel consumption. Possible cost: hard to guess, but potentially as high as $2 billion.

Coal conversion. Factories and electric utilities would be converted to using coal instead of oil and natural gas by a system of regulations and tax penalties. Potential cost: $15 billion to $20 billion.

Now, these are all very rough estimates. It could not be known, for example, whether gasoline consumption would rise sufficiently to trigger the full 50-cent tax, or how soon the auto industry would improve auto fuel consumption sufficiently to avoid the "gas guzzler" tax. It could not be known what coal conversion would really cost, given the physical limitations on operating new coal mines, building new railroads and rail cars to haul the coal, buying scrubbers and other antipollution equipment to cleanse coal burning emissions, and obtaining space and preparing sites to dispose of all the sludge that would result from the coal-cleansing operations. It was not known how much the extra demand might inflate coal prices (a potentially new area for federal regulation). Appallingly, the energy planners had little more idea of potential consequences than the public.

The gas-guzzler tax might cost less than $50 billion, coal conversion perhaps more than $20 billion. But these were only a part of the far-ranging package, and it was even harder to divine what some of the other parts might cost. For example, subpart 2 of Part E proposed a federal takeover of the role of state public utility commissions in setting electric utility rates unless the states were willing to convert to "marginal pricing." No one was quite sure what this meant, least of all the energy planners, but it probably meant that large users of power at hours when utilities normally experienced their highest loads would have to pay higher rates to cover the cost of installing electrical generating capacity to carry these "peak" loads. Joseph C. Swidler, a Washington consultant with long experience as a utility regulator, estimated that in one rate case alone, involving Commonwealth Edison in Chicago, marginal pricing, depending on how you did it, might raise rates to industrial and commercial customers by anywhere from $111 million to $493 million.[1]

The idea of federal rate making had a twofold purpose, both parts of which were based on ideas that had been kicking around in Congress for some time. It would prevent utilities in the various states and regions from competing with each other to attract industrial customers, a process that some Congressmen felt has hastened the migration of industry from the North to the South and Southwest. It would transfer electricity costs from homeowners to industry, where, of course, they would be hidden in the higher prices of consumer products. Consumers would thus think that Congress had done them a favor.

But there was more involved here than mere cost transfers. There would be big conversion costs. "Time-of-day" electric meters would be needed for marginal rate making, since rates would vary during hours of consumption. Apartment houses could no longer have a single meter; each apartment would need one. Utilities would be required to conduct home-insulation programs. Such costs to the consumer, of course, would represent bonanzas for the insulation and electric-meter industries.

The plan looked as if it had swept together every idea, tested or untested, that anyone had ever thought of for manipulating the energy market. The government would buy vans to transport federal workers to and from jobs as a "demonstration project"; there would be big ERDA expenditures on such doubtful projects as use of solar energy for large-scale power generation; the federal public-service employment program (CETA) would supply workers to help with insulation and weatherization efforts; and so forth, and so forth.

Now, the point here is not to make judgments on whether all these ideas were good or bad. Some might be good, some bad. The judgment that needs to be made is whether it is wise to take a large package of untested energy conservation ideas and write them into federal law, thus making necessary a further huge expansion of the regulatory bureaucracy to implement such laws.

Consumers are, after all, natural conservationists simply because, with only few exceptions, their resources are limited. They make choices daily of the type the government was proposing to make for them en masse: whether it is cheaper to insulate or pay an extra $200 a year for fuel oil, whether the cost savings from a car pool justifies the inconvenience, whether to give up a vacation trip in the old car in order to afford replacing it with a new car. The variations are endless, and each is made on the basis of a set of individual circumstances and value judgments. Businessmen make the same kinds of choices to maximize their profits. Is it wiser to buy a new truck that would be utilized 70% of the working day or to rely on an outside hauler who would have larger utilization and thus lower costs? Is it cheaper to use coal and pollution-control equipment or to switch to oil and gas?

Had the government simply freed the energy market of regulation and price controls, all these individual decisions would have been made on the basis of the true costs of various forms of energy, which in turn would reflect their relative scarcity. Conservation would take place naturally as the choices reflected the natural scarcities. And all the silly talk about running out of energy would be meaningless because the gradual process of adaptation and substitution would make that impossible. ERDA has identified no fewer than 250 different potential energy technologies, proving that substitution possibilities are almost endless.

Instead, the Carter energy team and the President himself chose to profess that the world-market system had been destroyed by a group of oil-producing states and that the only possible response was for the United States government to make a vast energy plan to protect its people. The market system had indeed been damaged, although certainly not destroyed, by seven years of the kind of federal market intervention that the plan represented. But the planners in this case had an even less clear idea of what complex effects their plan would produce than the planners who had gone before them. They did not know, most specifically, whether or not it would bring the economic recovery screeching to a halt with its new tax burdens, its new income transfers from the productive to the unproductive, its economic inefficiencies, and its drain on scarce capital.

The plan did indeed promise to rebate much of the taxation to the public or possibly to use some of it to bail out the Social Security program (Mr. Carter's Social Security plan involved using general funds from the Treasury to supplement Social Security taxes, and some of these funds would no doubt be generated by the energy taxes). The combination of supplementing Social Security with energy taxes and weighing energy-tax rebates in favor of low-income earners would further expand income transfers, a subject we discuss in a later chapter with regard to its effect on economic productivity.

But aside from its expansion of national economic planning and its tacit acceptance of the "limits to growth" ethic, the energy plan had another disturbing element. Seldom in American history had a President presented the people with an economic program so larded with moralism and so accusatory in tone. For example, this line: "Overseas, there is no greater symbol of American energy waste than the heavy, powerful, accessory-laden American automobile."[2]

"Waste" is not only a pejorative word but also a subjective judgment. Burning wood in the fireplace of a modern home is "waste" in a sense since it uses wood and supplies very little heat. Drinking wine is a "waste" since it provides very little nourishment. Going to a movie is a "waste" since anyone can live without movies. In short, what is one man's "waste" is another man's comfort. But here was a government document, proposing over 100 new laws that would be just as legal as the laws against murder and rape, based on the judgment that Americans were "wasteful" in their choice of automobiles.

Now this idea, as with most of the others in the energy plan, is not new. For years, social critics have been deploring the nation's taste in automobiles. The automobile has not only reshaped the American culture and economy, but is the center of profound emotions. To its owner it provides mobility and freedom, privacy, a sense of individuality and style, and the joy of controlling power, even when the owner has very few other sources of power. It is no accident at all that nations where governments exercise the most rigid control over people—Russia is the best example—also have the fewest automobiles. Critics of the automobile hate it for the very reason that most people love it: its unique contribution to the individual's sense of freedom and individuality. It offends the intellectual elite who find such individual expressions by ordinary people crude and, of course, "wasteful."

Milton Friedman, the Nobel laureate in economics, examined this kind of paternalistic attitude in a *Newsweek* column on June 13, 1977. Referring to a media report that described residents of an affluent suburb as "The nation's most careless squanderers of energy," Professor Friedman wrote: "Are the residents of the suburb (and the reporters writing the story) also 'squanderers of food, housing, clothing'? Is it either an actual or desirable policy that everyone should consume all items at some minimum sustainable level? At the same level as everyone else? What has happened to pride in our success in improving the living standards of our people? Today's lower middle classes live at levels that would have been affluent 'squandering' a century ago; and today's 'squanderers' will set the pace for the less advantaged tomorrow—if ill-considered government meddling does not kill the goose that lays those golden eggs."[3]

Indeed, Americans do not buy only large cars. They buy all kinds of cars, trucks, vans, motorcycles, mopeds, bus tickets, subway tokens, airline tickets, train tickets—a vast variety of forms of transportation. And there can be little doubt that most of these choices involve serious economic considerations. A sizable station wagon, of the type the President apparently deplores, has great utility for that typical suburbanite who has three children, a dog, school-band instruments or football teams to haul around, the need to buy lumber to improve his home, an obligation to take his family to visit the grandparents in some distant town at least once a year, and so forth. The station wagon will allow him to do all those things in comfort and safety. His large car has great economic utility and is far from being a "waste" in any economic meaning of the word.

The only accessory that represents any significant energy cost is his air conditioner. It is doubtful that European motorists are any different from Americans in wanting to stay cool in the heat. But most parts of Europe do not suffer the long, hot summers that most parts of the United States experience.

In other words, the energy document had a preachy tone. To be sure, there probably is a fundamental human need to be accountable for giving way too much to the comforts of the flesh, but in a free society that exercise is best conducted by the church, not the state.

If the tone of the energy plan sounded very much like a Jimmy Carter Sunday School lecture, the substance reflected the personality of his chief energy adviser, James R. Schlesinger. Mr. Schlesinger was described by *Time* magazine (April 4, 1977) as a systems analyst, "a member of a special American priesthood that has grown up to cope with the many questions concerning the effectiveness of government and business strategies."

The complex system of penalties and rewards in the energy package reflects the systems analysis approach. Mr. Schlesinger has defended the plan on grounds that it was not intended to thwart the market system but to put the market system to work on behalf of conserving oil and gas and converting the nation to coal and other energy sources. The argument is not totally implausible and is certainly the best that could be made for the plan. But the question arises: if it was intended to put the market system to work, why not use the real market rather than attempting to invent one? Even a systems analyst, however brilliant, would find it impossible to simulate the complexities of a fairly simple market system, let alone one as huge and complex as the energy market.

Mr. Schlesinger developed his systems-analysis approach to problems during the 1960s as a senior fellow at Rand Corporation, one of the nation's foremost "think tank" research organizations that analyze policy problems for government and business for a fee. In 1969 he came to Washington as assistant director of the Bureau of the Budget. In 1971 he was appointed chairman of the Atomic Energy Commission. A short while later he was moved to the Central Intelligence Agency, where he conducted a tough internal shake-up. And in 1973 he became Secretary of Defense.

At Defense, Mr. Schlesinger was not only a hard-nosed administrator but also one of the nation's foremost hawks. His quarrels with Secretary of State Henry Kissinger, over what he regarded as a soft policy of detente and strategic weapons accommodation with the Russians, finally led to his firing by President Ford. There were also rumors that Mr. Ford resented his Defense Secretary's patronizing attitude, but Mr. Schlesinger himself attributes the firing to his foreign-policy views and opposition to military budget cuts.

In addition to being tough, Mr. Schlesinger has been accused of being arrogant. The *Wall Street Journal* (July 8, 1977) quoted Mr. Schlesinger's wife Rachel as saying, "He came home the other day and said, 'They're saying I'm arrogant. They're right. Goddamn it, I am arrogant. I can't stand stupid questions."

But whatever Mr. Schlesinger's personality characteristics might be, the energy plan was not so much a reflection of his own limitations as a planner as a reflection of the inherent conflicts and contradictions that arise when anyone attempts to manipulate a vast market. The other problem, and a fatal one, was that the whole plan was based on the false premise that energy resources were being exhausted. And for a clue to where that notion may have originated, we turn to still another top member of the Carter energy team, S. David Freeman.

Lewis H. Lapham, editor of *Harper's,* described Mr. Freeman as a "fervent advocate of environmental reform" in a brilliant article in the August 1977 issue of his magazine. The article, titled "The Energy Debacle," described how Mr. Freeman's limits-to-growth ideas came to dominate the "Energy Policy Project" conducted under Ford Foundation sponsorship at a cost of $4 million from 1971 through 1974.

The product of the project was a report, published in October 1974, titled "A Time to Choose." It could hardly have been more hysterical in its "sky is falling" rhetoric. As Mr. Lapham described the Freeman thesis: "His report recommended a policy of energy conservation and suggested that the United States could reduce its demand for energy by as much as 50% if only it would establish a federal agency large enough and forceful enough to impose rationing (on heating fuels as well as gasoline), allocate resources, rearrange the international oil market, set prices, raise taxes, issue energy stamps, and redistribute income. The report also asked for the manufacture of more efficient automobiles, for government subsidy of anything that might conserve energy, for a schedule of pollution taxes, and for the raising up of a tribunal that could award supplies of energy (on the basis of need and moral worth) among major industries and geographic regions."[4] An apt summary indeed.

Mr. Lapham continued: "As might be guessed from Mr. Freeman's presence in the White House, many of these same proposals, together with the social doctrine implicit in the report, appear in President Carter's energy plan."

Indeed, "A Time to Choose" apparently impressed Mr. Carter so much when he read it in 1974 that he invited Mr. Freeman to help him with energy policy during his 1976 campaign. It did not, however, impress some of the nation's leading economists. The Institute for Contemporary Studies in San Francisco published a rebuttal, titled "No Time to Confuse" in 1975, in which 10 leading academicians including futurist Herman Kahn of the Hudson Institute and energy expert Morris A. Adelman of MIT took turns at hacking the Freeman study to pieces. In the introduction, Armen Alchian of UCLA, a leading market economist, said the book deserved a place in the Guinness Book of World Records for the most errors of economic fact and analysis in one volume, including misinterpretations of the simple law of supply and demand.

The Ford Foundation, it is said, was so troubled by the academic outrage that it conducted its own internal analysis of the Freeman report. But it never saw fit to publish it.

Mr. Lapham, in his *Harper's* article, drew an interesting contrast between Mr. Freeman and William Tavoulareas, president of Mobil Oil Corporation, a member of the energy project's advisory board, and an internal antagonist of Mr. Freeman's when the report was being prepared.

He described Mr. Tavoulareas as representing the "merchant class" on the project board. "Most of the people associated with this class endorsed the notion of an 'energy crisis' because it was good for business: if oil could be made to seem in scarce supply, then everybody could maintain a posture of innocence while selling it for high prices."

Mr. Freeman, he argued, represented the "technocratic class" that "aligned itself with the academic and bureaucratic interests, with government regulation in all markets, with the host of ambitious mandarins (city planners, professors of social science, journalists, foundation officials and university presidents) who talk of building a New Jerusalem on the slum of capitalism. Although as self-interested as the older class, the new class is less forthright about its desire for political influence. Its publicists seldom point out that a policy of 'zero growth', whether computed in terms of energy or anything else, rewards people who explain, categorize and interpret things at the expense of people who make things. In a stagnant society, the bureaucrat holds sway. His taxes, regulations and moralisms replace the market mechanism, and, like the grocery clerk in command of a limited inventory, he finds himself invested with the wisdom of Solomon."[5]

In an interview with Mr. Freeman, Mr. Lapham learned that the Freeman report did not trouble itself inordinately with inputs from the Tavoulareas crowd: "I could take it or leave it," Mr. Freeman was quoted as saying. "What none of them seemed to understand . . . probably because they were board-of-directors types used to ordering people around . . . was that I had the power. I had the power and it didn't matter what any of them said."[6]

Some of Mr. Freeman's ideas were finally to be translated into real power, backed by the might of the United States government, in the energy plan. There was only one hitch. Before that could happen, it had to get through Congress. And as Congress gradually woke up to what it was being asked to deal with, that proved to be a difficult process, although perhaps not difficult enough.

Mr. Carter launched the energy plan on television with that now-famous phrase borrowed from William James, calling it the "moral equivalent of war." He predicted before his speech that his popularity would fall after announcement of the energy plan.

He was right. But whereas he obviously felt he was making a noble sacrifice, asking the public to face up to harsh reality and necessity, his loss of popularity derived from somewhat different causes. A lot of people thought the energy plan was sheer madness. They wondered if the "moral equivalent of war" was actually being waged against the American people by Mr. Carter and his tough Energy Secretary who had so recently been waging a cold war against the Russians. The energy plan began a steady decline in public confidence in the new President. Even environmentalists of the moderate stripe didn't like the plan because of its focus on returning the nation to a coal-based energy economy.

It was not lost on the public that the President, who had promised in his campaign to make government more lean and efficient, was starting his term by creating yet another government department, The Department of Energy, with 20,000 employes and a $10.6 billion budget. Chevron U.S.A., an oil company, noted in its newsletter that $10.6 billion was more than twice the cost of all United States oil imports from Saudi Arabia in 1976. It didn't help much when Mr. Carter and Mr. Schlesinger argued in reply that the DOE's budget and personnel were mainly drawn from activities already existent in government. The public hadn't been overly impressed with some of the agencies that were folded into the DOE—the Federal Energy Administration, for example.

Yet another bone of contention was the plan's proposal on

natural gas. Mr. Carter had said in a letter to governors of gas-producing states just before the 1976 election that he favored gas deregulation. The support of such men as Governors Dolph Briscoe of Texas, David Boren of Oklahoma, and Edward W. Edwards of Louisiana helped swing the election to Mr. Carter. But his energy program called not for deregulation but expanded regulation, with intrastate gas sales in the producing states brought under the federal price ceiling. The fact that the ceiling was to be raised to $1.75 from $1.42 was hardly reassuring to these men, considering the fact that contracts for most intrastate gas were being written at prices above $1.75. Governor Edwards, in particular, was so furious that he practically threatened to secede from the union.

Similar outrage came from other quarters. Thomas A. Murphy, chairman of General Motors Corporation, described the plan's proposal to impose excise taxes on large cars and rebates on small cars "one of the most simplistic, irresponsible and shortsighted ideas ever conceived." For one thing, the tax rebate would make foreign-built small cars more attractive, costing United States jobs. For another, the plan would represent discrimination against families with five or more people—23% of all American families—who can't fit into four-passenger cars.

The petrochemical industry complained that a proposed "user" tax on petroleum would drive the costs of its feedstocks to $3 above the world-market levels by 1985, forcing much of the $40 billion industry out of the country and costing many of the 395,000 jobs the industry provides.

Appliance firms objected that the plan's energy efficiency standards for home appliances would sharply increase prices and reduce industry competition by forcing some companies to drop lines where volume did not justify the retooling costs.

Carl Bagge, president of the National Coal Association, which supposedly would have benefitted from the plan, said on "Meet the Press" that industry did not have the money to pay for both the cost of converting plants to coal and of installing required antipollution equipment.

The research agencies of Congress also challenged the plan. A Library of Congress study said natural-gas production would decline under the plan and oil imports would continue to rise. Further, it contended that "it is highly unlikely that the coal utilization goals of the administration will be reached."

The staff of the Joint Economic Committee thought the taxes and price increases inherent in the plan would have "destabilizing economic potential if not compensated for or rebated in a timely and nondisruptive fashion. These measures give greatest cause for concern because they involve substantial income transfers."

The General Accounting Office offered the opinion that "based on the administration's own estimates, with a few exceptions, the plan will fall far short of its goals."

The first victim of this reaction in Congress was the gasoline tax. It was killed in the House Ways and Means committee, thus eliminating one of the major tax- and income-redistribution threats. However, the House, through some adroit engineering by Speaker O'Neill and his hand-picked ad hoc energy committee, went along with many other parts of the plan after watering some of them down. The "gas guzzler" tax was retained although the mileage standard for tax penalties was lowered. Industry taxes for oil and gas use were retained, although weakened, as was the ban on new industry facilities burning oil and gas. The controversial electric-rate takeover was accepted. The wellhead tax on crude oil was approved, but Mr. O'Neill stuck in a tax exemption to benefit heating-oil users, a subsidy that would not be lost on his home state, Massachusetts, a heavy heating-oil consumer.

An attempt, again led by Representative Krueger, to deregulate natural-gas prices was again defeated in the House, and the White House proposal to bring intrastate gas under controls was accepted with some modifications, mainly a more liberal interpretation of what "new" gas would receive the higher $1.75 ceiling price.

In other words, the House, hurrying along on the rigid timetable set by Mr. O'Neill and with very little idea of the broad implications of what it was approving, embraced a major chunk of the energy plan after the gasoline tax had been removed. Congress then adjourned for its August recess.

After the recess there was a different mood in Congress. Mr. Carter's popularity in the public-opinion polls had continued to slip during the summer. Consumers, with gasoline plentiful, were asking what all this "energy crisis" talk was about. Interest groups, such as the utilities and the environmentalists, had more time to study the implications of what remained of the plan.

When the Senate took up the plan in September, it killed the gas-guzzler tax. It retained deductibility from federal income taxes of state and local gasoline taxes, which the House had voted to eliminate. It sharply reduced the scope of the oil- and gas-user taxes, although it retained the new facilities ban with some broad exceptions. It rejected the electricity rate takeover. It rejected the wellhead tax on crude oil. And it voted, once again, for deregulation of newly discovered natural gas, although with a temporary cap on interstate gas prices.

As the Senate went about gutting the energy plan, it was the President's turn to react violently. At a press conference on October 14 the President alluded to his early statement about the "moral equivalent of war," saying:

"But as is the case in time of war there is potential for war profiteering in the impending energy crisis. This could develop with the passing months as the biggest ripoff in history."

He went on to make a highly misleading statement by saying that the oil and gas industry, under his plan, would have an annual "income" of $100 billion by 1985. "What the oil companies and gas companies are now demanding, and making some progress, is $150 billion." "Income" in the lexicon of most people means profits; what the President apparently meant was total revenues, although that projection, in itself, was debatable.

The oil industry was indignant. Herman J. Schmidt, vice chairman of Mobil, replied that "from 1973 to 1976 the profits of the 30 largest oil companies increased by only 11% while their capital spending increased by 85%. The industry has had to borrow substantial amounts of money in order to finance these expenditures. . . . We can find no basis for the President's assertion that by 1985 the industry's annual income would be about $100 billion under his proposal."

On November 3, a full-page advertisement, sponsored by the National Taxpayers Union and signed by 46 leading economists, including Milton Friedman, Paul MacAvoy, Armen Alchian, and Ezra Solomon, appeared in major newspapers. For so academic a group, it carried an embittered headline: "Demagoguery at the White House." It objected to the use of the term "war profiteers" by the President.

"As responsible economists of all parties, we deplore discussion of important national issues in these terms," the ad said. "We believe the President's intemperate language reveals the essential weakness of his case.

"The issue is not oil companies versus the people. And one does not need to be a fan of the oil companies to recognize that. Every signer of this statement has been critical of the oil industry. We strongly oppose the current system of controls and import subsidies that adds millions of dollars to the income of oil refiners. We believe in a competitive oil industry, free from monopoly.

"We think the best way to achieve the goals of energy conservation and limited imports from OPEC is to let the market set prices—with regards to those who serve consumers most efficiently. Mr. Carter wants the bureaucracy to set prices and to distribute the rewards politically."

That most political of bodies, the United States Congress, was obviously still some distance short of agreeing with the market economists, but the Senate at least was a long distance from agreeing with the President. The next step was for the Senate and the House to try to reconcile their differences in conference, and as the year 1977 drew toward a close, that is what they set about to do.

By this time the energy package had been broken into six separate bills by the Senate. Speaker O'Neill sent his hand-picked pro-Carter forces to the conference, but Russell Long countered with well-chosen conferees who could be expected to resist some of the more important provisions of the Carter program.

The conferees had little trouble with a "catch-all" bill that provided various incentives for energy conservation, such as encouraging home insulation and installation of energy-saving devices. There was a provision for government loans to low-income families for energy conservation. And the mandatory federal standards for home appliances survived the conference. Work on this section was completed October 31.

Agreement on the "coal conversion" section was tougher, mainly because of the costs and environmental risks of converting large power plants to coal. But finally, on November 11, the conferees came up with a much watered-down conversion plan, requiring existing power plants and other large installations to convert to coal only if they could do so with little expense and without violating environmental laws. That was a big, and fortunate loophole, if coal conversion should become law.

By December 1 there was agreement on federal involvement in the setting of electric utility rates. And here again, the Carter proposal had been beaten down to a shadow of its former self. It merely asked states to "consider" federal rate setting guidelines.

There was also conditional approval of a watered-down tax on "gas guzzling" cars.

It was on the natural gas price ceiling and the proposed wellhead tax on crude oil that the committee broke down. Senators from gas-producing states particularly objected to Mr. Carter's proposals for extending controls to intrastate contracts. And it was beginning to dawn on some members of the committee that taxing crude oil was a strange way to encourage production.

Although there were hints at times that the conferees were close to a compromise, possibly involving increases in the proposed ceiling on natural gas to somewhere above the $1.75 level proposed by Mr. Carter, the conference finally adjourned without completing action on the energy package. It would remain for the second session of the 95th Congress to tussle some more with the energy bill.

This outcome was hardly a victory for the forces who would like to see energy decontrolled. Natural gas in interstate commerce remained controlled at $1.48. The entitlements and allocation system on crude oil and oil products remained in place, continuing to encourage imports and to discourage domestic development and production. The new Department of Energy with its vast bureaucracy was still muddling in the energy market. For example, it blocked a deal by American companies to buy natural gas from Mexico in late 1977 and was posing a threat to imports of liquefied Algerian gas.

In short, the nation's energy problems, born out of federal market intervention, were tangled in a political debate over who gets what. The only hopeful sign was that few people still believed that there was a genuine energy "shortage." Even the International Energy Agency in Paris, with its aspirations to make energy bureaucracy worldwide, was forced to admit that there would likely be a crude oil surplus into the 1980s. That was progress but the energy debate is far from ended. It is part of the continuing and crucial debate over what kind of national economy the United States will have, one that relies on markets or one in which government attempts to control economic forces.

CHAPTER TEN

LIBERTY VERSUS EQUALITY

"I want all to have a share of everything, and all property to be in common; there will no longer be either rich or poor; no longer shall we see one man harvesting vast tracts of land, while another has not ground enough to be buried in. . . . I intend that there shall only be one and the same condition of life for all. . . . I shall begin by making land, money, everything that is private property, common to all. . . . Women shall belong to all men in common."

MOST OF THE CHAPTER OPENING DECLAMATION, ASIDE FROM the commonality of women, would sound fresh today in any political debate between socialists and free-marketers, but in fact it is uttered by the lady communist, Praxagora, in the comic play *Ecclesiazusae* written by Aristophanes in 392 B.C. Will Durant quoted it in *The Life of Greece*, part of the epic historical work *The Story of Civilization*, to demonstrate that in politics there is nothing much new under the sun.[1] The punch line comes, incidentally, when a character named Blepyrus asks Praxagora, "But who will do the work?" and Praxagora replies, "The slaves."

Aristophanes was having some fun with communism and the Athenian version of Women's Lib. But wealth and income redistribution was a major political issue, maybe *the* major political issue, in ancient Athens, just as it is today throughout the world. Mr. Durant noted that while hardly anyone was so radical about equality as to advocate freeing the slaves, young impoverished Athenian citizens, joined by intellectuals eager for new ideas and the applause of the oppressed, were frequently in a state of rebellion.

Wrote Mr. Durant: "They point out how unreal is the equality of the franchise in the face of mounting economic inequality . . . they are resolved to use the political power of the poorer citizenry to persuade the Assembly to sluice into the pockets of the needy—by fines, liturgies, confiscations and public works—some of the concentrated wealth of the rich. And to give a lead to future rebels they adopt red as the symbolic color of their revolt."

Indeed, not only is there nothing much new under the sun, but as the late Polish-born scientist Jacob Bronowski made clear in the "The Ascent of Man," the celebrated BBC television series, much of history can be interpreted as a war between the haves and have-nots. Even in primitive societies, when well-organized communities were able to build food surpluses, they were in danger of raids from feckless nomadic tribes. And so it has been through much of history, whether it be the sacking of Rome or the Twentieth Century German envy of its neighbors that produced such cataclysmic results. (It should also be noted, however, that decline and weakness of the attacked states or political orders has played an important role in such events. Inflation, for example, was a significant factor in the Athenian unrest.)

The struggle between the haves and have-nots is no less evident today. An underlying theme of the Democratic platform and of "liberal" philosophy in the 1960s and 1970s was that government social and economic policies could and should bring about greater equality in living standards.

It is an appealing philosophy that attracts adherents not only from the poor but from the more compassionate members of the comfortable middle and upper classes. It does not seem to be an overstatement to say that it has been the dominant political philosophy throughout most of the world, including the United States in the post-World War II era.

It also forms the ethical base for modern Soviet and Chinese socialism and their ultimate goal of worldwide communism in which all men would live in equality and harmony and the state would "wither away." The fierce conflicts between these two huge nations are not over this fundamental ethic but are based on traditional jealousies and suspicions born out of centuries of Russian expansionism and China's bitter memories of the many times it has been a victim of military and economic conquest from outsiders. It is also a conflict over the means of achieving the communist nirvana, the belief by Chairman Mao that the Russians had corrupted the ideals of communism. He saw communism as needing constant nourishment from a revolutionary fervor of the people in order to flourish and succeed as a political and social philosophy. The Russians, with centuries of central rule behind them and 30 years' more experience in struggling unsuccessfully with the communist ideal, regarded the Chinese view as naive and dangerous but also possibly threatening to Soviet aspirations to provide the dominant moral and intellectual leadership to the world communist movement.

Both the Russians and the Chinese had made a subtle change in the Marxist principle, "From each according to his abilities, to each according to his needs." Until the ultimate communism is achieved, both have recognized that an economic system, socialist or capitalist, can hardly function without incentives, so the slogan has become "From each according to his abilities, to each according to his *work*." In fact, that is a great deal closer to the philosophy of Russell Long and the American Republican Party, with their preference for "workfare" over welfare, than to the communist ideal.

Indeed, it could be said that the Soviet political and economic system of the 1970s has become one of the most highly conservative in the world, particularly in its unwillingness to accommodate dissent or change. The Soviet march toward communism, if it is progressing at all, is moving by inches, rather than miles. The Chinese, at least until Mao's death in September 1976, still represented revolutionary idealism but also are a long way from the state's withering away.

But despite all the contradictions of state socialism, the egalitarian ethic is the appeal it offers to the Soviet and Chinese peoples and the peoples of the world, in much the same way that other powerful social-political-religious movements have done through history. The have-nots, who still outnumber the world's haves in overwhelming numbers, are promised a share of the economic pie.

That same appeal is also working in the market democracies, in some ways more powerfully than in the socialist states. Indeed, developments of the last decade or so suggest that there was something to the theory of the early 1960s that the market democracies and the socialist autocracies might be "converging," becoming systems with more similarities than differences. The theory came about in part because the Russians in the 1960s were trying to invent a sort of market socialism, in which state enterprises were encouraged to innovate and become more efficient through introduction of profit incentives. It didn't work very well for the fundamental reasons that the central planning agency, Gosplan, was, like all bureaucracies, reluctant to give up its power and more importantly, because, the Soviet regime was not willing to give up control over prices, thus denying themselves the key to a genuine market system.

The Soviets, in true doctrinaire style, hotly denied that there was any such thing as convergence. The Soviet Union was certainly not going to move in the direction of capitalism, they argued; their goal was communism, which is antithetical, in their view, to capitalism. And the only way the market democracies could move their way was through adopting that goal for themselves.

And indeed, it seems that most of the movement toward convergence is taking place in the market democracies, although it is possible to argue that this doesn't represent convergence but the evolution of something distinct and more viable than Soviet socialism has been. It is hoped that is true.

Whatever direction the movement, it is founded as well on the egalitarian ethic. The market democracies have become what is popularly known as "welfare states," with the central government assuming an ever larger responsibility for income redistribution, taking from the rich and the middle class and giving to the poor. At least that is the theory. In actual practice, the redistributive mechanisms are not all that efficient. They also give part of what they take from the middle class to other members of the middle class and to the rich, as for example when contractors earn a bounteous living putting up public housing or when doctors and nursing-home operators reap bonanzas at the expense of taxpayers through unnecessary services to Medicaid patients.

Evidence that redistributionism has become a powerful political force in the United States in the 1960s and 1970s is seen in the fact that it has prevailed under both Republican and Democratic Presidents. It has accounted in large part for the fact that public spending in the United States has quintupled over the last 20 years and that governments at all levels now spend over $700 billion annually, about 37% of the GNP, compared with about 26% in 1958.

An editorial in the *Wall Street Journal* on October 24, 1977, referred to what had happened since John Kenneth Galbraith wrote his best-selling and influential book *The Affluent Society* in 1958, bemoaning "private opulence and public squalor" and arguing that the United States should devote more of its resources to the "public sector." Mr. Galbraith's place in literary history may rest on whatever role he played in persuading the country to do just that.

But the *Journal* editorial noted that despite the enormous expansion of government spending the services rendered by the public sector still leave a great deal to be desired. Some 900,000 miles of highways and streets are urgently in need of repair or upgrading, public transportation is often creaky, the crime rate has risen rapidly, and so on.

The final explanation of where all that public sector money went "reflects the change in government from a deliverer of services to something much more ambitious," the *Journal* said, "an instrument for reordering society. Government transfer payments, the taking of substance from one person and giving it to someone else, have climbed eightfold since 'The Affluent Society.' And this is an understatement, since some government services, such as education, involve transfers that are not registered in the statistics."

In the process of growth, redistributionism has picked up a powerful political constituency, or it might be said more accurately that the support of a diverse constituency has been responsible for the rapid growth of redistribution. President Lyndon B. Johnson, who may have contributed the most of any President to this process with his "Great Society" programs, was a master at building constituencies, which accounts for his success in winning passage of legislation both as a Congressman and as President.

President Johnson knew out of long experience that bills do not get passed in the United States Congress without the support of a reasonably broad spectrum of the hundreds of interest groups that bring varying degrees of influence to bear on Congress. So he designed Great Society programs for the poor—who by themselves are not a particularly powerful interest group—that would also have a considerable appeal to the nonpoor. It is no mere accident that farm-state Congressmen could see a great deal of merit in a food stamp program that might yield rewards for food growers as well as added protection against poverty for the urban tenement dweller. Or that the AFL-CIO, even though most of its members have long since moved into the middle class, could see a great deal of promise in public housing programs that would expand jobs for construction workers or in welfare programs that would expand the roles of unionized public employes. Or that many doctors and druggists could not be too annoyed about the sharp expansion, through Medicare and Medicaid, in public spending on medical services, even though it carried the taint of "socialized medicine."

In addition to this type of constituency with a direct interest in redistribution, the movement picked up another kind of backing from a force that has taken on a substantial significance throughout the world. For lack of a better definition, it might be called the "limits to growth" movement, which had its modern impetus from an organization called the Club of Rome, formed in Geneva in 1968. The guiding spirit of the Club was Aurelio Peccei, an Italian industrialist, but it pulled together a collection of thinkers and philosophers from several nations, including the United States.

The seminal product of the Club of Rome was a study, published in 1972, called *The Limits to Growth*. Employing MIT's computers, the authors of the study concluded that the population of the world was rapidly using up the earth's resources and that the earth would reach its maximum capacity to sustain human life within a hundred years. Although English economist Thomas Robert Malthus had made similar dire predictions 200 years earlier and civilization had not only managed to survive but had even made enormous economic progress, the Club of Rome study attracted worldwide attention and a large measure of belief.

It happened to support the thinking of another group, the environmentalists, who were arguing, in a similar vein, that mankind was rapidly destroying his own environment. Fred Hoyle, the English scientist and author, theorizes that fears about the environment got their primary impetus from the first photographs of our planet taken from outer space, which impressed upon mankind the idea that we are all passengers on a single spaceship Earth, and that at this point in our evolution, that is all we have. So we had better take care of it.

Although the Club of Rome was to modify its no-growth position at a meeting in Philadelphia early in 1976, the modifications were hardly noticed. The no-growth ethic was off and running in 1972, no doubt in part because a short while after *The Limits to Growth* was published Americans found themselves waiting in lines at filling stations to buy scarce gasoline. The idea that this was merely the result of the foolish economic policies of their government, which we discussed in earlier chapters, was less persuasive than the apocalyptic notion that maybe, indeed, we had begun to use up the world's resources of energy.

There is, however, a corollary to the limits-to-growth philosophy. It is simply that since we can't afford further economic growth, it is imperative that we establish mechanisms for distributing the existing economic pie more equitably. In short, redistribution. So the no-growth people and the environmentalists are united with the redistributionists.

Finally, there is the group defined by Irving Kristol, a member of the *Wall Street Journal*'s Board of Contributors, as the "new class," the entire body of college intellectuals, government employes, lawyers, and others, who, along with the other private-interest groups, have thrived on what the French call *dirigisme,* the direction of the economy by political authority. The planning and execution of economic redistribution keeps their services in strong demand.

The pressures for more and more income transfer and redistribution also impinge on the United States from abroad. The international corollary to the battle over redistribution in the United States is something called the North-South dialogue. Conducted under the auspices of the United Nations, it is, in simplest terms, a demand by over 100 less developed nations that income and wealth be transferred to them from the developed nations. They argue, in terms not altogether unrelated to those of the domestic debate in the United States, that their demands are justified by past "exploitation" at the hands of the colonial powers. It was proposed at the UN in 1976 that the developed nations should contribute .7 of 1% of their GNP by 1980 to aid the LDCs. The United States, which has become increasingly less susceptible both to UN overtures and this kind of argument, has actually been reducing its foreign aid. In 1975 it contributed only .23 of 1% of its GNP to the LDCs, down from .49 of 1% in 1965. President Carter has proposed that the allotment be increased.

But the United States has not stinted at home. It is hard to find any substantial spending program devised in Congress over the last decade that does not have some element of redistribution. The federal income tax is, of course progressive, with the larger earners paying higher rates than low-income taxpayers. The threshold for paying any tax at all has been raised in recent years. Social Security benefits, particularly at the minimum level, have been raised. Unemployment insurance has been expanded. Welfare programs have proliferated so much that Senator Abraham A. Ribicoff of Connecticut noted recently that there are 1150 separate agencies throughout the United States, "administering every conceivable type of welfare program." Federal law requires that a certain percentage of government contracts of various types be awarded to firms owned by minority groups. The list goes on and on.

Despite all the effort at redistribution, there have always been serious questions about how much redistribution really takes place. Vilfredo Pareto, an Italian-Swiss engineer and economist who died in 1923, argued in what came to be known as Pareto's law that through history and in every place the pattern of income distribution has been and will remain constant, despite the best efforts of welfare economists. Or in other words, the plight of the poor can only be improved by raising the income and wealth of the economy as a whole.

Although Pareto's law has always been challenged by welfare economists—and indeed, it is a rather startling proposition—there is modern evidence to support it. In a trio of articles in *The Wilson Quarterly* (Autumn 1977), historian Edward Pessen and economists Robert J. Lampman and Helen H. Lamale discussed the rising American standard of living in the post-World War II period, which has pulled more and more Americans out of poverty. But as a chart at the beginning of the series shows, income distribution has not changed appreciably. Wrote Professor Lampman:

"The past three decades of progress and change were not marked by any increase in inequality in the overall distribution of income or wealth. While some individuals' fortunes rose and some fell, economic progress was widely shared. Interregional and some 'intergroup' (e.g., black and white) differentials in family incomes narrowed. That part of the population living in what is now defined as poverty fell from almost a third in 1947 to 12% in 1975 when . . . the median family income was $13,719. In 1975, 60% of families were clustered in the narrow range between $6,914 and $22,037. The fifth of families below this range received only 5.4% of total incomes, while the fifth above it received 41% of the total. The top 5%, whose incomes started at $34,144, had 15.5% of all family income in America. . . .

"There appears to have been only a slight change in the degree of income inequality in the postwar period in spite of the rising levels of income and the changing composition of the population. However, inequality in the U.S. per capita distribution of income may have dropped more sharply. Family size declined more for the lowest fifth of the families than for other families, and unrelated individuals increased as a proportion of the population. This decline in the size of poorer families was due to older people and young adults leaving the family unit to live alone.

"About half of the income of this 'lowest fifth' consists of transfer payments—welfare, Social Security, unemployment insurance, workmen's compensation and the like."[3]

Some of the failure of income redistribution may result from simple inefficiencies, not to mention the fact that in-kind income transfers of various descriptions, such as medical care, often are not included in income distirbution calculations. Whatever the reason, Paul W. MacAvoy, former member of the Council of Economic Advisors under President Ford, noted once that in terms of sheer spending, "we are spending more than enough to bring above the poverty line every member of the population who is considered poor."

The problem of inefficiency and agency proliferation has brought about strong arguments for eliminating all the multitudinous forms of income redistribution in favor of a simple cash system.

Among such advocates have been such diverse thinkers as Richard Nixon and George McGovern. Writing in *Across the Board,* a publication of the Conference Board, University of Michigan economist Paul W. McCracken, former chief economic advisor to President Nixon and now a member of the *Wall Street Journal's* Board of Contributors, had this to say:

"A more sensitive concern about sharing equitably the fruits of our affluent economy must be high on the agenda of national policy, but it must not be a cynical Robin Hood exercise through which politicians keep themselves in power by taking away from the affluent to buy the votes of recipients. What we do need in this country is an explicit, systematic, generalized income maintenance or income distribution program. It should be the analogue of unemployment compensation, which steps in and provides income when incomes are too low because of interrupted employment—except that this generalized program should step in when an income is too low for whatever reason."[4]

Professor McCracken may, however, have put his finger on the reason we don't have such a program. The political process is such that it is very attractive for politicians to be able to offer specific programs that give some benefit, or at least seem to give a benefit, to some interest group. That is why President Johnson's Great Society, with its bounty for so many interest groups, was so successful in a political sense.

It has been less than successful in a social sense. There has been created the sense that government favors some privileged groups more than others. There is, for example, the complaint that the nonworking poor receive, through Medicaid and other welfare services, better medical care, diets, and in some cases, housing than the working poor. There is the fear of some economists that we are approaching the point where income transfers are discouraging high-producers from working harder and low-producers from working at all since they are not well equipped to earn much more than they can receive on the dole. In a survey of food-stamp recipients in Westchester County, New York, for example, Economist Bette K. Fishbein of the Institute for Socioeconomic Studies found that 37% of those surveyed said that if they didn't have food stamps they would find ways of earning more money. "This is an important finding," she wrote in the Institute's *Journal*, "and demonstrates the work disincentives inherent in the program."[5]

Finally, there is a fear that the constant efforts to plug income transfers into federal programs are seriously distorting the market economy. Wrote Professor McCracken in his *Across the Board* article: "Lacking a systematic, generalized program giving expression to our concerns about income distribution, we then tend also to paralyze our capacity for using the pricing system to do what it does sensitively and well—namely, to guide the allocation of productive resources. There is strong sentiment for price control, in spite of its frequently demonstrated tendencies toward economic arthritis and moral degeneracy, because of what inflation means for those with low incomes. We cannot pursue a rational energy strategy today because pricing energy, to be consistent with today's cost realities, would have an adverse effect on those with lower incomes."

Nobel Laureate Friedrich A. Hayek believes that the redistributionist movement has confused the principle of equality of opportunity by attempting also to achieve equality of result. It is not only impossible to achieve equality of result, it is even impossible to determine what it is, he argues. In Volume 2 of his series of books published under the general heading of *Law, Legislation and Liberty,* Professor Hayek wrote that equality of opportunity could be guaranteed by a set of laws or rules but equality of result could not be. "What the rules, and the order they serve, can do is no more than to increase the opportunities for unknown people. If we do the best we can to increase the opportunities for any unknown person picked at random, we will achieve the most we can, but certainly not because we have any idea of the sum of utility of pleasure which we have produced."[6]

To this he added: "As is becoming clear in ever increasing fields of welfare policy, an authority instructed to achieve particular results for the individuals must be given essentially arbitrary powers to make the individuals do what seems necessary to achieve the required result. Full equality for most cannot but mean the equal submission of the great masses under the command of some elite who manages their affairs. While an equality of rights under a limited government is possible and an essential condition of individual freedom, a claim for equality of material position can be met only by a government with totalitarian powers."[7]

Professor Robert Nisbet of Columbia struck a similar theme, quoting Tocqueville to the effect that "Every central power that follows its own natural tendencies courts and encourages the principle of equality, for equality singularly facilitates, extends and secures the influence of the central power."[8]

Professor Nisbet went on to say: "I take the time-honored phrase, 'equality of opportunity' to mean, basically, equality of access to the law, to the rights and privileges and freedoms guaranteed by law. Certainly, this is what equality of opportunity meant to the Founding Fathers, including Jefferson and has meant until very recently.

"Today, however, equality of opportunity has increasingly become subtly fused with equality of result or condition. And this kind of equality—equality of result—lies at the heart of the egalitarianism that confronts us in government, the media, the universities and other habitats of the political intelligentsia—or, to use a term I prefer, the clerisy. Redistribution of income, property and other goods through taxation has become an honored aim. Once the purpose of taxation was simply to raise enough money to meet government expenditures. Today it is aimed at reconstruction of economic and social conditions.

"The point is, equality has become more than a time-honored

value—one among a plurality of values. It is by now tantamount to religion, carrying with it (at least in the minds of many intellectuals, leaders of special-interst groups, and a rising number of politicians and bureaucrats) much the same kind of moral fervor and zeal, much the same sense of crusade against evil, and much the same measure of promise of redemption that have historically gone with religious movements. The difference is this, however: whereas the religious movements I speak of have traditionally had man's spiritual condition principally in mind, the new religion of equality and the clerisy of power that serves as the church for this new religion have nothing spiritual in mind—only the economic, social and political. It is one thing to declare Everyman a priest as Luther did, or to declare men created equal in the highly limited sense Jefferson intended when he drafted the Declaration of Independence. Expectations are not aroused, or do not become consuming. It is an entirely different matter when equality of economic and social condition becomes a god for the intellectual or politician. Expectations cannot do other than increase exponentially. Envy—of all passions the basest and most destructive of personality and society alike—quickly takes command, and the lust for power with which to allay every fresh discontent, to assuage every social pain, and to gratify every fresh expectation becomes boundless."[9]

President Carter, caught in the income-redistribution maelstrom and not at all out of sympathy with the distributionists despite his conservative leanings, set out to make some sense of it all in his first year. His concept was that it was mainly a task that better organization would deal with. He was soon to learn differently when his Social Security, welfare, energy, and tax proposals hit Congress and the public prints, arousing deep emotions both from the distributionists and free-marketers. In fact, he was dealing with a conflict as old as mankind, not merely with ways and means. Aristophanes would have understood it perfectly.

CHAPTER ELEVEN

WELFARE REFORM

The uniform, efficient welfare system of the economic textbooks is nothing but a mirage.—Doolittle, Levy and Wiseman in *The Public Interest*.[1]

IN CONTRAST TO THE FRIGID WEATHER OF JANUARY, WHEN President Carter took office, much of the country was sweltering under a prolonged spell of hot, humid weather in July 1977. In New York City, on the evening of July 13, thousands of air conditioners were trying to combat the 90-degree heat when, at about 9:30 P.M., the big blackout of '77 began. Lightning had struck several power plants to the north of the city, and one by one the overloaded generators that supply the Big Apple shut off. People were stranded in subways, theaters and restaurants; in hospitals emergency treatment was given by the light of spotlights; television transmitters went dead, and newspaper presses halted.

Blackouts, of course, are nothing new to long-suffering New Yorkers. Tales are still told of the camaraderie, Good Samaritanism, and near-absence of crime in the famous blackout of November 1965. This time, however, there was a dramatic difference. Within minutes of the power failure the streets of low-income neighborhoods from Harlem to Brooklyn were filled with mobs on a rampage. In a holiday mood, with shouts of "It's Christmas in July," tens of thousands of people, most of them black or Hispanic, smashed into stores and carried out whatever they could lay hands on. Jewelry, clothing, groceries, appliances, and cameras were openly carried through the streets. In the Bronx new Pontiacs were driven away from a car showroom. All through the night and most of the next day, with the power still off, the looting and burning continued. Twenty-five hours after the blackout began, when electricity was finally restored, more than 3700 looters had been arrested, 1037 fires had been fought, some 2000 stores were in ruins, and losses were estimated at $155 million.

Two days later, mulling over the causes of the riot, the *New York Times* said in an editorial, ". . . we must begin to understand that, at least in some measure, these scars are self-inflicted. We did not spend enough of our ingenuity and our affluence to solve the problems the riots of the 60s made evident."[2]

Expanding this theme editorially on the following Sunday, the *Times* declared, "We may continue to ignore the terrible problems of poverty and race, but we must do so aware of the risks to both justice and peace."[3]

Evidently this was too much even for normally-liberal *New York Times* readers, who responded with a torrent of letters that ran 20 to 1 against the views of the editorials. Among the less vituperative letters subsequently printed in the paper was this comment: "I know of no group who has received more time, attention, and money in recent years than the poor of New York. They are one of the main causes the city is in financial difficulty."[4]

The blackout of '77, the *Times* editorials, and the indignant letters help dramatize the problems of understanding and dealing with poverty in the United States. Such problems pose paradoxes that are reflected in public-opinion polls, as well as in differences of opinion between equally honorable public officials. Polls taken in 1977, for instance, showed that most Americans are rather antagonistic to the concept of public welfare, yet strongly support what welfare programs do. In other words, they are against the abstraction of wasteful government spending but for the concrete substance of programs like aid to dependent children, medical, food, and housing help to the poor. In like manner, two members of the same political party can agree on the abstract concept of requiring work in exchange for welfare benefits but disagree on the specifics of implementing that concept, the prime current examples being President Carter and Senator Russell Long of Louisiana.

These were the problems and paradoxes that the President was to take up less than a month after the blackout, when he announced at a Saturday morning press conference in Plains the details of his much-heralded program to cure the "welfare mess."

During his campaign for the presidency Mr. Carter had repeatedly pledged that he would completely overhaul the welfare program by shifting the welfare cost away from the local governments altogether; introducing strong work incentives, job creation, and job training; encouraging family stability by eliminating penalties that force men to leave their families; and streamlining and simplifying the entire welfare system.

To launch this sweeping program, President Carter chose Joseph A. Califano, architect of much of Lyndon Johnson's Great Society programs and the Carter Secretary of Health, Education, and Welfare. Sticking as usual to a tight schedule for preparing and introducing sweeping legislative innovations, the Carter team got cracking with Mr. Califano's announcement, on January 26, of a public forum on welfare reform so that groups outside the department could toss ideas into the HEW pot. For three months, at weekly sessions, the welfare-reform consulting group pored over the mishmash of current welfare programs. The group included representatives from most major government departments, Congress, the National Governors Conference, state legislatures, and counties and cities who had grappled with the welfare monster and could concur with Mr. Califano's summary that "Given the vast resources this nation spends on income assistance, it is appalling that our programs are so poorly coordinated . . . unfairly exclude millions from adequate aid, contain absurd incentives to break up families or discourage work . . . and are an administrative jungle, incomprehensible to legislators, administrators and the American people alike."

Even defining the "mess" is a task to defy Webster. There has been such a welter of overlapping programs and so many different yardsticks to measure needs and costs that definitions tend to vary as much as the blind men's description of the elephant. The Congressional Budget Office, for instance, reported in a June 1977 background paper on poverty that during the decade 1965–1975 public expenditures of all kinds for social welfare had grown fourfold—from $77.2 billion to $286.5 billion—while the number of families in poverty had declined by only 30%. "Social welfare," however, is a sweeping phrase that covers nearly all domestic nondefense spending by government, from education to housing, from Social Security to food stamps.

What has been commonly thought of as "welfare" is public assistance to the poor, made up of five programs: Aid to Families With Dependent Children (AFDC); Supplemental Security Income (SSI), which is aid to the needy aged, blind, and disabled; Medicaid; food stamps; and general assistance. Those five together cost local, state, and federal governments about $42 billion in 1977, up from $4.2 billion in 1965. General assistance, the smallest of the five, is the one major program financed and administered only by states and localities. The federal government finances all of the food stamp program and sizable percentages of AFDC, Medicaid, and SSI.

These five programs, with their ballooning costs, duplication, inequities, vulnerability to fraud, and mushrooming bureaucracies, have been the target of public ire and repeated attempts at reform.

A glance at two of the programs as they existed in 1977 should be sufficient to illustrate the problems. With AFDC, for example, each state and the District of Columbia determines the amount of money needed monthly by families to live. The level varies enormously from state to state, from $187 a month for a family of four (three children) in Texas to $497 in Hawaii. (It should be remembered that the federal poverty level was considered to be about $5500 in fiscal 1976 for a family of four. Thus Hawaii was above the federal level at almost $6000 annually, while Texas was well below at about $2300.) But only 18 states actually pay families the difference between their income, if any, and the amount the state says is needed to get by. The other states pay less than the monthly standards they themselves have set because of an almost infinite number of ways to measure eligibility. About half the states do not make AFDC payments to families with unemployed fathers. The federal share of each state's AFDC costs is computed on that state's per capita income and ranges from a minimum of 50% up to 79%. For every dollar spent by such wealthy states as New York, the federal government also spends a dollar, but in Mississippi every state dollar is matched by $3.76 from Washington.

The Medicaid program of expenditures also varies widely from state to state. The federal government has established a list of basic medical services (hospital care, nursing-home care, doctor services) that each state must provide to persons eligible for AFDC or SSI in order to receive federal Medicaid funds. States also may provide Medicaid for people not eligible for AFDC or SSI, and 28 states do so. Some states pay for more services than others, and most of these additional costs are matched from Washington. In the first quarter of 1976 HEW reported that the average monthly Medicaid payment per recipient was $846 in Alaska and $265 in Minnesota but only $64 in Missouri and $66 in Mississippi. The federal government pays from 50% to 78% of the Medicaid costs incurred by the states.

The chief charges against this tangle of programs in 1977 were that (1) they often failed to provide relief for people in poverty while benefitting people who earned more than the so-called poverty line, which was raised to about $5900 in April for a nonfarm family of four, $3000 for individuals; (2) they tended to break up families; and (3) they were a disincentive to work.

For a decade the public has been treated to thousands of stories in the media that bear out these charges. A few random examples:

● In Oregon the combined value of AFDC and food stamps is $5724 a year for a family of four. In New York it is $5592. In 22 states the value of the AFDC food-stamp benefits would exceed the earnings of a full-time worker paid at the minimum wage (then $2.30 an hour).[5]

● In Michigan an AFDC family of four with a mother employed at $7000 a year continues to draw more than $1200 in cash benefits plus food stamps worth nearly $300 and Medicaid. In Michigan, however, a two-parent family of four with a father working at the same wage gets no assistance except food stamps.[6]

● In Chicago hundreds of government employes were suspected of drawing welfare payments along with their regular salaries. Among the 92 indicted in 1977 were persons employed by the Postal Service, police department, public library, and Internal Revenue Service.[7]

● In Washington, D. C. two clergymen withheld hundreds of thousands of dollars from food stamps sold through their church and used part of the money to subsidize a privately owned ice-cream parlor.[8]

● Some doctors were discovered bilking Medicaid funds. In a cleanup drive launched by HEW there was one who charged the government for 26,000 treatments in a single year, another claimed to have performed six tonsillectomies on one patient, and still another sought payment for several abortions on a woman for whom the doctor had previously performed a hysterectomy.

The foregoing merely highlight the mess that President Carter had promised to clean up. The first thing to be said about the sweeping new welfare plan that he introduced on August 6 (waiting purposely until the House had approved his energy bill and gone home for vacation) is that it was an earnest, good-faith attempt to deal with most of the abuses, frauds, and overlapping. Calling on Congress to abolish the existing welfare system which is "neither fair or rational," he declared that the measures he was introducing would ensure that work would always be more profitable than welfare, that there would be strong incentives to keep families together, reduce fraud and error, and give significant financial relief to states and local governments. The highlights of the lengthy message to Congress were:

1. *Job Opportunities.*   The Federal government would take on the task of helping workers from low-income families find jobs in the public and private sectors. Measures would be taken to ensure that work would always be more profitable than welfare and that a private or nonsubsidized public job would always be more profitable than a federally funded public-service job. When employment could not be found, up to 1.4 million public-service jobs would be created. The jobs would pay at least the minimum wage.

2. *Work Benefit and Income Support.*   AFDC, the food-stamp program, and SSI would be completely scrapped and replaced by a

new work-benefit and income-support system. Two-parent families, single people, childless couples, and single parents of children above the age of 14 would be expected to work full time and required to accept available work. The basic benefit for a family of four in this category would be $2300. To encourage continued work, benefits would not be reduced at all for the first $3800 of earnings and would thereafter be reduced by 50 cents for each dollar earned up to $8400.

3. *Other Income Payments.* Aged, blind, or disabled persons would receive $2500 a year; couples in this category would get $3750, a slight rise from current benefits. Unemployed singles would receive $1100 and childless couples $2200, but both would have to accept a job or training or lose all benefits. A family of four under certain circumstances—young children or incapacity, for example— would receive a basic benefit of $4200 a year with benefits reduced 50 cents for each dollar of earnings, and benefits would be phased out entirely when the family's earnings reached $8400 in outside income.

4. *Earned-Income Tax Credit.* The current earned-income tax-credit program would be expanded to provide more tax relief to the working poor. The new program, which would apply to private and nonsubsidized public employment, would continue the current 10% credit on earnings up to $4000 a year, allow a 5% credit on earnings between $4000 and $9000, and phase out the credits at $15,600. The credits would be paid by the Treasury Department with a maximum of over $600.

5. *State Role and Fiscal Relief.* Each state would save at least 10% of its current welfare expense in the first year of the program, with substantially increased fiscal relief thereafter. Each state would be free to continue supplementing the basic benefits.

Although the President had insisted early in the year that any new welfare program must not cost more than the current expenditures, he gradually gave way to pressures from various groups, particularly from mayors and governors who insisted on immediate fiscal relief. In his press conference at Plains he said that the new program would cost $30.7 billion, which he said was $2.8 billion above the present level of spending. In addition, the expanded earned-income tax-credit program would cost $3.3 billion.

Before considering the pros and cons of the President's reforms, it might be useful to take a closer look at some of the statistics involved. Perhaps one measure of the welfare mess is the public confusion over how much is currently being spent and how many people receive benefits, a confusion often shared by journalists. Mr. Carter placed current welfare costs at $27.9 billion. *U. S. News & World Report,* in an article about the plan, reported current spending at $37.8 billion.[9] One *Time* magazine story said "welfare payments" were $11.4 billion;[10] a front-page story in the *New York Times* pegged the cost at $25 billion.

Similarly, the number of people receiving benefits, depending on what publication one reads, is placed anywhere from 23 million to 11.5 million, a figure that an article in the widely read Gannett newspapers declared was the all-time United States high.[11]

The whole purpose of the welfare program, of course, has always been to aid people who are in financial distress and who cannot, for whatever reason, help themselves. When Lyndon Johnson launched his War on Poverty in 1965 it was estimated that 33 million people, or 19.1% of all United States families (including one-person families) lived in poverty throughout the nation. A decade later, after a tidal wave of money had flowed out of Washington, the number of poor had been reduced less than a third, to 26 million people or 13.8% of families.

Why wasn't poverty eradicated, or at least cut more drastically? The Congressional Budget Office undertook to answer that question and, after some sleuthing that would have done credit to Hercule Poirot, reported, in the previously mentioned background paper on poverty, some answers that deserve more attention than they have received. One of the major problems, the CBO discovered, is that enigmatic "poverty line," which determines who is eligible for assistance and who is not. That figure is set by the Labor Department from data supplied by the Census Bureau, which periodically sends interviewers out to question a demographically selected 50,000 families about their incomes. The replies are supposed to give reliable figures on all revenues from jobs, dividends, rents, pensions, and cash welfare assistance, that is, money income before paying taxes and not including the value of "in-kind" transfers. And therein lies the rub. Those in-kind transfers include all sorts of valuable benefits that have spilled from the government cornucopia: food stamps, housing assistance, medical care, and so forth. In fact, the CBO reported that although cash assistance in 1976 amounted to $18 billion, the cumulative perks in the form of in-kind transfers cost government $41.1 billion.

How does such selective bookkeeping affect the welfare rolls? The CBO was curious and decided to hire an independent source to obtain the same sort of information that the Census Bureau collects. This unidentified research team asked more searching questions to spot nonreported and underreported income and to determine just how much those in-kind transfers affected total income.

The answers resulted in some startling conclusions, which the CBO report states starkly: "In fiscal year 1976, without any public transfer payments or taxes, approximately 21.4 million families would have been poor . . . roughly one out of every four families. When public cash transfers are counted—the Census concept of income—the incidence of poverty is halved to 10.7 million families (13.5 percent of all families.) *If in-kind transfers are included and taxes are taken, 6.6 million families remain in poverty* (8.3% of all families). . . . Including Medicare and Medicaid benefits, this represents about a 70 percent reduction in the number of families who would be considered poor using the pre-tax pre-transfer concept" (italics added).[12]

Heigh-ho, as Glencora Palliser, the leading character in a popular 1977 television series, might have said. Glencora, wife of a fictional nineteenth century British prime minister, was a pragmatic woman whose valuable advice to her sensitive, aristocratic husband was to listen to his critics as well as his friends in making up his mind about an issue. Maybe Jimmy Carter needed Glencora to point out that things were not as bad as some of his advisers were saying.

As with most of the Carter proposals in 1977, critics were in abundance on the welfare-reform plan. The AFL-CIO Executive Council said that it "falls far short of what is needed to provide the poor with decent jobs or adequate income. It also fails to provide the immediate fiscal relief which states and cities so urgently need."[13]

A favorite phrase revived from the early 1970s was frequently quoted in the media, to the effect that the proposals were too stingy for the liberals, too expensive for the conservatives. Such was the pronouncement also on the death in 1973 of Richard Nixon's Family Assistance Plan, which called for national minimum-income guarantees for all families as well as work requirements. One reason for its defeat was that liberals in Congress were pressured into voting against it by welfare-rights lobbyists whose favorite word for welfare recipients was "clients." On the other hand, conservatives rejected the concept of a guaranteed annual income and feared that costs would be uncontrollable.

The most vocal critic then, as again in 1977, was Senator Long of Louisiana, head of the Senate Finance Committee, who favors piecemeal changes in the present system with emphasis on a more stringent work requirement than either the Nixon or the Carter plans contained. That concept of "workfare," insisting in essence that every welfare recipient work for his or her benefits, probably administered the coup de grace to the Nixon plan, fostering in the minds of many the picture of children left untended while mothers toiled in servitude. The enormous surge in the number of women working in recent years has somewhat blurred that particular fear. Public attitudes, too, are increasingly swinging toward approval of requiring work in exchange for public assistance wherever possible.

It would seem that President Carter and Senator Long were not too far apart in their wish to tie welfare to work. Actually, however, the Senator was spearheading the legislative assault on the White House program on both practical and ideological grounds, warning that costs would be prohibitive and that even more people would become dependent on welfare. Mr. Long told one group that the original estimate for Medicaid had been $238 million in 1965 and that it had risen to $2.3 billion by 1969 and $20 billion in 1977, adding, "with some of our past experience to serve as a guide, we'd better be prepared for an actual cost of $60 billion or even $120 billion."[14] Asserting that it was unrealistic to assume that the Carter program would eliminate fraud and dependency, he cited vast increases in the numbers of persons who have claimed total disability since programs to aid the disabled were expanded. In a similar vein other critics cited the rise in unemployment figures in 1972 when the Talmadge Amendment became law, requiring that all welfare recipients must actively look for work, which may have led many who weren't looking to claim that they were.

While the President's welfare program was being sidetracked in Congress by more pressing business, Senator Long's power was strong enough to get a pilot workfare project through Congress as one of the riders attached to the Social Security amendments passed in late 1977. This rider authorized states to use AFDC program funds to experiment with special work projects for welfare recipients. The experiments could last two years and would pay participants prevailing wages. Other welfare riders that became law through the same ruse would: (1) provide state and local governments with an additional $187 million in fiscal 1978 to help them pay welfare costs, (2) establish financial incentives for states to reduce welfare payment error rates, and (3) give states access to wage record information maintained by the Social

Security Administration and employment security agencies for AFDC recipients.

The whole welfare reform concept was moving like molasses through a special House subcommittee, which endorsed most of Mr. Carter's plan, including the guaranteed annual wage and earned income tax credits, with some provisos that would add a billion here and subtract a billion there. When the first round of deliberations ground to a halt in mid-December, the subcommittee put off until 1978 the sticky question of how to create jobs for the poor.

One problem that all the proposed work requirements posed was the kinds of public-sector jobs that could be filled by poor, unskilled workers. The President's proposal was to create 1.4 million new jobs, the largest public jobs program since the Depression. He said that jobs would be created in areas such as public safety, recreational facilities and programs, facilities for the handicapped, environmental monitoring, child care, waste treatment, recycling, cleanup and pest and insect control, home services for the elderly and ill, weatherizing of homes and buildings, teachers' aides, and cultural arts activities. Whether such jobs could be filled by unskilled workers or would duplicate services already being performed by state and city employes is in doubt.

A case in point was the workfare program underway in Milwaukee in mid-1977. The WPA-type program there, as described by the *New York Times,*[15] offered single people without dependents who applied for welfare aid a choice: take a job, when available, doing such chores as sweeping streets, cleaning parks, or doing clerical work—or receive no benefits. Wages were $2 per hour for a 32-hour week for the welfare employes, who often worked alongside civil-service employes earning twice as much. Several complaints have been filed against the program by municipal unions, charging that its members are being put out of work, replaced by the $2-per-hour employes. The same concern has prompted the national AFL-CIO to fire a salvo of criticism of the Carter plan, charging, among other things, that it would form a "pool of second-class citizens" and would undercut the nation's wage structure. Workers in the Milwaukee program had mixed views: some resented doing the same work for less pay; others felt that the work was more satisfying than receiving mere handouts.

Another problem confronting any kind of minimal-pay workfare program was voiced before a House committee by none other than Labor Secretary Ray Marshall, who told the legislators that many Americans today feel that manual labor is distasteful: ". . . many people in our society have a monumental bias against work, especially manual work and the people who do it . . . that it's somehow degrading."[16]

Secretary Marshall's comments were borne out two days later by an article in the New York Times[17] on a bitter controversy between apple growers in Winchester, Virginia and Mr. Marshall's own Labor Department. The apple growers have been importing pickers from Jamaica because, they claim, few domestic workers want that kind of job. One of the growers told a tale of frustration: He had hired a dozen professed apple pickers from the region to harvest the fall crop; five actually showed up at 7 A.M. the first day of picking. By 10 A.M. only two were left, and at 3 in the afternoon he didn't have any workers. Such shenanigans caused a group of apple growers to bring suit against the Labor Department to force it to certify the importation of foreign workers. Similar stories are told by mushroom growers in Pennsylvania, grape growers in California, and a host of other employer groups to justify hiring illegal Mexican immigrants.

To return for a moment to the July blackout in New York City, the lessons learned from prosecuting the arrested looters were perplexing. According to the district attorney of Brooklyn, hardest hit of the five boroughs of the city, 176 persons were indicted of the 1004 arrested during the blackout. Of those 176, almost half—48%—had full-time jobs. One was a $372-a-week meat cutter. Others included a U.S. Navy man and eight city or federal employes. Eleven percent were students. Of the 41% classified as unemployed, most of them were enrolled in paid poverty or training programs. Only 8.5% were on welfare. In fact, most of them, the DA said, were simply thieves.

In spite of such figures, J. Bruce Llewellyn, a member of a group called 100 Black Men and himself a victim of the looters, said in an Op-Ed article in the New York Times[18] shortly after the blackout that one of the real lessons to be learned from the catastrophe was that "present Government programs—welfare, jobs, housing, etc.—are wholly ineffective and cannot prevent a repetition of the disorder."

The foregoing figures and illustrations are not meant to be a diatribe against the poor or a case history of welfare failure. They are cited to illustrate our original premise that the welfare situation is indeed complex and that people of good will can and do frequently disagree on the best way to improve it.

Hundreds of scholarly studies have been done on these welfare complexities, and hundreds of proposals have been made for change. Recently, the thinking on welfare improvements has fallen into two broad categories: comprehensive reform, which would scrap most or all of the current system and replace it with something completely different; and "incrementalism," which basically means to tinker or fine-tune the present system to improve it.

President Carter's plan was more in the nature of the first category, as he himself indicated in the first sentence of his welfare message: "I am asking the Congress to abolish our existing welfare system and replace it with a job-oriented program for those able to work and a simplified, uniform, equitable cash assistance program for those in need who are unable to work by virtue of disability, age or family circumstance."

Part of the trouble with the President's ideas was that they were anything but "simplified." Representative Barber Conable of New York called the plan "unduly complicated," adding that parts of it were so confusing as to be incomprehensible. For example, at one point it said that only one job or training slot would be allowed for one adult per family, but elsewhere it said that other family members would remain eligible to participate in other training or youth programs. Another example: the concept was supposedly designed to keep families together. Yet apparently the basic yearly benefit of $2300 for families in which someone was deemed fit to work would go up to $4200 if that person (presumably the father) were no longer with the family.

As to the broad concept of comprehensive reform, the oldest and best-known idea is probably that of the negative income tax, a principle promoted by economist Milton Friedman. At first glance the idea is simplicity itself. Abolish all current welfare programs, except possibly Medicaid. In their place, make a straight cash payment to any family or individual whose income is below the poverty line. In other words, people whose income is above that line would pay "positive" income taxes into the Internal Revenue Service, which in turn would pay out "negative" tax money to those in need. Eliminating AFDC, food stamps, SSI, and so forth would reduce administrative costs, the argument goes, and replace a hodgepodge of inequities with a single, uniform system of payments made by the federal government. Former Representative Martha Griffiths, a strong proponent of such a uniform system, has urged that welfare checks be dispensed just as federal payments to postal workers, veterans, or Social Security recipients, with no geographical disparities.

The last attempt before 1977 at comprehensive reform of welfare was in 1969 when President Nixon introduced the Family Assistance Plan (FAP), a variation of the negative income tax idea. It held enough appeal to be passed twice by the House, in 1970 and 1971, but was defeated both times in the Senate because of the liberal–conservative split we cited before. Some of the features of President Carter's 1977 welfare plan are very similar to those of the Nixon FAP: flat payments to families of proven need, work incentives, public-service jobs, elimination of AFDC.

In a thoughtful article on welfare reform, three University of California analysts pointed out some of the obstacles the FAP ran up against and the political lessons they held for President Carter or any other architect of sweeping change. Writing in *The Public Interest*,[19] Messrs. Frederick Doolittle, Frank Levy, and Michael Wiseman said, "From a political perspective, the current welfare system is a web of vested interests; any program change will be met by political opposition." Enlarging on that theme, they wrote that the delicate balance of interests in welfare politics included such diverse elements as Russell Long, black welfare mothers in Los Angeles, mayors, governors, social workers, and the United States Chamber of Commerce.

They might have added that HEW itself is an administrative monster of 346,000 employes that controls the largest slice of the federal budget (35%) and that the whole welfare apparatus is well on its way to becoming, as in Great Britain, one of the country's major industries.

One of the misunderstandings that undercut the Nixon plan was whether benefit levels should be uniform in all states with no adjustments for variations of living costs. Critics attacked the FAP because its annual payment of $1600 was below the AFDC payment in more than half the states. Mr. Nixon had confused people by insisting that the grants be uniform throughout the country, but when he added that state supplements would be used to make sure no one lost benefits, his reassurance was either ignored or not heard.

The Carter plan was open to the same criticism, although it is extremely difficult to say yet which states would gain and which would lose. The President would abolish AFDC; his level of yearly benefits for a family of four fitting the AFDC description would total $4200. In 1976 federal and state AFDC benefits in Mississippi were $720 a year. Even with the value of food stamps added in, that state's benefits amounted to less than $2000. On the other hand, Hawaii currently pays the highest AFDC benefits of all—$5964—and with the value of food stamps added, an AFDC family in those palmy islands can draw well over $6000 a year. Obviously, in some states the new federal floor would be much higher than current welfare benefits, whereas in others it would be lower.

Mr. Carter said that each state would be free to supplement the basic benefits with matching federal payments available for the extras. He also said that each state would be required to pay 10% of the basic federal income benefits provided to its residents except where it would exceed 90% of its prior welfare expenditures. This would mean that the states to receive the most relief would be those with the highest current benefits. New York, Massachusetts, Illinois, and a few others would receive relief of 25% or more of their current outlays. Thus the reforms would most benefit those states that are now overly generous with their benefits and have created their own fiscal problems. It is estimated that the average relief under the plan is 18%, but 21 states would receive only around 11% relief.

Samuel T. Francis, a policy analyst for The Heritage Foundation, has pointed out a large number of anomalies and controversial features of the Carter proposal.[20] For one, he noted that adding singles and childless couples would expand the numbers on welfare at a time when most people want to reduce the welfare rolls. For another, he noted that the complicated two-tier benefit structure could lead to fraud and evasion and that the only penalty for someone in the upper tier who refused a job was to be dropped to the lower tier.

Mr. Francis had two caveats about the new standards of filing that should be considered. One was that, unlike the present system, the filing unit could be a nuclear family regardless of whether they lived with other nuclear units, a rule relaxation that could promote illegitimacy, he believed, as well as crowding in low-income housing. The other was about the assets test, which he said would make it possible for welfare recipients to own a house, expensive appliances, and a family car and still receive benefits from the federal government.

The main trouble with the Carter plan, the FAP, and other comprehensive welfare reforms is always one of arithmetic, whether it is the percentage of costs that the states pay or the actual level of benefits. It has been pointed out again and again by critics that a negative income tax, with its base payment plus deductions for work expenses plus low tax rates, could mean that families earning far above the poverty line could be eligible for some government support. Thus if you want to pay a substantial amount of money to those who have no other income and you also want to reward work, you have to pay small amounts even to people with relatively high incomes. President Carter's plan would completely phase out benefits to a family of four only when its income reached $8400. And tax credits would continue up to an income of $15,600.

Indeed, the more we think about comprehensive welfare-reform plans, the more we tend to agree with the Doolittle–Levy–Wiseman conclusion that "the uniform, efficient welfare system of the economic textbooks is nothing but a mirage." Judging from past experience, any sweeping reforms will almost certainly open a Pandora's box of new complexities, new inequities, and new expense.

What to do? After exploring the alternatives, we fall back reluctantly on the tinker's approach, more formally called incrementalism. As Richard P. Nathan of the Brookings Institution has said, in one sense the FAP has already been enacted: the food-stamp program provides more aid to the working poor than FAP would have; SSI has been established to provide payments to the aged, blind, and disabled; various work requirements, however, spotty, have been written into law; and job programs aimed to assist the poor already exist.[21]

The Agricultural Act of 1977, which gives food stamps to those who need them without charge, can be regarded as another incremental reform, albeit a dubious one. In typical helter-skelter fashion, the President had recommended early in the year that, under tighter, eligibility standards, food stamps should be free. While Congress was weaving this proposal into the agriculture bill, the President was recommending the complete abolishment of food stamps as part of his welfare reform. But the new food-stamp law was at least temporarily on the books and was being hailed as a boon to the working poor who could not previously scrape up the cost of the stamps. It can be regarded as a mini-negative income tax, even though it might mushroom into another vast giveaway program that will attract several more millions of recipients than is intended.

All things considered, further tinkering with the present system—solving the problems that can be recognized—is preferable to setting up a whole new scheme that would pose problems we haven't even thought about. To that end, syndicated columnist George F. Will tossed out an appropriate parable: A town's electricity generator failed and various engineers were unable to fix it, so an elderly professor was summoned. He examined the generator carefully, then tapped it lightly once with a hammer, and power was instantly restored. He submitted his bill for $1,000.02 and itemized it: "Tapping—$.02. Knowing where to tap—$1,000."[22]

CHAPTER TWELVE

SOCIAL SECURITY COSTS

When older Americans sneeze, Congress runs a fever. That's the most reasonable explanation for the mess both houses of Congress are making of Social Security reform.—New York Times editorial.[1]

IN THE 1950s THE CIVIL RIGHTS MOVEMENT LED TO SWEEPING changes in the way this country treats its black minority. The success of that movement led to the birth of powerful lobbies to promote welfare rights in the 1960s and Women's Rights in the early 1970s. Now in the late 1970s a potent new political force is coming to the fore to expand the rights of the elderly. In 1977 this movement burst into the headlines and into the lobbies of Congress with surprising suddenness.

Time magazine took notice of the surge of "gray power" with a cover story titled "Now, the Revolt of the Old."[2] The *New York Times* printed an article about the new and vociferous movement of the elderly with the headline, "The Old-Age Lobby Has a Loud Voice in Washington."[3] Throughout the country old people were asking, and getting, such benefits as reduced property- and income-tax rates, less-expensive medication, bargain electricity rates, group taxi service, hot-lunch programs, and low-cost public housing.

And in Washington, where respect for any sizeable bloc of voters is paramount, gray power was stampeding Congress into more of the act-now-think-later brand of legislation that has played such havoc with the nation's finances for the last decade. The twin goals of the oldsters in 1977: extend the mandatory retirement age and bolster Social Security.

Raising the mandatory retirement age from 65 to 70 was an idea that took root and blossomed so quickly that legislation was well underway before anyone had more than a hazy notion of how it would affect youth unemployment, sex discrimination, or the Social Security system itself. And its swift passage through the House of Representatives was an indication of how powerful the lobby for the elderly had become.

In April 1977 Representative John Brademas thought he was going out on a limb by predicting that Congress would outlaw mandatory retirement before the end of the decade. When he said that no one had ever lobbied him on the issue, Harriet Miller, executive director of the American Association of Retired Persons, said that she would have her lobbyists on his doorstep the next morning. Whether Ms. Miller made good on her promise is not known, but somebody must have been lobbying hard: a bill raising the mandatory retirement age to 70 was passed by both houses and sent to a conference committee, which prompted Brookings economist John Palmer to warn, "It's incredible that Congress would be moving so fast to replace one retirement system with a new one it knows so little about."[4]

Incredible was the best word, too, to describe the tortuous passage of the other major goal of the elderly, major Social Security reforms, from the White House through the House, through the Senate, and through conference committees before the first session of the 95th Congress wound up.

Although outlawing mandatory retirement was relatively new and untried, Social Security reform was like a revolving door in Washington, passing in and out of the halls of Congress with monotonous regularity. What made it pressing in 1977 was the fact, widely disseminated by the media, that Social Security was going broke by paying out more than it was taking in to the tune of $4.3 billion—that it was, in other words, threatening the lifeline of 33 million Americans who received Social Security benefits.

The message to do something was being sent, in thousands of letters, to the White House, and to every Senator and Representative and was being reinforced by the lobbyists of the American Association of Retired Persons, The Gray Panthers, Concerned Seniors for Better Government, the National Council of Senior Citizens, and the National Association of Retired Federal Employes. The result was the mess to which the *New York Times* editorial referred.

To understand the Social Security crisis of 1977 and the anxiety it engendered it is necessary to review briefly some history, and we do it with some arbitarary leaps in time and space, starting in Germany in 1884. It was then that German Chancellor Otto von Bismarck initiated the idea of a public pension system, setting the official retirement age at 65, which at that time sounded like a very advanced age, because the life expectancy was only 37. The relatively modest Social Security Act of 1935, which launched the system in the United States, copied Bismarck in making 65 the age of retirement, even though the average life expectancy in this country at that time was only about 60. The intention of the original act was a modest one. J. Douglas Brown, one of its architects, wrote recently that the system was not intended to be an enlarged private insurance scheme run by the government. It was, rather, to prevent hardship in old age by providing "the most adequate protection possible within the limits of available funds."[5]

In 1937 workers in commerce and industry began paying into the system 1% of the first $3000 of their salaries, and employers contributed a like amount. In 1940 Miss Ida M. Fuller of Vermont became the first beneficiary, receiving a payment of $22.54. Miss Fuller, by the way, died in 1975 at the age of 100, having contributed $22 to the fund and received more than $20,000 in benefits over 35 years.

The money paid to Miss Fuller and 220,000 other beneficiaries in 1940 had been collected into the Old Age and Survivors Trust Fund from those Social Security taxes deducted from paychecks. It was called an "intergenerational transfer"; that is, workers paid into the fund in order to support old people already retired, and in turn they would eventually collect pensions from younger workers paying into the fund.

The system was simple and Americans of modest means, who had faced the poorhouse when they became too old to work, now were building a retirement nest egg.

But over the years that simple plan got more and more complicated. Gradually it was expanded to cover more workers and more dependents with a greater variety of benefits. Domestic and farm workers were added. So were the self-employed, permanently disabled workers and their dependents, as well as a host of retirees' dependents and survivors, including full-time students. Government workers could join voluntarily. Reduced benefits for workers who chose to retire at 62, as well as their dependents, were granted. Medicare was added to provide hospital insurance for those over 65. The snowballing effect kept picking up momentum. In 1947 less than 2 million people collected benefits—one for every 22 workers. By 1967 the beneficiaries had reached 24 million—one for every 3.1 workers. Today, with 33,000,000 Americans receiving benefits, there are less than three workers for every beneficiary, and by the year 2035 the ratio is expected to be about 2 to 1. Only about half of those 33 million presently receiving benefits are retired workers.

How has all of this been financed? A comedian would reply, "with great difficulty." More precisely, the answer is that it has not been adequately financed, and that is why President Carter and Congress were being pressed so hard in 1977 to save the Social Security system from what looked like certain bankruptcy.

Although payroll taxes have gone up steadily and so has the wage base, benefits have far outstripped them. From the original 2% tax, divided equally between worker and employer, the rate in 1977 was 11.7% or 5.85% each, and the wage base was $16,500. But even though one dollar out of every four the federal government collects comes from the Social Security tax, the trustees of the Old Age and Survivors Trust Fund were predicting that the fund would be exhausted by 1984, if not earlier, and that the Disability Fund would be out of cash by 1979. In 1977 those two funds were expected to pay out about $80 billion in benefits, some $4.3 billion more than they took in.

Like so many other threats to the government's solvency and to the stability of the dollar, the Social Security muddle of 1977 was a product of those heady days of the 1960s and early 1970s when Congress seemed to be operating under the illusion that government's capacity to grant benefits to the public was virtually unlimited by any need to consider cost. This was the political corruption of Keynesian economics and one that the great British economist would almost certainly have rejected out of hand. When President Nixon declared in 1972 that "I am now a Keynesian," it was not a declaration that he had read and understood Lord Keynes' general theory but rather an acknowledgment that as a shrewd politician he had come to recognize the political benefits that accrue to anyone who can seem to endlessly divide loaves and fishes for distribution to the multitudes.

There is no area of legislation where the act-now-think-later mentality of Congress is more evident than Social Security. One of the flaws in the system that partly accounts for the rapidly growing deficit came about as the result of a gross miscalculation by Congress in a 1972 amendment to the Social Security Act. At that time the lawmakers decided that benefits for both current and future retirees should be adjusted periodically to allow them to keep pace with rises in both prices and wages. The unintentional effect of this law has been to "double-index" benefits, causing them to rise about twice as fast as the rate of inflation. The law was intended to protect workers already retired, and it did. But it was much too generous to workers who were to retire in the future. By the year 2050, according to one calculation, the average retiree could receive $34,000 a year in benefits.

The assumption on which Congress acted was that wages would continue to keep pace with prices, as they had since 1952. Since the maximum-wage base on which Social Security taxes were calculated rose automatically with national average wages and those wages were expected to keep abreast of prices, Congress reasoned that no increase in the tax rates would be necessary. However, the situation soon began changing rapidly. Unemployment rose, and many fewer workers and employers than expected were paying Social Security taxes. Many of those laid off chose to retire earlier and began drawing benefits from Social Security. At the same time inflation began to spurt upward, causing benefits to rise much faster than anticipated.

Compounding the error was a major miscalculation of the birth rate. Gazing into their crystal ball in 1972, Congressional statisticians predicted that women would bear 2.5 children for the foreseeable future and assumed that there would be enough workers paying into Social Security to keep things balanced. The birthrate, however, continued its 20-year slide downward, and by 1976 the prediction on which Social Security relies was that there will be only 1.9 children per woman for the next 75 years; in Social Security parlance that means two workers for every beneficiary.

Another misjudgment in calculating benefits concerns the number of people claiming disability, a figure that has risen far more than was anticipated. In 1957, the first year that disability benefits were paid, only 150,000 workers received them. The number had risen to 1.5 million by 1970 and to 2.7 million at the end of 1976. The sharp rise has taken everybody connected with administering the program by surprise, and no one has a ready explanation of the reasons in the absence of medical evidence that disabilities are truly more widespread. One possible explanation is that the law provides no middle ground: either an employe is able to work or he can be judged completely disabled, and there are no nationwide standards for determining that dividing line. Standards vary so widely from state to state that when 221 claims that had been ruled on in one state were submitted to 10 different states in a random test, there was complete agreement on only 48 of the claims.

"There is no disability decision that is simple," according to Professor Monroe Berkowitz, a Rutgers University economist who specializes in Social Security matters. But, commenting about public attitudes, he added, "To be disabled has become a socially acceptable role."[6]

To be sure, the United States was not alone in grappling with mounting Social Security problems. It was a worry to most Western societies where benefits had risen faster than the public's ability (or willingness) to pay for them. Great Britain claimed a surplus in its government Social Security funds, but the pensions paid out were often so small that retirees were forced to ask for outright welfare. West Germany was juggling billions of dollars worth of taxes and trust funds to keep its system from going bankrupt in 1978. In Italy, employers were rebelling against an enormous 35% Social Security tax on workers' wages.

President Carter had promised, during his campaign, to get down to business quickly in restoring Social Security to something approximating soundness without reducing benefits or raising taxes paid by low- and moderate-income workers. In early May of 1977 he made a series of proposals, the major points of which were:

1. Employers would be required to pay taxes on the whole of their payroll instead of on only the first $16,500 of each employe's wage. This "uncapping" would take place in three stages, starting in 1979 and ending in 1981.

2. The $16,500 present maximum-wage base for employe contributions, already scheduled to rise to $23,400 by 1982, would go up to $25,800 instead, with a scheduled 1% tax-rate hike coming sooner.

3. General funds from the Treasury would be transferred to Social Security coffers whenever unemployment exceeded 6%.

4. Double-indexing would end, and benefits would be geared only to wages. This is called "decoupling."

As with Mr. Carter's energy package, the Social Security plan did not get a universally warm reception. And as with the energy plan, that was just as well, because it contained some basic flaws that might have caused as much trouble as did the 1972 amendments, rather than rescuing the system from those earlier misguided efforts.

Among the early critics of Mr. Carter's plan was David Ranson, a young Englishman who had issued warnings five years earlier about the potential effects of the 1972 amendments to the Social Security Act. Mr. Ranson, a consultant to the Treasury in the Ford Administration, had some succinct comments on the Carter proposal, calling it "largely cosmetic and an enormous lost opportunity." The plan, he said, did essentially nothing to reduce the enormous growth of outlays, but was a broad-gauged plan to increase taxes, especially on upper-income groups, and contained accounting gimmicks that if effective would temporarily alleviate the cash-flow problem but would merely divert attention from the serious economic problems.

Mr. Ranson wrote: "High-wage employes do not go unscathed when taxes are imposed on employers. A tax on the use of any resource is the same as a tax on the resource itself. It makes no difference from whom the tax is collected in the first instance. A payroll tax reduces take-home wages and raises unit labor costs. It curtails employment. This is especially true in this instance where the higher-wage burden does not carry with it increased benefits. . . . In effect, the plan adds work disincentives to the economy in exactly that area where they are apt to cause the largest discouragement to work effort and production."

The business community was alarmed at what it viewed in the Carter plan as a thinly disguised surcharge on business profits. Albert H. Cox, Jr., chief economist for Merrill Lynch & Company, said that the proposed increase in employer contributions to the system would be tantamount to a tax surchage of 12% on business profits by 1981—the biggest such increase in 30 years.

HEW Secretary Califano had suggested blandly at a White House briefing on the proposals that increasing employer labor costs would not inhibit hiring. Rather, he said, corporations would absorb the extra cost out of profits. Edward H. Kay, Jr. of Sears Roebuck, representing the Council of State Chambers of Commerce, testified before the House Subcommittee on Social Security in July 1977 and had a different view from Mr. Califano.

Mr. Kay said, "The criterion under the administration's total payroll is not whether the business is profitable or large or small, but the number of higher paid employes. This, we believe, will produce very capricious and regrettable results. Generally, business in the long run will not absorb the increased costs of taxing total payroll out of profits—but to the extent it does it will reduce funds available for capital investment—thus having an adverse effect on the creation of jobs. To the extent that the market permits, increased costs will be passed on to the consumers in increased prices and that will be inflationary. Also, since payroll taxes are viewed as wage related costs, applying the employer tax to total payroll, to the extent it is not passed on to the consumer, will tend to depress wages and fringe benefits. A marginal company is unlikely to be in a position to pass on the costs; therefore, taxing total payroll would create a harsh and unfair situation for them."

Still another objection to raising the employer share of the tax was that it would have increased the incentive for state and local governments to recommend that their employes withdraw from Social Security, an option that workers in the private sector do not have. Some 10 million state, city, and county workers now participate in the system, but over the last few years there has been a slight but noticeable trend for these government employes to leave the system after giving the required two years' notice. The Washington Post in 1976 quoted an employe of Fairfax County, Virginia, just across the river from Washington, D.C., as saying, ". . . you could have a beautiful retirement system if you didn't have to pay Social Security. We'll definitely study [the withdrawal option] and I think when things get rolling you'll find a lot of groups getting out."[8] With such government employes accounting for about 9% of the total system, their withdrawal would create new actuarial problems for Social Security. The enviable role and influence of federal employes, who are not covered by Social Security, are discussed later.

Mr. Carter's proposal for dipping into general revenues was not viewed with much enthusiasm either. The most typical response was to ask, "What revenues?" To many it bordered on the ludicrous to borrow money from the Treasury, which had a fiscal 1977 deficit of some $45 billion, in order to reduce another deficit that was, for the moment at least, "only" $4.3 billion. Representative Ullman, chairman of the House Ways and Means Committee, seemed to sum up the general resistance to this idea in his comment that "we just can't continue loading everything onto income taxes."

A deeper philosophical concept was at issue as well in the debate about borrowing from general revenues. It was the concept Americans have, however slenderly rooted in fact, that Social Security is a pay-as-you-go plan, a benefit already paid for by taxes that everyone shared equally. The complete and true financing of benefits, it is believed, is evident in the deduction made from nearly every paycheck; if Congress raised the Social Security tax everyone would feel it immediately and could judge whether or not the raise was warranted. This would not be true if the financing was hidden away in the vast expenditures from general revenues. Social Security would become, in fact, just another welfare program.

Implicit in this concept, of course, is the notion that Social Security is like a private pension plan, which it is not. In a private plan a fund is built up through premiums and the money is invested in securities that yield returns and provide an assured source of benefit payments. In 1971, before the effects of double-indexing became a factor, the Social Security Administration cited an example of how a young person would fare in a private plan compared with Social Security. If a young man of 18 should start investing the same amount he paid in Social Security tax in a private plan that yielded a 5.5% investment return, it would grow to $107,983 when he reached the age of 65. If you added his employer's contribution, which must be regarded as a fringe benefit and part of the employe's contribution, the sum would come to $215,966. For that amount, the young man could have bought a private annuity that would pay him almost $22,000 a year beginning at the age of 65 for the rest of his life, based on the life expectancy calculated by the Social Security Administration. But the agency itself estimated that the man's total Social Security benefits would be $94,904, including possible benefits for his wife or widow. In other words, private pension benefits would have been more than twice Social Security benefits.

Since 1971, of course, rapidly expanding benefits for retirees have meant that those with middle-income earnings during their working years now see little decline in their standard of living during retirement and have less incentive to save during their working years. Commenting on this fact in *The Public Interest*, Harvard economist Martin Feldstein wrote, ". . . the typical retiree receives from Social Security alone more than he was able to earn in his 30's, 40's and 50's—when he had children to support, a mortgage to pay, and other expenses. It is ironic and sad that Social Security forces many families to cut their spending even when their income is low and the responsibilities are great, in order to have more to spend during retirement when their income is already as high as it has ever been."[9]

The loss of investment capital to the nation is sad, too. Robert L. Schuettinger wrote in a 1977 booklet published by the Council on American Affairs that "if these huge sums were invested in the economy, public or private, the whole nation would benefit from increased capital accumulation and growth. As things stand now, because the payroll taxes are spent almost literally as soon as they are collected the whole nation is worse off than it could be. Because of this present allocation of vast quantities of money the capital needed to ensure a high standard of living for the present generation upon retirement will have been dissipated. It is impossible to underestimate the importance to the economy of a national pension plan based upon *savings* (which will add to the GNP) rather than a pay-as-you-go plan, together with borrowing, which will only increase inflation and not add to economic growth."

One of the President's eight proposals that escaped controversy was his recommendation to halt the ruinous effects of double-indexing by "decoupling" benefits from both wages and prices, a move which he said would cut the long-term deficit in half. But this was only half a loaf; the other half was "the enormous opportunity lost" that Mr. Ranson mourned, cutting the ratio of benefits to previous earnings.

These "replacement ratios," as they are called by economists, were figured by complicated formulas, but in essence they boiled down to an example like this one cited by Mr. Feldstein: a married man who retired in 1976 and who always had median earnings (about $8500) would receive cash and Medicare benefits worth nearly as much as his preretirement wages. And, because the benefit schedule was progressive, a person whose earnings were below the median could have a standard of living that was higher after retirement than it was before. If the current benefit-replacement ratios were to be maintained, Mr. Feldstein said, the tax rate would have to rise to 16 or 17% from the current 11.7%. If worker productivity growth should be less than the 2% currently anticipated, the tax rate would have to rise even further.

Raising taxes and/or cutting benefits were the tough choices facing Congress as it wrestled with Social Security throughout the summer. With 1978 elections just around the corner the legislators had to summon the courage to adopt measures that were certain to upset one bloc of voters or another. Who was it to be? The elderly? Employers? Younger workers? Government employes? One show of bravado that surfaced briefly in the House Ways and Means Subcommittee withered quickly on the floor of the House under the fire of two of those blocs of voters. The subcommittee had decided that one way to ease the deficit and rectify a glaring anomaly would be to require all federal, state, and local government workers to join the Social Security System. Neither Congressmen nor those ubiquitous congressional aides who often draft bills nor 2.4 million other federal employes belong to Social Security, their own pension plans being far more lucrative.

This inequity was brought out forcefully by a news article in the *New York Times* at the very time the Social Security battle was still raging in Washington. The article announced that James B. Cardwell, Commissioner of Social Security, was retiring at the age of 55 with a Government pension of about $24,000 annually and for the first time in his life would begin paying taxes into the Social Security system because he was taking another job. The former commissioner criticized the retirement system that allows civil servants to draw an annuity at age 55 after 30 years' service or at age 60 after 20 years' service and declared that he did not intend to become a "double-dipper"—someone who draws both a federal pension and Social Security benefits. "I do think as a citizen, just standing back and looking at it, that the whole arrangement is not in balance," he said.

Apparently few of his colleagues in government service felt as dispassionate about the disparity. When the House began considering the measure in late October a blitz of mail from postal workers and other government workers all over the country as well as intense lobbying by federal employes in Washington caused the universal coverage proposal to lose by a lopsided vote.

The House chose to ignore the President's proposals to use funds from general revenues and to tax all of an employer's payroll, but it fashioned a steep tax rise of its own to cover the Social Security deficit. Under its bill the payroll tax would rise gradually for both workers and employers until it reached 7.10% in 1987 and the wage base would rise to $42,000. This whopping increase would mean that in 10 years the maximum Social Security levy would be $3,024.60 each for the employer and worker, compared with the current $965.30.

Another feature of the House bill, designed to appease elderly constitutents, would abolish, by 1982, the rule that persons between age 65 and 72 must forfeit part of their Social Security benefits if they hold a job and earn income above $3,000. This proposal has always been frowned on by Social Security actuaries who fear that ending the earnings ceiling would increase the flow of pension payments and further weaken the Social Security Trust fund. Some of this could be offset, of course, by continued payments into the fund by these workers.

A report in the *Wall Street Journal* on the House action summed it up this way: "Twice during the two-day floor debate, Congressmen faced the choice of rewarding sharply focused interest groups—elderly persons and government employes—at the expense of privately employed working-age people, whose clout is diffuse. Twice the result was a higher payroll tax."

It was already November when the Senate took up Social Security, and some members pleaded that the complicated and controversial measure should be held over to 1978 rather than being jammed through to quick passage. Senator Byrd declared, however, that he did not want Congress "to be subjected to the criticism of not having acted on a situation that cries out for action." He did not add that a tax hike of the proportions that seemed likely to be passed to rescue Social Security would be even more unpopular in an election year.

In less than a week, under Senator Byrd's firm hand, the Senate then passed a bill that differed from the House version mainly in the manner in which the enormous tax hike would be effected. Both chambers were willing to raise the payroll tax sharply as well as the wage base on which employes pay. But the Senate version was closer to President Carter's original proposal that employers be taxed on their entire payroll. The Senators would have raised the wage base on which employers pay from the first $16,500 of a worker's wages to the first $75,000 after 1985. The Senate refused to abolish a ceiling on all earnings for those over 65, as did the House, but did agree to raise the limitation to $6000 by 1979.

With everyone eager to quit Washington for the holidays, the fate of the Social Security measure became a cliffhanger for several weeks, first because of wrangling in the House over the appointment of conferees, and then, when the conference committee finally got underway, because of two extraneous riders the Senate had attached. Despite numerous differences between the House and Senate on the actual Social Security details, the committee settled them quickly. The sticking points dealt with welfare programs and college tuition tax credits. A compromise was soon reached on the welfare provisions, but it took the threat of a Presidential veto of the entire Social Security package before Sen. William V. Roth Jr. (R. Del.) agreed to give up his proposal to offer a credit of up to $250 a year for each child attending college.

Once that hurdle was cleared Congress quickly passed, and the President signed, the multifaceted bill that gave constituents as a Christmas gift a $227 billion tax hike over the next 10 years, the largest peacetime tax increase in the country's history. The final version bore almost no resemblance to Mr. Carter's initial proposals. Gone was the troublesome suggestion to borrow from Treasury funds. Gone, too, was the uncapped wage base for employers. In their stead, the new law provides additional funds for Social Security by sharp rises for everyone and by tripling payroll taxes for many workers and their employers over the next decade.

Carefully avoiding a large election year rise in the Social Security tax, the Congress decided to let already-scheduled increases stand for 1978. But from 1979 on through 1987, the payroll tax would rise to 7.15% each for worker and employer from the 1977 level of 5.85%. Over the same time period the maximum wage base would rise from the current $16,500 to $42,600. The impact will be particularly dramatic on workers earning the maximum taxable amount and on their employers. Each paid $965.25 into Social Security in 1977. By 1987 the worker who earns the maximum will be paying the government $3045.90 in Social Security taxes, an amount which will be matched by his employer.

To achieve the "decoupling" recommended by the President, the new act stabilizes the ratio of benefits to earnings slightly below current levels for workers retiring after 1983. The new ratio would give a worker who had average earnings a Social Security pension amounting to about 43% of his preretirement pay, plus another 22% if he has a dependent spouse. This change, it was claimed, would save the system about $2 trillion over the next 75 years. However, the benefits, which are tax-free, are still generous and the actual amounts paid out will still rise, particularly for those workers whose lifetime earnings have been near or above the maximum wage base, and for everyone in years when inflation causes upward cost-of-living adjustments.

The new law compromised differing opinions on the earnings ceiling for those over 65 by raising it gradually to $6000 by 1982 from the current $3000. Over that amount, individuals between 65 and 70 years of age would still lose 50 cents in benefits for every dollar earned, but anyone over 70 could earn as much as possible without penalty.

Two new provisions liberalize benefits for two special marital categories. To remove an incentive for the elderly to "live in sin," anyone over 60 who marries or remarries will be able to keep his or her previous benefits. And a divorced spouse would receive benefits after only 10 years of marriage, instead of 20.

The new law contained numerous provisions that seemed minor at the moment but may, of course, mushroom into unexpectedly new major expenses, as has happened so frequently with past Social Security legislation. It was being predicted, for instance, that raising the earnings ceiling for those over 65 would cost "only" a billion dollars, but no one seemed sure. Likewise, the remarriage benefits were initially expected to cost about $200 million a year, but as life expectancy rises so could these costs.

One big "if" in the new law concerns the 10 million nonfederal public employes in the Social Security system and the budgets of the states and municipalities for which they work. If the costs of the steep tax rises prove to be too much for already overburdened local budgets and if these public employes elect to leave the system, where does that leave Social Security bookkeeping? And while posing riddles, we might ask how churches, colleges, and other nonprofit organizations are to handle these large new expenses?

Indeed the ink was scarcely dry on the new Social Security laws when the lawmakers began to have second thoughts. Most were worrying that inflation and unemployment would rise more than expected, swelling the system's outflow and shrinking its income. The big tax increase itself could trigger such a chain reaction, some said, with employers either raising prices to offset the costs of the tax or laying off workers.

Representative Ullman startled some associates by predicting that some of the higher taxes would never take effect, adding that "a better financing mechanism" would soon be found. Although he did not say what alternative he had in mind, listeners assumed he was referring to a European-style value-added business tax, applied at each point in the exchange of goods and services, from first production to final consumption. This has been described as a "national sales tax."

With the real cost, both in dollars and in public confidence, yet to be measured, the situation reminds one, once more, of Mr. Feldstein, who has said, "As long as the voters support the Social Security system, it will be able to pay the benefits that it promises. It is therefore very important to prevent an increase in the tax rate or other changes that will undermine public support of the primary purpose of the system: providing basic income-related annuities that individuals otherwise could not or would not buy for themselves."

The pessimists in Washington wondered, at the end of 1977, if that point had been reached when a Harris survey showed that Americans were divided down the middle on the new law, with 43% favoring it, 43% opposed, and the rest undecided. It remained to be seen how public opinion would react when the next Social Security tax bite was actually reflected in the nation's paychecks.

Meanwhile, the extension of "gray rights" by raising mandatory retirement seemed close at hand as the year ended. But with final legislation still pending, observers were warning that a conflict between older citizens and those who are young or of a minority is inevitable. Gregory W. Smith of the Harvard Law School wrote that the consequence of raising or eliminating mandatory retirement "will be a freezing up of the job market and especially of opportunities for advancement. . . . This logjam at career's end will inevitably slow the assimilation of minorities and women into positions from which they have been most effectively excluded in the past."[13] Businessmen were beginning to protest that raising the retirement age would hamper them from clearing out the deadwood and making way for younger people without having to fire anyone.

Whether the measure would actually benefit or harm many people is still a matter of conjecture. But one nearly-65-year-old regards the idea as "mischievous." In his *Wall Street Journal* column,

Vermont Royster, wrote that the bill "reflects an attitude much preva-lent today about the making of law and universal rules that has already done us much mischief, and if continued will do much more."[14] The column went on to cite such universal rule-making problems as those caused by banning any substance suspected of causing cancer, ban-ning any building on land that may be flood-prone, and the affirmative action programs that have led to "a morass of rules and regulations."

One can only hope that sometime soon, before the elderly, the young, and the minorities actually square off against each other, the people in Washington will have the courage and good sense to reform Social Security in a way that does not unduly penalize any group or, for that matter, any worker.

CHAPTER THIRTEEN

THE NATIONAL HEALTH

Deciding on the correct quality and style of medical care requires involving the individual family and its own physician in the decision of how much they want to spend for medical care and how much for other things.—Harvard economist Martin Feldstein, writing in *The Public Interest.*[1]

ONE OF THE MOST POPULAR PLAYS ON THE LONDON STAGE IN the late 1960s was a satirical comedy called *The National Health*. The title is the phrase the British use when they talk about their program of tax-supported health care. Playwright Peter Nichol's London audiences obviously responded to his satirical thrusts at the impersonal and detached attitude of hospital doctors and nurses toward their patients.

The thrusts were not entirely fair, of course. British doctors and nurses are much the same as in the United States, mostly hard-working and conscientious. But there can be little doubt that when a third party, either government or a private insuror, becomes involved in medical decisions, doctor and patient by definition lose some of their individuality. This may or may not change the quality of care, but one thing is certain: it changes the economies of medical care, making overall costs harder to control, just as Professor Feldstein suggests.

"The national health" was one of the knottiest public policy questions confronting the Carter administration. In the United States, unlike Britain, the phrase can have several meanings. The most emotion-free, and least often intended, is merely the "state of the nation's health."

Although benign, this definition is worth discussing because it casts considerable light on the health issue, mainly in the sense of demonstrating that the nation's fundamental health and the availability of medical care may be less closely related than is sometimes suggested.

According to HEW estimates, in 1975 there were 4.8 million people working in the health industry in the United States, 375,000 of them—one for every 570 citizens—were physicians. Medical schools have doubled their capacity since 1960, and the number of paraprofessionals, trained in health care but lacking a medical degree, is also increasing.

On the whole, Americans have never had better health. Life expectancy is up to an average of 72.5 for both men and women; infant deaths are the lowest in our history; many of the killer diseases have been nearly eradicated. But are these heartening statistics due solely to wonder drugs, new medical technology, and more plentiful health care?

Dr. Eric J. Cassell of the Cornell University Medical College thinks not. In his book, *The Healing Art,* an excerpt of which appeared in the *Wall Street Journal*,[2] Doctor Cassell cited several convincing illustrations to back up his conviction that improved living conditions rather than modern medicine have been responsible for reducing the ravages of disease in the United States. He told of an extensive, five-year medical-team effort to improve the health of Navaho Indians in the 1950s. There were decreases in a few specific ailments, but at the end of five years there was virtually no change in the overall disease pattern or death rates. The investigators concluded, he said, that the disease and mortality patterns were a result of the way the Navahos lived and could not be changed until basic changes had taken place in the tribe's way of life.

In the country as a whole, Dr. Cassell reminded us, the death rate from tuberculosis, the incidence of typhoid fever, and the high infant mortality arising from diarrhea–pneumonia all were sharply reduced before effective drugs and vaccines were discovered. This occurred, he said, because standards of living, education, nutrition, and sanitation had improved.

Indeed, many of the menaces to health in the United States today are, ironically, symptoms of our affluent, sedentary lifestyle. Just as tuberculosis, typhoid fever, and infant infections of the early 1900s could be traced to crowded, unsanitary living conditions and bad nutrition, so obesity, some cancers, and coronary heart disease can be linked to overeating, tobacco, lack of exercise, and stress. Doctor Cassell thought it would be naive to expect that medical science by itself could erase these modern health problems, and added, "Medical care did not get us out of our past troubles, and it will not get us out of our present ones."

To return to the definition of "the national health," however, its more common meaning, and one that is filled with emotional overtones, is government-financed health insurance fashioned along the lines of the British system. The American Medical Association used to call this "socialized" medicine before doctors began to relax their opposition to certain limited forms of government intervention in the health-care industry. Still, during most of the postwar era, any suggestion that the government might devise a national health-insurance policy of its own has created intense public controversy.

The Carter administration came to office at an interesting time in the evolution of the national health-insurance issue. What had seemed to be an inexorable movement toward such insurance in the 1960s and early 1970s had been slowed by two facts. First, the United States government was running out of money, was, in fact, running chronic deficits largely as a result of the sharply rising costs of social programs it had undertaken in the 1960s and the continuing high rate of military spending. Congressmen were beginning to perceive that the only way the costs of a huge national health-insurance program could be contained would be through rigorous and probably unworkable government control over the incomes of every person involved in medical care, from surgeons to hospital orderlies. Furthermore, it would require a virtual big-brother supervision of every aspect of health care—where hospitals could be built, how many beds each could have, where physicians would be permitted to practice, who should have an appendectomy, who should receive eyeglasses, or even (perhaps carried to its not-impossible extreme) when and where one should get a bottle of aspirin.

The costs of health care in the United States were already getting out of hand. The total bill for America's health care in 1976 was $139 billion, up $62 billion in five years and $100 billion since 1965. Outlays for health were accounting for 8.6% of the GNP, more than was being spent for defense. In more human terms, in 1977 it cost $1020 a year to buy medical and hospital insurance coverage in San Francisco for a family of four, almost double what it cost four years earlier. But that figure only covered actual premium costs. It is estimated that actual medical costs for a family of four in 1977 were about $2500, the sum of doctor bills, insurance premiums, and taxes used for Medicare and Medicaid.

While all medical costs rose twice as fast as the overall cost of living from 1950 to 1976, the most dramatic part of the increase was in hospital expenses. In 1950 the average daily cost per patient was only $16. By 1976 it was about $175, an increase of more than 1000%.

Many reasons were being given for the spiraling hospital costs. One was that too many hospitals had been built. The claim has been made that out of 930,000 hospital beds in the country, up to 100,000 are surplus. It costs an average of $60,000 to provide one hospital bed and half that to maintain it each year. Another reason often given is that too much money is being spent on expensive equipment. A favorite example is the proliferation of CAT-scanners, $500,000 sophisticated X-ray machines that picture soft internal body tissue.

Too much government and red tape are also contributing factors. Alex McMahon, president of the American Hospital Association, lashed back at HEW critics in August 1977 when he told the AHA convention that government officials who want to stop escalating costs of health care should realize that they are "part of the problem." Eight new federal regulations issued earlier in the year would add an average of $22 to the bill of each patient in the nation's hospitals, he said. Other hospital officials say that hospitals must cope with as many as 1000 regulations enforced by up to 100 overlapping agencies.

Still another cause of rising medical costs is the fear among doctors generated by a proliferation of malpractice suits, a fear that can lead to excessive and costly treatment. According to a survey reported in *Dun's Review* in May 1977,[3] physicians now order an extraordinary number of tests and X-rays to forestall a patient's suing in the event something is overlooked. Premiums for malpractice insurance rates have risen spectacularly in some states.

But the heaviest blame should be laid at the door of the government and private insurance plans, which issue virtual blank checks to cover expensive treatments and facilities. An article in *U.S. News & World Report*[4] stated that Americans pay less than one tenth of their own hospital bills and one-third of their physicians' fees directly.

"Furthermore," the article continued, "under many insurance policies a patient can run up a big hospital bill and never pay a cent for treatment that would cost him hundreds of dollars if performed in a doctor's office. For this reason, patients sometimes are hospitalized even for routine convalescence or diagnostic checkups, health officials say. Various studies contend that 8% to 20% of all patients in hospitals should be sent home or put in nursing facilities—a move that would reduce their bills by 75%."

The spectacular rise of health care costs has been matched by the growth of third-party medical insurance to pay for them. In 1976 over 90% of hospital payments and 60% of doctors' fees were covered by either private or public insurance plans. In a scholarly study on that subject, Harvard economist Feldstein has pointed out that with the vast increase in insurance coverage since 1950, the net out-of-pocket cost to the patient, in real terms, has hardly changed at all. Mr. Feldstein wrote: "I think this is the essence of the hospital-cost inflation problem: Increased insurance has induced hospitals to improve their product and provide much more expensive care."[5]

A critic of the health care industry, Professor Clark C. Havighurst of Duke University, said in an interview at the university that a good case could be made that the private sector's failure to control cost lies in the influence that doctors and hospitals have exerted over the design and operation of health-insurance plans.

"Health insurance was blocked by the medical establishment for years. It was only when hospitals and doctors themselves came to sponsor—and control—third-party payment programs such as Blue Cross and Blue Shield that they became an accepted medium of financial protection."

According to Professor Havighurst, the "Blues" created the principle of comprehensiveness and shallow coverage "in order to help health care providers collect their bills, not because it made sense to the consumer." The Blues also set up an effective deterrent to cost controls "because they took the position that, if a doctor ordered something, it should be paid for unless it was absolutely unjustifiable medically. Commercial insurers found themselves subject to intense criticism and pressure if they sought to impose limits on what they would pay for."

Anxiety over health costs has been growing throughout the 1970s, in government, in business and industry, even among the private insurers themselves. Ford Motor Company said that its medical insurance bill rose to $298 million in 1975 from $68 million a decade before, and it has been estimated that by 1979 automobile manufacturers will be paying $3000 per worker for health insurance.

The 20 largest private group health-insurance companies have reported underwriting losses in four of the years between 1969 and 1976 and are meeting stiff resistance from customers angered by the rise in insurance premiums. Illustrative of their concern about costs and their own struggle to survive is a remark made by Robert D. Kilpatrick, president of the Connecticut General Insurance Company: "If the private sector cannot show that it is able to control these rapidly rising costs, business managements, unions and everyone else concerned may well throw in the towel and seek a government takeover out of despair."[6]

Judging from past government performance, that would indeed be an act of despair. To its credit, the federal government has been just as anxious as everyone else over mounting health costs and has spent $11 million on studies since 1972 to try to find out what is wrong. But it shouldn't really have taken $11 million to discover that, as the AHA president said, government itself is part of the problem.

Presumably, part of that money was spent on a study reported in a Congressional Budget Office background paper on federal medical programs. The paper, published in August 1977, contains this statement: "Since the enactment of Medicare and Medicaid, the rate of inflation in the health-care sector has been disproportionately high, both in absolute terms and relative to the overall rate of inflation."[7]

In 1966, the last year before the two Medis came into existance, the public portion of all health care costs was 25%. In 1976 it had become 42%. Most of the public expenditure was for federal and state Medis. The federal portion alone in 1976 was $26 billion, up threefold in six years, and if present trends continue it is expected to be $32 billion in 1978, a 40% spurt in two years.

Medicare provides coverage for hospital and some home health-care costs for 99 out of 100 Americans over the age of 65. An optional extra that has been elected by about 96% of aged people provides further insurance for fees for doctors, tests, and ambulance service. Since Medicare came into being, the number of hospital days accounted for by the elderly has risen by about half.

The costs of Medicare are financed entirely by Social Security taxes and are managed at the federal level. Medicaid, an adjunct to the welfare program, is jointly financed and managed by federal and state governments and, as in many such joint programs, responsibility and control over expenditures are often ill defined.

In the mid-1970s Medicaid was beset by charges of overpayments to certain doctors and nursing homes said to be running "Medicaid mills" to take advantage of slipshod administration of Medicaid money. In 1966 the poor of all ages saw doctors less frequently than the nonpoor did, but by 1974 the poor were using physicians' services at a slightly higher rate than other groups. Some of those visits were probably unnecessary, a fact that became apparent when 1976 Senate hearings on Medicaid fraud uncovered such practices as "ping-ponging" patients through batteries of unnecessary tests, "kiting" the real-estate value of nursing homes, and billing for nonexistent patients.

After three years of consideration, Congress passed a bill in October 1977 to curb such scandals by increasing penalties for fraud and abuse, strengthening the oversight responsibilities of Professional Standards Review Organizations made up of physicians, and generally tightening administration.

The scandals, as well as the overall costs, illustrated the comment of medical writer Harry Schwartz, in his book *The Case for American Medicine*,[8] that "The whole history [of Medicare and Medicaid] is a classic example of what happens when government acts without really understanding what it is doing, or what the impact of its actions will be."

Although the 1976 Democratic party platform called for national health insurance and Mr. Carter had endorsed that plank, when he took office he was faced at once with the task of trying to get better control over the plethora of programs that government had already created. For the moment, then, there was little time or inclination to carry out the national health-insurance pledge and thus bite off a bigger chunk of the health-care business. But pressure was mounting on all sides to find some remedy for containing medical costs. What to do? Mr. Carter did what Presidents always seem to do when they run out of ideas—he opted for direct controls.

Direct economic controls are not so much a policy as an admission of policy failure. They are what government does when it can't think of anything else to do. And they almost never "work" in the intended sense. The reason is that although prices can be controlled, costs can't be, or at least not entirely, which is almost the same as saying not at all. To control agricultural prices in the strictest sense, for example, you would have to be willing to put some farmers out of business because their costs are subject to forces no one can control—bad weather, for example. Hospitals buy food. Some costs—heating oil, for example—are set by world markets, which an individual sovereign nation can't control. Hospitals use a lot of heating oil. And labor unions don't like to stand still for wage freezes when their members experience inflationary pressures. Hospitals use a lot of labor.

In spite of these considerations, the Carter proposals, introduced in April 1977, limit annual rises to 8.3% on total revenues received for inpatient treatment at acute care hospitals. A second proposal would require hospitals to obtain government approval for any capital expenditure above $100,000. However, to soften the impact of the revenue "cap," and avoid union complaints, there was a provision for the "passthrough" of nonsupervisory wage increases.

As it happens, none of these proposals was really new. Hospital-cost regulation had been tried during President Nixon's controls fiasco in the early 1970s and had caused mounting difficulties. From 1971 to 1974 a special subcommittee of the Cost of Living Council tried various formulas for keeping costs in check. At first, only wages and such services as X-rays and lab tests were controlled. But increasingly sophisticated tests and equipment were being developed, and costs needed to be absorbed somehow. Finally, controls were changed to a comprehensive limit on the overall increase in the cost per patient-day, but the AHA filed suit against the Cost of Living Council, charging that such control of the quality of hospital care went beyond the legislative mandate. The problem was still not resolved when controls were lifted in 1974.

As Mr. Feldstein pointed out, it may seem natural to regulate hospitals in the same manner as public utilities, but the two services are entirely different; direct regulation of the costs of hospitals would make their service completely unresponsive to the preferences of patients and their physicians.

Stating that the only limits on health care a patient can be expected to tolerate are those he sets for himself, Mr. Feldstein continued: "Although imposing an arbitrary limit on the increase in hospital costs might be beneficial for a few years, in the long run it would make the quality of hospital care completely unresponsive to the preferences of the patients. How would a regulatory agency decide whether real hospital costs should rise at an annual rate of 4%, or 6%, or 8%? After adjusting for the increase in wages and in the prices of things that hospitals buy, should costs and therefore quality be allowed to increase at a rate of 2%, or 4%, or 6%? An arbitrary choice would eventually mean that the quality of hospital care will be very different from the level that patients and their physicians would choose."[9]

Another apparatus for trying to deal with capital expenditures and medical costs was created by the federal government in 1974 when Congress passed the National Health Planning and Resources Development Act, authorizing states to organize Health Systems Agencies. Some 200 such agencies, called HSAs, have been set up around the country to review hospital expenditures and develop area health systems. Some seem to have clout and others do not, but the United States Chamber of Commerce, which usually opposes federal economic planning, has been encouraging businessmen around the country to get themselves appointed to HSAs, and many have done so. Their rationale is that if they can halt construction of hospitals where no clear need is evident, they can better contain their own company insurance costs. The same 1974 Act of Congress requires each state to set up Certificate of Need machinery by 1980 to approve new health-care facilities and capital expenditures. About half the states so far have established such machinery, and those that have often rely on the advice of the regional HSAs.

In the acronymic jungle of Washington's health efforts, one that offers more promise of efficiency than most is the HMO, short for Health Maintenance Organization. Under this plan, individuals and families would enroll at a community clinic to receive complete health care for a fixed yearly rate. The emphasis would naturally be on preventive medicine. The idea had caught the eye of President Nixon because it seemed to be a way of (1) improving incentives to both doctors and patients to reduce hospitalization; and (2) breaking down resistance of medical societies to a potent, more efficient corporate practice that would, in effect, provide competition for more traditional methods and thus lower the cost of medical care in general.

The shining example among HMOs has long been the Kaiser–Permanente Medical Care program, created in the late 1930s by the innovative builder, Henry J. Kaiser, to provide medical care for the 5000 men who were building Grand Coulee Dam. Mr. Kaiser and other contractors paid doctors a lump sum in advance to treat workers for on-the-job accidents in the remote Columbia River fastness of Washington state. Unions and workers paid additional advance fees to cover other medical fees for themselves and their families.

The plan was extended to the Kaiser shipyards and steel mill on the West Coast during World War II; after the war it was opened up to anyone who wished to join. Today the plan has 3.1 million subscribers and numbers among its clients government agencies, labor unions, and such corporations as Ford, General Motors, and Ohio Bell Telephone. It operates 26 hospitals and 66 outpatient clinics and employs 3000 doctors and 25,000 other medical employes. The doctors work for a salary, but if they provide care at less than budget they get a share of the surplus. Conversely, if they go over their budget, they have to make up the difference.

The money-saving appeal of HMOs has caught on with a number of corporations and unions around the country during the '70s. But Congress has fallen short of its own expectations in trying to promote HMOs with federal subsidies. Legislation authorizing subsidies was loaded with requirements for such high benefits that subsidized HMOs often have not proved financially feasible. Some doctors, moreover, say that the concept of HMOs for the general public is faulty because they doubt that medical checkups are sufficient for keeping people well. They argue that the financially successful HMOs serve mainly healthy people, not the elderly and disabled who require frequent medical service.

Still another government initiative to control medical costs was the creation of PSROs—Professional Standards Review Organizations—by the Social Security amendments of 1972. The

PSRO amendment was sponsored by former senator Wallace F. Bennett (R., Utah) as a compromise between those forces who argued that the government should set up a bureaucracy at HEW to determine what care, at what cost, should go to federally insured patients, and those who argued that doctors and doctors only should judge how much treatment a patient should receive. The PSRO amendment provides that doctors' decisions made in caring for federally insured patients be reviewed by other physicians appointed as members of the PSRO panels under federal administrative control.

Since 1972 HEW has started 108 PSROs, and 64 more are in the planning stage; the program is expected to cost around $275 million yearly when fully in use. Each team is supposed to review Medicare and Medicaid cases and decide what services are unnecessary. However, five years after its authorization and still only half developed, the PSRO concept has run into a big snag. In November 1977 an HEW study declared that the review-board system had not saved money or reduced the length of time patients remain in the hospital, and added, "Modest reductions in hospital occupancy rates produced little if any reduction in staffing and fixed costs."[10] Another idea down the drain.

But private companies, perhaps more earnest in their efforts to save money, have been sponsoring peer review boards themselves to try to curb lengthy and costly hospital stays among their employes. In Akron, Ohio, such a screening panel, set up by the Goodyear Tire & Rubber Company, discovered that six doctors out of 300 were responsible for more than half the extended stays. Appropriate measures were taken to crack down on the six. After another such review sponsored by the company in Freeport, Illinois, stays of Goodyear employes at the local hospital dropped from an average of 4.8 days to 4.2 days.

PSROs are not popular with doctors. The most important objection is that they consume physician hours that could be spent treating patients. This costs money. The second is that even the most rigorous and detailed review of a physician's medical decisions does not often turn up compelling evidence that he was wrong, and the doctors on the PSRO are reluctant to say that he was in the absence of compelling evidence. This is particularly so when the only consideration for doing so is to save the government some money.

Professor Havinghurst of Duke has written that PSROs "are subject to little oversight and to no significant competitive pressure to lower costs."[11] In the case of the government-sponsored PSROs this is probably true. But the contrast between the government's experience with PSROs as well as with HMOs, compared with those of private industry, is striking. It points up dramatically a fact that Washington seems to have completely lost sight of. And that is that costs can be better controlled by the private sector than by the public sector. When there is a dollar-and-cents saving available to a company or an individual, it will be taken. But when the saving is to be made from the public purse, the incentive is missing.

President Carter's hospital-cost-control proposal was stalled in Congress, at least for the first session, while the legislators tended to the energy and Social Security measures. It is quite possible that, with those two major bills out of the way, the focus in Washington will widen from merely containing hospital costs to that ultimate goal of social dreamers—national health insurance.

The President himself was indirectly sending up conflicting smoke signals on health insurance late in his first year of office. At a press conference in late October he mused before the television cameras about major innovative proposals that might be forthcoming during the rest of his term, and said that he couldn't think of any. "I think we've addressed all of the major problems already."

Yet at his next conference, only two weeks later, he was saying that he had just had his first exploratory talk with Cabinet members on the subject of national health insurance, and that "I think by early next year, the principles of the national health program will be outlined to the American people."

He might have added that HEW Secretary Califano was already hard at work on such a comprehensive insurance program and was committed to coming up with a proposal early in 1978.

The drift toward national health insurance has been inexorable throughout the 1970s, spurred on by Senator Edward Kennedy, the HEW bureaucracy, and the social action lobbies. It was put on the back burner for a few years while Congress tended to other pressing matters, but the growing awareness of rising medical costs has brought it to the forefront of national attention again. In Congress, a number of plans for NHI have been simmering and are likely to be brought forward if the trend gains momentum.

So far, the main deterrent to NHI has been the threat of horrendous costs to the government. Five of the six plans that have received the most attention in Congress would try to limit the federal share of spending by cost-sharing—that is, patients would pay part of medical bills out of pocket. Under the current system of third-party payments, the patient has little incentive not to overuse the health services. Cost-sharing would require the patient to pay something to make him aware of the costs involved. The sixth plan, introduced in the 94th Congress by Senator Kennedy and Representative James Corman (D., Calif.) with the firm support of organized labor, would abolish all deductibles, grant unlimited hospital stays, and pay for drugs, dental care, and even housekeeping services. It would rely on stringent federal controls to prevent runaway costs.

Charles Schultze in his Godkin Lecture at Harvard in 1976, put his finger squarely on the chief problem of the Kennedy–Corman bill when he said, ". . . social intervention often fails, not because it relies unnecessarily on regulation or other command-and-control devices, but because in other ways it ignores the properly structured economic incentives for achieving social goals. One of these ways involves the perverse and antisocial incentives that some social programs themselves set up. Another is the failure to recognize how existing institutions channel private economic activity in the wrong direction.

"The federal Medicare and Medicaid programs have historically reimbursed hospitals in a way that promotes, rather than discourages the escalation of medical costs. Hospitals were reimbursed individually on the basis of the costs each incurred. As a consequence, there was no incentive to take measures to reduce costs, and given the sources of prestige in the medical profession, there was a positive incentive to add high-cost technology and services. More recently, improvements in reimbursement policy have been undertaken to move the system gradually away from an after-the-fact reimbursement of costs toward one that does offer some incentives for cost control. But progress is slow. *And one concomitant of an under-emphasis on economic incentives is an overemphasis on centralized controls that attempt to hold down costs by an ever-growing body of detailed regulations*" (italics added).[12]

President Carter, during his presidential campaign, endorsed certain aspects of the Kennedy–Corman plan. He said he supported a mandatory program that would provide comprehensive benefits, financed through payroll taxes and general revenues. He offered no cost estimates but said he would impose quality and cost controls. One might hope that during his first year as President he has been paying more attention to Mr. Schultze than to Senator Kennedy. But his initial efforts to control health costs by proposing further controls do not augur well.

If and when he does get down to brass tacks on NHI, he also would do well to pay attention to Martin Feldstein, who has devoted much time to studying and writing about hospital costs and national health issues. In the previously mentioned article in The Public Interest, Mr. Feldstein pointed out that health costs rise very rapidly even under government health programs with extensive direct controls such as those of Britain, Canada, and Sweden. In this country, he said, paying for national comprehensive health insurance, even if expenditures did not rise, would require a substantial tax increase. He estimated that it would require $44 billion to replace current private expenditures on physician and hospital services and an additional $34 billion if drugs and other personal health care were included. Such a $78 billion increase in government spending would require that the personal income tax of everyone be raised by more than 50%.

Mr. Feldstein's article stated a proposal he had tailored to meet six objectives: (1) it should prevent deprivation of care; (2) it should prevent financial hardship; (3) it should keep costs down; (4) it should avoid a large tax increase; (5) it should be easily administered; and (6) it should be generally acceptable.

To meet these objectives, he continued, "My proposal is extremely simple: Every family would receive a comprehensive major-risk (MRI) policy with an annual 'direct-expense limit'—i.e., a limit on out-of-pocket payments—that increases with family income. A $500 direct-expense limit means that the family is responsible for up to $500 of out-of-pocket medical expenses per year but pays no more than $500—no matter how large the total annual medical bill. Different relations between family income and the direct-expense limit are possible. For example, the expense limit might start at $400 per year for a family with income below $4,000, be equal to 10% of family income between $4,000 and $15,000, and be $1,500 for incomes above that level. . . . The key feature is an expense limit that few families would normally exceed but that is low relative to family income."[13]

Mr. Feldstein said that major-risk insurance is the most important type of health insurance for the government to provide because it concentrates on those families for whom medical expenses would create financial hardship or preclude adequate care. Once a family had exceeded its direct-expense limit and become eligible for MRI, it would have no incentive to limit its spending for medical care. To ensure that relatively few families would exceed their direct-expense limit, Mr. Feldstein recommended that the MRI policy make use of a co-insurance feature instead of a deductible. Co-insurance simply means cost sharing by the patient and the insuror.

As he explained it, "The annual direct limit of $1,500 for families with incomes over $15,000 could be achieved by using a 50% coinsurance on the first $3,000 of medical bills. Fewer than one family in 15 had medical expenses of more than $3,000 in 1976 (including of course, the expenses now paid by insurance). Therefore, fewer than one family in 15 would reach an expense limit that is based on $3,000 of spending. The co-insurance rates could be cut at lower income levels to keep the direct expense limit to 10% of income, e.g., a 33% co-insurance rate at an income of $10,000. At some income level it would probably be desirable to cut the $3,000 base so that the co-insurance rate did not have to fall too drastically. It is encouraging in this regard that fewer than one family in five had 1976 expenses exceeding $1,500; a 30% co-insurance rate would produce a direct-expense limit of $450."[14]

Mr. Feldstein believes that such a plan would avoid a large tax burden, would be administratively simple and would be acceptable to physicians, hospitals, and the general public. It would eliminate the hassle of controls or fee schedules, and it could be administered by the same companies that provide health insurance now, with only a small increase in their total premium.

The Feldstein plan is one of several, of course, that would remedy what many regard as the major defect of most existing health-insurance plans: the catastrophic medical bills for prolonged illnesses that are not covered. Another such plan, one of the six proposals for national health insurance that has already been introduced for congressional debate is the Ribicoff–Long Catastrophic Health Insurance and Medical Assistance Reform Act. It has the virtue of being the least costly, by current estimates of the six proposals now in the hopper, at $9.8 billion.

Health insurers who are fighting hard both to prevent financial losses incurred by high medical costs and to protect their very existence from government encroachment also are beginning to support the idea of cost-sharing as a means of survival. Robert F. Froehlke, president of the Health Insurance Association of America, has said, "We already know how to give monetary incentives to the patient. It is called cost sharing, and we do it with the deductibles and co-insurance. Unfortunately, we long ago answered the siren cry of the marketplace and allowed too many policyholders to become accustomed to full coverage. It is time we begin the process of educating the public that they cannot afford this illusory benefit called 100% coverage."[15]

CHAPTER FOURTEEN

ANALYZING UNEMPLOYMENT

Our social goal ought to be zero for socially significant involuntary unemployment.—Charles L. Schultze, chairman of the Council of Economic Advisers.

MR. SCHULTZE, WHO MADE THE CHAPTER-OPENING STATE-ment at a confirmation hearing before the Senate Finance Committee in January 1977, was as good as his word. A "jobs" program was a major feature of the economic stimulus program the Carter team proposed to Congress shortly after Mr. Carter's inauguration. And there was no particular complaint when the Congress took the jobs part of the package, after turning up its nose at a proposed tax rebate, and built it into a $21 billion appropriation.

When Mr. Carter signed this massive spending bill on May 12, he called it a "major move in the right direction." The bill called for an immediate $4 billion for public-works projects, twice the amount the President had asked. It appropriated $8 billion for "public service" jobs, ostensibly earmarked for the chronically unemployed by the local governments that administer the program. There was another billion dollars for youth-employment programs. And finally there was $7 billion in revenue-sharing money for states to use at their own discretion.

The jobs program was the first major piece of legislation passed under the new Carter administration, and, aside from the successful pressures on the President to drop the tax rebate, there was a harmony that would not be repeated with any other major Carter program in 1977. That should not be too surprising. Although the unemployment rate had dropped sharply in January while President Ford was still in office and was, at 7.3%, well under the May 1975 recession high of 9.2%, it was still high by nonrecession standards.

One of Mr. Carter's main themes in the campaign had been a promise to bring unemployment down to 6%. He was under strong pressure from the AFL–CIO, which was unhappy with the jobs part of the stimulus package because it wasn't large enough. The unions wanted a $30 billion outlay. There were a variety of other forces to be appeased with the $21 billion bill. It would make governors and mayors of financially pressed states and cities happy, for interesting reasons that we go into a little later. It met some of the demands of black groups, although most, as with the unions, didn't think the package was large enough. In short, there is always a lot of political support for any spending bill that will produce jobs, and Mr. Carter promised at the signing of the $21 billion bill that it would provide a million new jobs. In addition, as part of the tax bill passed in early 1977, Congress had approved a novel program giving tax credits to encourage private employers to add workers.

The jobs bill had a special concession for black groups in that 10% of the spending for public works, or $400 million, was set aside for minority enterprises. The provision, introduced by Congressman Parren J. Mitchell of Maryland, described a minority business as one "at least 50% of which is owned by minority group members or, in case of publicly owned business, at least 51% of the stock of which is owned by minority group members." Minorities were defined as American citizens who are "Negroes, Spanish-speaking, Orientals, Indians, Eskimos and Aleuts." The act specifically earmarked 2.5% of the $4 billion public-works portion for Indian tribes and native Alaskan villages.

Congressman Mitchell, in arguing for his amendment, had said that although the government was spending a great deal of money to encourage minority enterprises, mainly through the Small Business Administration, and although there was a declared policy in favor of awarding government contracts to minorities, the number of contracts actually awarded rarely exceeded 1%. This amendment was no doubt generously motivated, but it too would cause trouble later, as we discuss in this chapter.

The jobs program fell $10 billion short on what the AFL–CIO would have liked. It had proposed spending $10 billion for public works, $8 billion for public service, $8 billion to expand housing programs, $2 billion for youth employment and training, and $2 billion for "countercyclical" aid to state and local governments to help them offset the recession that by organized labor's reckoning, we were still in.

But labor learned a long time ago to set its sights high and then settle for something less. And after labor also won a big victory later in the year with a bill that would raise the minimum wage by 45% by 1981, George Meany could say on a television interview show that labor had not fared at all badly in the first year of the Carter administration.

But a good many people who had seriously studied the unemployment problem may have wondered what the "jobs" package really had to do with unemployment as they understood it. To them the bill looked, not like a program based on careful analysis of the problem itself but one fashioned through the political process to respond to the special needs and wants of certain unions, such as the building trades and public employes, and of state and local governments, New York in particular, which were having serious troubles balancing their own budgets and trying to gain access, by whatever roundabout means possible, to the federal Treasury and the federal government's unique power to create money out of thin air.

None of these analysts would be likely to disagree with Mr. Schultze's goal of a zero rate of socially significant, involuntary unemployment. Despite the claims of Marxists, the idea that any policymaker or serious economist would welcome a certain level of hardship unemployment as a means of holding organized labor in check does not ring true in today's world. Indeed, full employment had been a stated goal of United States economic policy since the Employment Act of 1946, and there has been very little debate over that goal. The debate has been over what types and levels of unemployment can be regarded as "socially significant" and over how best to deal with the problem when and where it exists.

It is at this level of debate that the jobs program of 1977, plus some other laws passed by Congress in 1977, raises some questions. A fundamental question is whether some of these programs might actually contribute toward increasing unemployment rather than decreasing it.

Had the Congress applied some genuine analysis to this problem rather than merely responding to political pressures, it might have noticed several things. It might have asked how it is that some 12 million illegal aliens have come flooding into the United States in recent years, attracted by the availability of jobs at the low end of the pay scale. Or why fruit growers in several parts of the country argued, in a head-on struggle with the United States Department of Labor in 1977, that they would not be able to find workers to pick their crops if they were not allowed to bring in imported labor. Or why the United States Army, which usually provides an outlet for young men and women who can't find civilian jobs, reported in the spring of 1977 that it was having trouble meeting its recruiting goals. Or why, according to Labor Department estimates in August of 1977, some 4.6 million people in the United States—a record number—have not only been able to find one job but are "moonlighting" with two or even, in some cases, three jobs. Or why *Business Week* was able to report on August 8, 1977, that there was a new shortage of secretaries and people to fill other clerical jobs. Or why the Conference Board's index of help-wanted advertising had climbed from below 75% of the 1967 base during the 1975 recession to 140% by December 1977. Or why the unemployment rate did not respond to economic recovery to the same degree as did most other economic indicators. Or why it remained relatively high at the 7% level, when both total employment and employment as a percentage of the working age population were at record highs.

There are some fairly simple answers to these questions and some fairly complicated or speculative ones as well. The simple answer is that although the United States economy was generating more jobs than ever before in history, it was not satisfying the demands of people who were looking for jobs or who were on record as *saying* they were looking for jobs. The job demand was coming from women, an ever-rising segment of the work force, and from teenagers, particularly numerous in the mid-1970s because of the baby boom that had hit its peak in 1957.

A Conference Board study by economist Fabian Linden in February 1977[1] noted that 1.7 million newcomers had been entering the labor force each year since the later 1960s, up from less than 1 million a year in the 1950s and early 1960s. He noted that women accounted for about 60% of the growth in the United States work force during the last two decades. "More than 45% of all women are now working, compared with only 25% after World War II."

Mr. Linden went on to say: "For the next two or three years at least the labor force will continue to expand at a rapid pace and there will be no significant tapering off until the end of the decade—which means that more likely than not unemployment will continue as a major problem for some time—probably for the rest of the decade." He noted that unemployment had become more and more a characteristic of the middle class as opposed to the poor. According to his research, some 25% of all married men who were out of jobs during the 1975 recession had earned more than $15,000 in the preceding year. In the late 1950s, the comparable figure was only 7%, after adjusting for inflation.

Even during the recession, as research by Martin Feldstein of Harvard for a Brookings study shows, only a little over half the workers who were out of jobs were actively looking for a new one. The remainder were mainly waiting to be hired to their old jobs after business picked up again. Other research has shown that most of these were relatively comfortable, living on unemployment compensation, food stamps, and savings, and sometimes earning money through odd jobs for neighbors or saving themselves money with work on their own homes.

By January of 1977, with the economic recovery 20 months old, persons out of work more than 15 weeks were only 2.4% of the labor force and the unemployment rate among heads of households was down to 4.8% from 6.1% in May 1975. Less than half the unemployed had been fired or laid off. The others had quit or were new entries or re-entries to the labor force. By May, unemployment among married men was only 3.6% of the work force, down over two points from the recession high.

In short, it was clearly evident during the early months of 1977 that not only had unemployment numbers dropped but that they were a far less reliable guide to actual economic hardship than they had been in the past. The number of families with two earners or more had risen; unemployment compensation, food stamps, and other forms of temporary support were readily available; not at all insignificantly, the unemployed were spared the income-tax burden they would be carrying if they were actually working.

Indeed, Jean M. Lovati had written in the monthly report of the St. Louis Federal Reserve Bank in September 1976 that "One very important difficulty encountered with the unemployment statistics is that questions concerning wages are not part of the survey. Persons reporting that they believe no jobs are available are not asked at what wage jobs appear to be unavailable. Thus no information is gathered on the extent to which unemployment results from an asking wage which is too high."

This can result, she noted, either from workers not finding themselves hard-pressed enough to accept a lower wage than they feel they are worth or from artificial restrictions, such as the minimum wage, that prevent them from asking for a low pay that would be commensurate with their productive ability.

And two economists at the Law and Economics Center of the University of Miami came up with perhaps the most startling challenge to the unemployment statistics of anyone. Drs. Kenneth W. Clarkson and Roger E. Meiners argued that the stated unemployment rate published by the Bureau of Labor Statistics had been inflated by more than two percentage points by the requirements, written into federal laws in the early 1970s, that recipients of welfare benefits and food stamps must register for work.[2] The result, the two economists said, was that many people had claimed to Bureau of Labor Statistics surveyors that they were seeking work when in fact they were not and in some cases would find it very difficult to look for jobs because of their having young children to care for or because of various disabilities. Such people, argued Drs. Clarkson and Meiners, do not fit the traditional definition of the unemployed. A two-point error in the unemployment statistic, raising it from 5 to 7%, would be the difference between a reasonably acceptable rate (4% has traditionally been regarded as "full employment" because of the normal job turnover in the work force) and a rate that is by historical standards unacceptably high.

The BLS, not surprisingly, did not take kindly to the Clarkson–Meiners contention that the agency was putting out a key economic statistic—one that could unseat a President and generate tens of billions of dollars in presumably remedial federal spending—that could be two points or more in error. A rebuttal by Richard Devens of the Office of Current Employment Analysis called the Clarkson–Meiners research "a superficial analysis" and little more than a "polemic rather than an analytic effort." The BLS charged that the two Miamians had failed to take sufficient account of other factors that would account for the persistently high unemployment rate in the mid-1970s in the face of record employment, such as the general rise in demand for jobs. The Clarkson–Meiners reply was that they had, indeed, taken account of such factors but still came up with the discrepancy. And circumstancial evidence, in the form of an interesting correlation between the unemployment bulge and the work-requirement amendments to welfare and food stamps, was at least on their side.

In the end, the argument seems to boil down to a question of whether a welfare mother, for example, would be likely to tell a BLS interviewer she was looking for a job out of fear that if she said otherwise the welfare and food-stamp people would get wind of it and cut off her benefits. Drs. Clarkson and Meiners think she would indeed; the BLS thinks she wouldn't or that her answer to the interviewer's question wouldn't be changed, necessarily, by the new work requirements.

Whichever side is right, there can be little doubt that a good many people in the American economy are unemployed by choice, even though they are registered for work. The *Wall Street Journal* editorial page in early 1977 sought out some of those people, young men in their early twenties, and found that they represented a group of indefinable size with very little motivation to work as long as they could live with family or friends and draw unemployment compensation, veterans' disability payments, or some other income sufficient to provide spending money. One of them, 23-year-old Mark Rinaldi of West Hartford, Connecticut, said he was confident he could get some sort of job if he tried, but since unemployment compensation was available, "I'm not going to work my head off."

Some social scientists see in this attitude a fundamental departure from the work ethic. Jerome M. Rosow, president of Work in America Institute, Inc., a research group in Scarsdale, New York, had this to say: "Our post-religious society brings different attitudes toward work. In the Judeo-Christian view, as developed by Calvinism and the Protestant ethic, work was an atonement for sin; thus, people would tolerate hard work, deferred gratification and sacrifice for rewards in the after-life. But with the new generation's disenchangment with religion, and with its challenge to arbitrary authority, a newer value system regarding work has evolved. We live in an age of hedonism in which younger people no longer accept work as a sacrifice; they either want more fulfillment at work or they will make a minimal effort. They respect authority only when exercised with restraint and rationality."[3]

He cited as support for this contention a Daniel Yankelovich survey of youth attitudes that showed that in 1975, when a group of American students was asked "Does hard work pay off?", 75% answered "no." In 1967, of a group asked the same question, 69% had answered "yes." Mr. Rosow noted some evidence that the work ethic is still alive. For instance, 8 out of 10 responded that "it's very important to do any job well" in a 1973 Yankelovich survey. But he believes that however you interpret the results, the attitude toward work is changing.

Of course, one solution to the attitude puzzle shown in the Yankelovich surveys would come to mind just from another look at the questions. "Does hard work pay off?" might well have elicited quite literal answers, referring specifically to money. There is a whole body of economists who would say that such a response has less to do with the work ethic than with a cool-headed appraisal of the relative rewards for working or not working. In other words, like Mark Rinaldi they can see no particular point in working when the state provides them with the means to live as well, or maybe even better, by not working. We discuss this work-incentive question at the end of this chapter.

Indeed, a good many people seem to find it worth their while to work only part-time. Over 15% of the work force is now on a part-time basis compared with just over 12% a decade ago. Employers find part-timers a good way to fill hiring slots because they usually don't receive the expensive fringe benefits other workers get. The short hours allow women to look after children and a home and keep any part-timer in a relatively low tax bracket.

Whatever the reason for the trend, it, too, may be distorting the unemployment statistic to some degree. A job seeker looking only for a part-time job obviously doesn't represent the kind of hardship case that would be represented by someone in need of a full-time job to support a family.

All of the above is not meant to suggest that unemployment is a minor problem. It certainly is not in personal terms, with its damaging effects on families and individuals who have come to depend on a certain level of income to meet present needs and future plans. It can have a demoralizing effect on those youths who genuinely want to work and advance but who have difficulty finding jobs that match their intelligence and meet their psychic needs for something worthwhile or meaningful to do. This group has come to include not a few college graduates who have taken liberal arts degrees only to find that they are, essentially, unskilled workers.

And unemployment is a serious problem in economic terms as well. For one thing, unemployment compensation is becoming a major cost. A 1976 federal law expanded the number of people covered by unemployment compensation insurance by 9 million, giving coverage to 93% of the civilian work force. In addition, maximum benefits have been expanded to 65 weeks. Joseph M. Becker, S.J., writing in *Across the Board* in February 1977, estimated that expansions of the program in recent years have quintupled its cost under normal conditions of unemployment, to $15 billion.

Moreover, many state trust funds and the federal funds for unemployment originally intended for administrative costs and loans to states with temporary deficits, are heavily in debt. The burden of this cost, as with so many others these days, is being loaded onto business. The unemployment compensation tax on employers in some states averages over $200 per employe a year. When you add that to rising Social Security taxes, the direct cost of employing a worker, just in terms of payroll taxes, is becoming a significant deterrent to hiring in itself.

Of concern to many economists and serious students of unemployment as well is the use of the unemployment statistic to lobby through programs that have shown only limited success in actually reducing unemployment. The best of the package that President Carter signed into law in May 1977 was probably the public-works program. At least it will mean that some public facilities will be built or improved that might not have been so otherwise.

But whether it will mean new jobs is problematical. Major construction projects are built by machinery and skilled labor, usually union labor or labor that under the Davis–Bacon act must be paid union-scale wages. A *Wall Street Journal* story by James C. Hyatt on July 21, 1977, examined what this meant in Baltimore, which received $5.7 million in January of that year from the $2 billion federal appropriation for public works in the preceding year. The money was allotted to 10 projects, including $388,000 to pave roads around Pimlico racetrack, $597,000 to turn a closed school into a neighborhood center, and $2 million to convert a group of old buildings into apartments.

But Marion Pines, who administers the city's manpower programs, says that so far "our experience in Baltimore really hasn't presented a great deal of new employment opportunities. We've met with the contractors. They've all said this money means they don't have to lay off any more."

Of 420 workers currently employed on the projects, less than 10% weren't already working. The Congressional estimate that its $2 billion would generate 300,000 jobs works out to about $14,000 a job. But the Baltimore jobs are costing about $36,000, or some two and a half times the Congressional estimate. Considering the small numbers of unemployed workers who had gotten jobs, the impact on unemployment does not sound impressive.

"We are very anxious to legislate results, but apparently do not really care whether the programs work," said Representative Bill Frenzel (R., Minn.) during the 1977 House debates on the public-works bill. Projects "which produce temporary jobs costing the taxpayers $25,000 to $40,000 each can hardly be considered a sound or responsible way to try to improve the economy," he said.

Part of the reason federal public-works programs are no more successful than they are has to do with the red tape the federal government itself has created, having to do with environmental protections, safety rules, and the like. Congressman James C. Cleveland (R., N.H.) complained to the House in early 1977 about the tangle surrounding the Water Pollution Control Act of 1972, which authorized $18 billion in federal spending for sewage treatment projects. "As of January 31, 1977, more than four years after enactment of the 1972 act, unobligated balances stood at $6.3 billion, while actual outlays were only $4.2 billion. Actual translation of paperwork into projects has been hampered by a morass of red tape and bureaucratic delay well documented by our subcommittee on Investigations and Review."

One thing stalling the 1977 public-works appropriation is that requirement we mentioned that 10% of the contracts go to minority firms. The requirement was challenged in courts as "reverse discrimination" by the Associated General Contractors, a national trade association of construction companies. Until the issue could be settled it was unlikely very much of that $4 billion would be generating jobs for the unemployed or anyone else.

Similarly, that big appropriation by Congress for "public service" jobs was coming under critical scrutiny in 1977. Called the CETA program (for Comprehensive Employment and Training Act of 1973), the public-service jobs program was described as the fastest growing part of the federal budget in 1977 after the $8 billion appropriation from Congress. It was scheduled to grow even faster if President Carter could get something resembling his welfare program through Congress in 1978, since it would attempt to take people off welfare and put them into CETA jobs.

But James Ring Adams wrote in the *Wall Street Journal* on November 3, 1977, that "if the present performance is any indication, this money will have far less of an effect on hard-core unemployment than Washington thinks it will. Slots that the Senate intended to go to poor blacks, Hispanics and welfare mothers are being used in some large cities to rehire municipal employes laid off in budget cutbacks. The current CETA expansion is supposed to be providing temporary 'entry-level' jobs to give a leg up into the work force for people without much training or 'work experience.' But local projects actually being launched often call for workers with sophisticated skills." In New York City, for example, CETA funds were going for 5 "assistant lawyers," 22 registered nurses, a systems and procedures analyst and 6 "fiscal records analysts."

David E. Rosenbaum of the *New York Times* wrote on November 6, 1977, that of Detroit's 5700 police officers, 1120 were being paid with federal money intended to stimulate the economy. "So are 350 of Detroit's 800 garbage collectors and 160 of the 1,470 firefighters.

"The situation is similar from coast to coast, in other cities in financial difficulty. In Boston, for instance, 15.5% of the municipal employes are paid with federal job funds. In New York, the figure also exceeds 15% and in San Francisco it is 12%."

Most of this money comes from the CETA and from countercyclical revenue sharing, those programs that President Carter said would play such a vital role in creating 1 million new jobs.

Alan Fechter, in an American Enterprise Institute paper in May

1975, had prophesied this development. Said Mr. Fechter, then a senior research economist at the Urban Institute: "The effect of public employment programs on unemployment and on increasing public services turns out to depend on the extent to which federal funds displace state and local funds. A review of the evidence suggests that in the long run 60% to 90% of public employment program funds would merely displace state and local funds. The short-run displacement effect ranges from 40% to 50%. Apparently, public employment programs add considerably fewer jobs than the nominal number of slots they fund."

Mayor Raymond L. Macomber of Attleboro, Massachusetts testified before the Joint Economic Committee of Congress in 1977 that federal manpower programs had not met the needs they were intended for. Participants had been trained in public-service positions only to find these jobs dead-ended after a year of service and themselves faced with total unemployment again. He added:

"A major contributor to the already bulging unemployment rolls is the unemployment checks doled out by the Department of Employment Security. Employers offering gainful employment find themselves in competition with the Department. This problem is most acute in the area of unskilled labor. These people find themselves in the position where many times it is more profitable to stay home rather than accept a job.

"With the advent of worker militancy, food stamps, Social Security, unemployment security, low income housing, rent supplements and low cost medical care and education we have removed the economic motivation for working hard from our lives. The traditional relationship between effort and compensation has deteriorated. Millions of workers are compensated more for showing up than for producing quality and quantity.

"In summary I recommend: First, closer monitoring of all unemployment compensation recipients. Second, a shorter time period to collect benefits. Third, change benefits to maximum of $60 a week with $6.50 per dependent. Fourth, possibly tie payments to some sort of public service employment."

Aside from the fact that the federal "jobs" programs don't do what Congressmen and the President claim for them, there is another problem. They are, in fact, largely subsidies to organized labor and the cities, which helps explain why they are lobbied so strongly year after year despite their demonstrated failures.

Aside from the massive deception this represents, for the public it presents an inflationary threat that is often overlooked. Cities like New York and Boston are capable of soaking up a lot of money for nothing much more than to provide salaries and pension benefits to their employes. New York, in particular, incurred a large share of its budget difficulties through the pension promises it made to municipal unions in the 1960s.

States and cities are not legally authorized to run deficits, although New York City and New York State managed to do it under carefully designed guises that finally put both into fiscal hot water. But there has been a strong movement by both to try to find ways to transfer more of their burden to the federal government. The federal government can, of course, and does run deficits, so its ability to play fairy godmother to the hard-pressed states and cities appears unlimited. But as other chapters of this book have tried to make clear, that ability is not unlimited at all. Its excesses are merely translated into inflation, which ultimately defeats the whole scheme.

A great deal of the British government's budget difficulty has been caused by its inability to control the appetites for local city councils for larger and larger central-government subsidies. The $21 billion 1977 "jobs" program looked dangerously like that sort of transfer. If the British system were to be copied by the United States, it is hard to imagine how high the federal budget deficit could go.

Anthony M. Rufolo, an economist at the Federal Reserve Bank of Philadelphia, wrote in the bank's January–February 1977 *Business Review* that many citizens, faced with rapidly rising taxes, are beginning to ask whether the benefits of public services are being provided at a reasonable cost. He added:

"It used to be conventional wisdom that jobs in the public sector paid less than similar jobs in the private sector. This disadvantage was thought to be offset by more jobs security, better fringe benefits and less competitive pressure. But there is a good deal of evidence to suggest that, while fringe benefits, job security and work pressures still favor the public sector, the municipal worker now holds an edge in wages too.

"The shift occurred as public sector wage gains began to out-distance those of the private sector during the 1960s. According to the Bureau of Labor Statistics, certain sizable groups of urban government employes averaged larger annual wage gains than the corresponding groups in private industry and only slightly smaller ones than those of federal employes. Both groups gained with respect to inflation, which advanced at an annual rate of 3.3%, but public workers' wages clearly were growing faster. At first public employes were trying to catch up, but by 1971 the percentage gains were so great that nine of eleven cities studied by labor economist Stephen H. Perloff had public sector clerical employes averaging higher dollar wages than their private sector counterparts. Two other groups studied by Perloff—data processing and maintenance/custodial personnel—also showed higher wages in a majority of the 11 cities.

"The figures for the 1970s don't show public sector workers continuing their clearly higher rates of wage growth, but neither do they indicate any significant lag behind the private sector in wage increases. Indeed, during the first half of the 1970s, while federal employes have had their salaries growing less rapidly than those of the private sector, local public employe groups have attained a rate of wage growth which is near the top of the range for private sector groups.

"Even if local employes obtain only the same wage-rate growth as private sector workers, they will maintain their relative wage advantage as long as they're starting from a higher base, as many are. A recent Pennsylvania Economy League study found that four groups of Philadelphia city workers made 11% to 38% more than their private sector counterparts while only one group made less (by 2.6%). This means that the city paid $1,070 to $2,884 more per year for the average worker in all but one group while paying $370 less per year for the average worker in the remaining group."

The rise in public employe wages can be attributed to the growing political power of public employes, in part because their numbers have expanded by some 75% in the last 15 years and, more importantly, because they have become increasingly unionized. Government employes have been the most rapidly expanding major segment of the AFL–CIO in recent years and now account for about 15% of that organization's membership.

Thus public employes have power both at the polls and at the bargaining table. Mr. Rufolo cited a study by economist Edward M. Gramlich showing the power of public employes in New York City. Mr. Gramlich had written: "If each [city government employe] was married, lived in the city and had one close friend or relative who would vote alike on city issues, conceivably 1,350,000 votes, 30% of the entire voting age population and roughly half the probable number of voters, could be marshalled in favor of making some strategic concessions to, or dealing leniently with, unions."[4]

Public-employe unions have also increasingly been exercising their right to strike, even though strikes are technically illegal in some states for certain public employes such as police or firemen. The laws have not been notably effective in controlling such strikes because of the difficulty of enforcing laws against large groups of voters and citizens. In outright confrontations with officialdom such as those that have occurred in Pennsylvania, Massachusetts, and San Francisco in recent years, the public employes have usually come out on top.

This rising power is reflected in the national policies of the AFL–CIO and accounts for its heavy lobbying in favor of increased public spending, despite the fact that the unions' members have to pay taxes that help support things like the $21 billion jobs program. A study by political scientist Dan C. Heldman for the Council on American Affairs in 1977 shows that the AFL–CIO consistently supports "liberal" initiatives in Congress, which, in modern parlance, means it consistently supports public spending. With the public-employe unions and building trades accounting for some 30% of its membership and representing the most politically potent part of that membership, this should not be particularly surprising.

Nor should it be surprising that Congress pushed through the jobs bill so quickly, despite doubts about its effectiveness in relieving unemployment. Or that President Carter, who had hoped for a much more conservative approach, ended up supporting the bill cheerfully. The AFL–CIO and the public employes, particularly when allied with majors and governors around the country, are a potent political force.

The early success of this lobby in the Carter administration has whetted its appetite for more. On Labor Day 1977 the AFL–CIO organized rallies all around the country to push for passage of the Humphrey-Hawkins bill or the Full Employment & Balanced Growth Act. We discussed one objectionable feature of Humphrey–Hawkins in Chapter Four: its efforts to move the country towards centralized economic planning. Its other goal is to bring the unemployment rate down to 4%, through "jobs" programs of course.

Certainly no one can quarrel with that 4% goal, which is one reason opponents of Humphrey–Hawkins are put on the defensive from the very start. Full employment is everyone's goal, but the above account should suggest that the political dynamics of this issue are not necessarily leading in that direction.

It should be noted again here that the AFL–CIO also lobbied hard for, and obtained, a 45% increase in the minimum wage over three years, even though there has been a growing consensus among economists of both right and left that raising the minimum wage will almost certainly exacerbate unemployment, particularly among teenagers.

As reported by the American Enterprise Institute, economist Robert Goldfarb in a 1974 article cited four studies produced between 1971 and 1974 indicating that a 25% rise in minimum-wage rates would lower teenage employment by around 3.5 to 5.5%. In a 1976 article, economist Edward M. Gramlich estimated that the same 25% increase would lower teenage employment by 1 to 6%.

Such studies cast a great deal of doubt on whether the AFL–CIO has a genuine commitment to full employment. As with every special-interest organization, its real commitment is to the improvement of the economic status of its members, in particular of its most politically effective members—politically effective both inside and outside the AFL–CIO. The minimum wage will do this, at the expense of some rise in unemployment, because it will tend to lift all pay scales as unions bargain for continued differentials between their pay and the statutory minimum.

The employment effect of the minimum wage is not a major macroeconomic problem. But the total and cumulative effect of expanding federal deficits, to the extent that these are enlarged by "jobs" programs, is a serious economic problem. As the federal Treasury seeks to finance its rising deficits it puts increasing pressure on the Fed to expand the money supply. There is one very simple reason for this. If the Fed tries to keep money growth restrained, it very often has to raise short-term interest rates. And since the Treasury is constantly in the market financing and refinancing federal debts, higher short-term rates can sharply raise the government's financing costs, which already are in excess of some $32 billion.

The federal government's heavy borrowing demands to finance large deficits thus bring pressure to bear on the Fed to follow an inflationary monetary policy. And inflation has a ruinous effect on any economy, destroying the value of savings, reducing public confidence in government, and generating antagonism between producers and consumers. It is the theory of Lawrence K. Roos, president of the Federal Reserve Bank of St. Louis, that much of the rise in unemployment in the 1970s stemmed from inflation.

Early in 1977 he said in a speech in St. Louis, "Inflation has had the effect of increasing the cost of living and thereby stimulating second members of families to seek jobs in order to supplement the in-

come of the principal breadwinner of the family." Thus "the inflationary policies of the past 10 years, some of which were designed to
decrease unemployment, have actually increased the rate of unemployment by creating more job seekers than jobs."

Some analysts feel that whether the Carter administration and
Congress will be able to resist the pressures for more spending could
be crucial to the avoidance of inflation and thus to the success or
failure of the administration. Norman Robertson, senior vice president
and chief economist at Pittsburgh's Mellon Bank N.A. told the American Petroleum Credit Association Conference in Dallas in September
1977 that this was one of his concerns:

"The key question is whether the administration and its supporters will patiently accept a rate of economic growth which at best will
make only slow and irregular progress toward the goal of full employment. Should mounting political and social pressures induce the
policymakers to engage in massive deficit spending, we would soon
find ourselves swept along on another boom-bust cycle of business
activity. The adoption of highly stimulative policies may temporarily
boost consumption and employment but the subsequent cost in terms
of accelerating inflation followed by rising unemployment illustrates
the futility of such a strategy. We must hope, therefore, that the administration can resist the temptation to seek the familiar short-run,
politically expedient remedies for unemployment, which over the
longer run prove counter-productive and self-defeating."

Mr. Carter showed some awareness of this problem in a speech to
the United Auto Workers convention in Los Angeles in May, 1977.
Said he: "We must attack both joblessness and rising prices—because
experience has shown that if we don't attack them together, we won't
be able to put a real dent in either."

But by September there could be doubt about how serious he was
about the attack on inflation. He and his economic team had pushed
the Fed for an easy-money policy with some success. And his Labor
Secretary, Ray Marshall, was urging further expansion of the CETA
program, suggesting that the $15 billion "shortfall" in the federal
budget deficit be applied to that end. (A shortfall in a deficit, by the
way, is where you don't go into the red as deeply as you expected.)
The federal government in fiscal 1977 suffered only a $45-billion def-
icit, whereas a deficit of $60 billion or so had been expected early in
the fiscal year.

Some economists think there is another element to the unemployment question that could have serious implications for the future. It is a more sophisticated economist's interpretation, called the "wedge model" of the problem Mayor Macomber of Attleboro sees in getting people to work productively.

Arthur B. Laffer, a young economist at the University of Southern California, explained the wedge model in a July 28, 1976 *Wall Street Journal* article in which he argued that the Humphrey–Hawkins bill would actually add to our unemployment problems rather than reduce them, hurting workers, consumers, and the truly needy who rely on other government programs.

Said Professor Laffer: "A firm's decision to hire is based, in part, upon the total cost to the firm of the employe's services. For most firms, the more it costs them to hire workers the fewer workers they will hire. Likewise, the less it costs firms to hire workers, the more they will hire.

"Employes' decisions to work are also, in part, based upon the amount of earnings the employe himself gets. The more the employe gets, the more willing he is to work, and vice versa. Employes are not concerned with the total costs to the firm. All employes care about is how much they get net . . .

"The difference between the wages firms pay and the wages employes receive is called the 'wedge.' This . . . consists of all taxes as well as such things as the market value of the accountants and lawyers firms hire in order to maintain compliance with government regulations.

"If the 'wedge' is increased, wages paid by firms must rise. Firms will hire fewer workers. Wages received by employes will fall. Employes will be less willing to work. Both the firm's desire to hire workers and the workers' willingness to work will be reduced as the 'wedge' increases. Output unambiguously falls and the level of total employment falls as the 'wedge' increases.

"In the United States, the wedge can be represented by either total government spending or by the total of transfer payments. Basically, transfer payments are real resource transfers from producers and workers to people based upon some characteristic other than work or production. As such, transfer payments reduce the amount of goods and services available to the people who produced them. Transfer payments are simultaneously a tax on production and a payment based upon a characteristic other than work. Transfers are often a payment explicitly for nonwork. Examples of this are agricultural subsidies, food stamps, . . . Social Security payments, . . . housing subsidies, . . . and, obviously, unemployment compensation itself.

"The Full Employment and Balanced Growth Act of 1976 [Humphrey–Hawkins] will increase the 'wedge.' In virtually every aspect, this act places additional burdens on producers and workers and simultaneously gives little in the way of final output in return. As such, this act would increase unemployment and reduce total employment. . . ."

What Professor Laffer was saying, in the very simplest terms, is that if the chief of a tribe should divide his tribe in half and tell those members on one side of the line that they must work to produce enough manioc root both for themselves and the members on the other side of the line, who would do nothing at all, he would probably have considerable trouble getting the working members to generate enthusiasm for the job. That is, unless he threatened them with water torture or some other cruelty. The productivity of the tribe would certainly fall sharply, which means its standard of living would fall, there would be social resentments, and ultimately the tribe might starve to death.

The United States would appear to be still a very long way from that fate with its 92 million employed and only 7 million unemployed. But some questions are being raised about how many of the 92 million are truly productive in the sense of producing genuine goods and services that the society wants and is willing to pay for.

In England, which probably has a larger wedge than the United States, even some unions are restive about the wedge. Jack Jones, head of the Transport and General Workers, Britain's largest union, was heard to comment in 1976 that he feels working men are growing tired of carrying so many public employes on their back. And the British Labor Government has in fact started trying to reduce the growth of public expenditure.

In short, the work ethic is more than a sociological or religious artifact; it is a fundamental component to a healthy economy and has been from the very beginning of tribal society. President Carter understands this and hopes to incorporate it into the jobs and welfare programs he has put forward, mainly by installing requirements that recipients of transfer payments perform some work in return.

But there is more to the problem than that. First of all, there is the administrative task of enforcing work requirements. Second, it is important that the work performed be in some way useful in relation to the cost of obtaining it. In a modern, complex industrial society it is not so easy to ensure that such a thing happens. But one good way to start, in the view of many economists, would be to reduce the share of the nation's resources controlled or managed by government and give the money back to the workers to spend on the things they themselves believe provide an improvement in their living standards and that thus are likely to motivate them toward harder work.

Mr. Carter had that as one of his goals, too; hence the move to cut the federal government's share of the GNP by two percentage points. But his first year in office has demonstrated how difficult, politically, that is to do.

CHAPTER FIFTEEN

GOVERNMENT VERSUS BUSINESS

When anybody calls up the Castle from here, the instruments in all the subordinate departments ring, or rather they would all ring if practically all the departments—I know it for a certainty—didn't leave their receivers off. Now and then, however, a fatigued official may feel the need of a little distraction, especially in the evenings and at night, and may hang the receiver up. Then we get an answer, but an answer of course that's merely a practical joke. And that's very understandable too. For who would take the responsibility of interrupting, in the middle of the night, the extremely important work up there that goes on furiously the whole time, with a message about his own little private troubles?"—From *The Castle* by Franz Kafka[1]

INDEED, THE MAYOR'S EXPLANATION TO "K" OF THE DIFFICUL-
ties of dealing with the all-powerful and enigmatic Castle
in Franz Kafka's nightmarish novel will not sound unfamiliar to
American businessmen. Increasingly, they complain, dealing with
government is coming to be like K's experience: the frustration of
trying to cope with hundreds of subordinate departments, mounds and
even tons of paperwork, runarounds and confusions. In short, it is
becoming Kafkaesque.

Businessmen have not been much encouraged by the Carter administration even though Mr. Carter said, in a message to Congress in
March of 1977, "One of my administration's major goals is to free the
American people from the burden of over-regulation. We must look,
industry by industry, at what effect regulation has, whether it protects
the public interest or whether it simply blunts the healthy forces of
competition, inflates prices and discourages business innovation.
Whenever it seems likely that the free market would better serve the
public we will eliminate government regulation."

Mr. Carter was no doubt sincere in this promise and he may yet,
with the help of a Congress that hears complaints daily about regulatory interference, do something about the regulatory burden. But early
in 1977 businessmen and free-market economists were looking more
at Mr. Carter's appointments to regulatory jobs than at his promises.
And they could see that former Naderites, consumerists, and public-
interest lawyers were well represented in these ranks. On past record,
at least, they could hardly be regarded as foes of federal regulation. In
his October *Fortune* article "Nader's Raiders Are Inside the Gates,"
Juan Cameron said that the new arrivals had "thrown open the doors of
the Executive Branch to people who were personae non gratae in the
past two administrations." Such people can already claim credit for a
tough strip-mining bill, a Department of Transportation decision in
favor of requiring air bags on future cars, and a fairly large chunk of the
energy program.

A survey by the Conference Board in mid-1977 of 86 business
leaders in 33 countries revealed that business-government relations
have worsened substantially since a similar survey in 1967. "Ten years
ago," said the Conference Board, "business executives expressed resentment at the trend toward controls but it was tempered with confidence that business-government cooperation would improve. That
optimism has disappeared." In other words, the fears and frustrations

of American businessmen are general throughout the market economics of the world.

The businessmen said that growing government controls were stifling investment, creating chaotic business conditions, fueling inflation, and damaging the individual citizens they are designed to protect. They cited a long list of the various forms of government intervention in market economies: price controls, income controls, profit limitations, statutory wage increases, credit limitations, foreign exchange controls, import controls, rent controls and subsidies, land-use planning, environmental regulations, consumer-protection regulations, industrial safety requirements, and government ownership, among others.

Although the United States is by no means the most regulated country in that group, it is catching up rapidly. A. Robert Abboud, chairman of First Chicago Corporation and the First National Bank of Chicago, noted in a speech to the American Petroleum Institute in June 1977 that from 1970 to 1975 there were 30 major regulatory laws passed and 24 new agencies created. There are now 90 federal regulatory agencies employing 100,000 people at a direct cost of about $4 billion a year.

"The most comprehensive estimates to date from the Office of Management and Budget," said Mr. Abboud, "are that government regulation of business costs consumers $130 billion a year, or $2,000 per family. Those who hope or believe that business can somehow absorb such costs might note that the sum is two or three times as large as total after-tax corporate profits."

William Lilley III, acting director under President Ford of the Council on Wage and Price Stability, and James C. Miller III, a former assistant director of that agency, offered some other numbers in the Spring 1977 issue of *The Public Interest*. For example, they noted that the number of pages in the Federal Register, where government edicts are recorded, tripled from 1970 to 1975, to more than 60,000. The number of pages in the Code of Federal Regulations climbed to 72,200 from 54,105. All this regulation costs Americans $40 billion a year in paperwork alone, the Commission on Federal Paperwork has estimated.

J. G. Vorhes, Vice President for Consumer Relations and Service Staff at General Motors Corporation, reported in July 1977 at a conference in Cambridge, Massachusetts, that GM spent more than $3.25 billion in calendar years 1974, 1975, and 1976 to comply with and prepare to comply with regulations imposed by all levels of government. "That amount does not include the cost of any equipment added to GM products to meet government standards," he said, "nor does it include any taxes or worker's compensation claims."

Standard Oil Company of Indiana recently totaled up the reports it files annually to federal agencies and found that they amount to 24,000 pages plus another 225,000 pages of supplementary computer printouts to the FEA. Dow Chemical U.S.A. says it spent $147 million in 1975 to comply with federal laws and regulations, or five cents for every dollar of sales. James Hanes, Vice President and general counsel, estimates that only $87 million of that amount could be termed necessary and appropriate. Of the remainder, $50 million were deemed excessive and $10 million questionable or worse.

Of the excessive expenditures, Mr. Hanes said, "It was money that simply fueled inflation. It could have been employed productively elsewhere by Dow and the ultimate victims, the consumers."

The costs are heading up, not down. Before coming to the White House, Charles Schultze, President Carter's chief economic advisor, coauthored a Brookings study in which he estimated that the cost of meeting air and water pollution standards could total $500 billion by the early 1980s and that annual outlays by the end of that period could reach $60 billion. The noise standards of the Occupational Safety and Health Administration (OSHA) alone will involve expenditures of over $15 billion in capital costs and $2 billion to $3 billion in operating costs in the years immediately ahead, wrote Irving Kristol in the January 12, 1977 *Wall Street Journal*. "If these noise standards are raised to the level recommended by the U.S. National Institute for Occupational Safety and Health—a recommendation endorsed by the EPA—the capital costs will climb over $30 billion."

The outpouring of federal regulation is matched in some cases by states. Donald H. Scott, president of the New Jersey State Chamber of Commerce, had this to say in October 1977: "In the State Chamber's offices adjacent to the bookcase rows which hold the state statute books, are shelves devoted to the state administrative code . . . Although publication of these many regulations has been mandated only since 1969 when New Jersey's administrative procedures law was enacted, the shelf space devoted to administratively imposed rules and regulations totals 8½ feet. The statute books themselves—laws enacted by elected representatives of the people and as interpreted by the courts—total only 10 feet, and the statute books date back to the colonial legislature."

Regulation at all levels has become so pervasive that in 1977 the

American Enterprise Institute, a free-market-oriented think tank in Washington, started a bimonthly journal called *Regulation* devoted solely to that subject. Wrote Editor Anne Brunsdale in the first edition:

"This journal is a response to the extraordinary growth in the scope and detail of government regulation. Surely this phenomenon is one of the two or three most significant political facts of our times. Yet, because the extension of regulation is piecemeal, the sources and targets diverse, the language complex and often opaque, and the volume overwhelming, much of this activity escapes public notice and therefore public debate. Partly in consequence, old regulatory agencies and programs remain and new ones are frequently launched with little analysis of the problems being addressed, of costs and possible side effects, and of alternative methods for achieving the same ends. . . .

"The editors of this Journal recognize that, in a complex industrial society, a substantial measure of regulation may be necessary. We are committed, nonetheless, to the ideal that this regulation should be sensible, cost-efficient, and as unburdensome as the nature of its objectives will allow. In the coming years, we hope to advance that ideal by stimulating informed public discussion."[2]

Indeed, many businessmen argue that they are not opposed to regulation per se, and that it is in fact sometimes useful to achieve social ends with rules that require all businesses to meet the same standards so that individual companies cannot obtain a competitive advantage through antisocial practices such as risking the health or safety of their employes with worn-out or outmoded equipment or by paying insufficient attention to the impact of their operations on the environment they share with their neighbors. But many businessmen are coming to believe that regulation has gone beyond the mere policing of the market and antisocial conduct and has become part of a generalized attack on business and the market system.

They have some allies outside the business world who see it as an attack on democracy itself. Robert H. Bork, Solicitor General of the United States in the Ford administration, told the annual general meeting of the American Philosophical Society in 1976 that democratic processes are becoming increasingly irrelevant. "They simply are not the processes by which we are ruled. And there is increasing acceptance of this condition, in part because egalitarians do not care greatly about process. Alexander Bickel [the late Yale law professor] noted that, for example, they prefer an activist Supreme Court as a means of displacing democratic choice by moral principle . . . ."

Mr. Bork continued: "So much law is made non-democratically, by bureaucracies, that no legislature can focus on more than a small fraction of the choices made. Moreover, the bureaucracies develop rather small but intense constituencies who often have more political influence than an electorate aggrieved by the total amount of regulation but rarely unified in opposition to any one.

"The prospect then is the increasing irrelevance of democratic government. What replaces it is bureaucratic and judicial government, which may be benign and well-intentioned, and may respond somewhat to popular desires, though not always, but cannot by definition be democratic."

In a speech titled "The New Deal is Dead," Congressman Elliott Levitas (D., Ga.) had this to say to the Woman's National Democratic Club in Washington in October 1977: "We have had administrative agencies or executive agencies from the first year after the Constitution of the United States was adopted. But in recent years, and particularly since the New Deal began—there has been an alarming increase in the rate of administrative agency responsibility for lawmaking.

"Now there will always be a need and place for bureaucrats to make and implement rules. I am not opposed to this, and most federal officials are honest, sincere, responsible and hardworking. But some are not. And they become a serious problem that must be checked by those who created the monster—Congress.

"Federal administrative agencies' rules, adopted under the provisions of the Administration Procedure Act have the force and effect of laws insofar as a citizen or a business is concerned. Many of them are even criminal in nature. I have pointed out to other audiences that a person who violates an act of Congress, which action is criminal in nature, can be arrested by a federal official, brought before a federal court, tried by a federal jury, and if convicted, sentenced by a federal judge and serve time in a federal penitentiary. Today, the same is true if a citizen violates an administrative rule—a rule, mind you, not a law—which has been adopted by no one elected by anybody.

"Now, as the number and scope and reach of federal administrative rulemaking increased, and as the bureaucracy itself increased in size and, in my judgment, became less responsive to public input, a problem began to arise that may not have existed during the early experiments in increased rulemaking. Today this cumbersome system of bureaucratic rulemaking encompasses so many areas of our lives and business, that I feel that time has come for it to be restructured and for the Congress to reassert its inherent, constitutional legislative responsibility. Administrative officials are too far removed from the public. We the people have no access to them—and, consequently, they are not responsive or responsible to us."

The argument that special-interest pressure groups, and very often business groups, have themselves played a major role in the perpetuation and expansion of regulation is hard to refute. It probably is a major part of the problem. Businessmen can hardly have credibility with the public, the bureaucracies, and Congress when they themselves have often been the first to ask for new regulatory protections and to lobby against removal of old protections. The airline industry, for example, has been in the forefront of the fight against efforts to reduce the regulatory powers of the Civil Aeronautics Board, which assigns routes and sets fares. The American Trucking Association leads the fight against curbing the powers of the Interstate Commerce Commission, often launching vitriolic attacks against proponents of trucking deregulation. The insurance industry has been heavily responsible for much of what passes for safety regulation. For example, it had a great deal to do with the decision last year by Transportation Secretary Brock Adams to mandate "passive restraint" systems for automobiles by 1984, a decision which means that unless a better restraint system can be found, future cars will be equipped with the controversial air bag, which is supposed to pop out of the dashboard and protect passengers if their car crashes head-on. The only trouble with that decision was that accumulating field data has shown that the air bag, in addition to being expensive, is not a very effective protection compared to the three-point seatbelt now in use, even taking into account the number of auto passengers who fail to buckle their seatbelts.

Many occupational groups have traditionally sought regulatory barriers to entry into their occupation, particularly at the state level, as a means of reducing job competition and thus raising their own incomes. In February 1973 Thomas E. Kauper, then an assistant attorney general in charge of antitrust, delivered a speech to the Town Hall of California in Los Angeles entitled "Regulation—Is Protection the Name of the Game?"

Said he: "While a case can be made for the licensing of certain professions which affect our health and safety, I would suggest that occupational licensing has gone too far. I would suggest also that the various licensing statutes may be abused by the favored occupations. Many statutes provide for licensing boards made up solely of members of the occupation to be regulated. This 'fox in the henhouse' approach carries with it a danger that the regulations issued by the board will be designed not to protect the public but to protect those in the industry from competition."

He cited a book by Jethro K. Lieberman that noted that a session of the Wisconsin legislature was once subjected to an onslaught of bills sponsored by caterers, canopy and awning installers, cider makers, car dealers, dancing-school instructors, egg breakers, frog dealers, labor organizers, meat cutters, music teachers, and beer-coil cleaners, all seeking the umbrella of state regulation. They failed, but others have succeeded. Economist Lee Benham of Washington University and his wife Alexandra did a study in 1975 of regulations against advertising and other competitive practices in the sale of eyeglasses enforced by boards of optometry in various states. The Benhams found that prices paid by individuals were about 25% to 40% higher in states with greater professional control. They also found that as a consequence of the higher prices approximately 25% to 40% fewer individuals in the more restrictive states obtained eyeglasses during a given year.

In recent years, federal courts have been taking a dimmer view of advertising restrictions as a bar to competition, on the grounds that commercial speech (advertising), as with any other form of speech, deserves some protection under the free-speech guarantee of the Bill of Rights. But there has not been a wholesale dismantling of state licensing boards as a result.

The proliferation of regulation also is leading more and more to regulators' coming into conflict with each other. The Environmental Protection Agency and the Nuclear Regulatory Commission were at odds in 1976 and 1977 over construction of the Seabrook nuclear power plant at Seabrook, New Hampshire. The NRC approved a cooling system that involved pumping seawater from the Atlantic Ocean and discharging it again through long tunnels into the sea. The EPA, claiming that the NRC-approved cooling system might harm marine life, favored cooling towers, and probably would have preferred no power plant at all. The resulting squabble delayed construction of the plant to the point where it and its owner, Public Service Company of New Hampshire, were in some danger of being scuttled themselves. Seabrook finally got a go-ahead in 1977, however.

The Employe Retirement Income Security Act of 1974 (ERISA), setting standards for private employe pension systems and setting up a fund, paid for by employers, to insure pension plans against insolvency, kept employers holding their breath while the bureaucracy tried to write firm regulations. Authority for enforcing the act was and is divided between the Department of Labor and the Treasury, which had a great deal of trouble getting their act together.

Sometimes, however, single agencies manage to exasperate business entirely on their own. A good example is the Occupational Safety and Health Administration (OSHA), established by Congress in 1970, which the American Conservative Union describes as "clearly the most controversial federal agency in the history of social legislation."

OSHA set about its task by drawing up reams of workplace standards and then sending its inspectors out to enforce them, whether they had any application to a particular workplace or not. The standards, which fill a full 800 pages in the Federal Register, often bordered on the silly, such as some 27 pages instructing on ladder safety and a warning to agricultural workers about the dangers of falling into manure pits. The OSHA bill passed the Senate by a vote of 83–3 and the House by 383–5. Who, after all, could be against protecting workers from job hazards?

In fact, most states already had extensive job safety standards. Workmen's compensation laws relating tax levels to safety records provided a genuine financial incentive for employers to protect the health and safety of their workers, not to mention the fact that some employers would choose to do that simply because it is the right thing to do.

So far, there is very little evidence that OSHA has protected anyone, but it has annoyed a lot of employers whose factories or stores have been invaded by OSHA inspectors with the power to levy fines for "violations." Some employers have simply locked the inspectors out and invited them to fine and be damned. The complaints to Washington have been massive, so massive, in fact, that President Carter has promised to let up on all the rule writing and snooping and concentrate only on those industries where a particular problem seems to exist. There is still, however, no convincing evidence that this policy is being implemented by the OSHA bureaucracy. Some of their efforts to "simplify" OSHA regulation sound more arbitrary to employers than their efforts to complicate it.

The costs of regulation are, of course, not entirely a dead loss. There can be little doubt about public support of some of the regulatory initiatives of the 1970s. Clean air and water are a public good, the same as schools or highways. It is not at all unreasonable for government to demand that employers provide workers with as much protection against job hazards as the inherent risks of the job allow. It is well within the purview of government to set standards designed to ensure that workers receive the pensions their employers promised. It is at least plausible that government should attempt to set certain safety standards for consumer products.

But the broad acceptance of these general principles has exposed some of the fundamental problems of trying to protect the public against a wide range of hazards through the legislative and regulatory process. One of the first problems is that experts disagree about what, in fact, constitutes a hazard. For example, do saccharin and cyclamates represent a serious enough risk of cancer to justify banning them from the market and thus denying the public their benefits as sugar substitutes for diabetics and people with obesity problems?

The so-called Delaney clause of the Pure Food and Drug Act leaves regulators little apparent choice, saying, as it does, that any substance found in experiments to cause cancer must be banned. Dr. George E. Moore of Denver General Hospital attempted in late 1977 to show the inanity of such a clause by inserting sterilized dimes into the peritoneal cavities in the abdomens of the type of rats used in experiments to discover carcinogenic substances. Sure enough, the dimes caused cancer.

Dr. Moore and his collaborator, Dr. William N. Palmer, published their finding in the *Journal of the American Medical Association* under the headline, "Money Causes Cancer: Ban It." Consumer protectionists were not amused. The Federation of American Scientists, a "public interest" group, complained that the two doctors were abusing laboratory animals to make a humorous point. But the two doctors were not kidding. Their point was clear enough, and important. The Food and Drug Administration had been banning or seeking to ban useful substances on the basis of evidence that was at best shaky, given the fact that any substance, implanted in or given in sufficient dosages to cancer-prone rats, might cause cancer.

Dr. Louis Lasagna of the Center for the study of Drug Development at the University of Rochester Medical Center conducted a different but equally interesting experiment. Choosing five commonly used, well-known, and somewhat controversial drugs—Ritalin, Equagesic, injectable B-12, Chloromycetin, and oral contraceptives—he asked 16 eminent medical and pharmacological experts, through a questionnaire, to rate them as to efficacy and risk for treating the conditions they are normally used to treat. He discovered, as he expected, that there was no unanimity among the experts.

Dr. Lasagna's point was that since experts disagree and since even a consensus of experts is often later proven wrong, it is unwise to try to introduce arbitrary and dogmatic legislation into the practice of medicine. "It was 'the experts' who told us that the Pill was 'safe,' that strict and prolonged bed rest was required for all patients with myocardial infarction, that calcium carbonate was the antacid of choice, that all digoxins or tetracylines were alike and that major tranquilizers could not possibly be antidepressants. In most cases, it was the poor benighted practitioner who was ahead of the experts and whose wisdom was eventually acknowledged. Our society wants to rely on experts, knowing (forgetting?) that they have been wrong in the past or that they may change their minds, or that they often disagree."[3]

A second problem with regulation is best represented by OSHA. Rules, in addition to being arbitrary, are necessarily universally applied, with little regard for special circumstances. Thus while it might be wise for a workman who deals with chemicals in their volatile state to have a special safety shower stall to use if he should become exposed, it is hardly necessary for an employer to undergo that expense for a worker dealing with the same chemical in a non-volatile state or in small quantities. That becomes simply a waste of money. But rules seldom make such distinctions.

And finally, there is the problem, best represented by environmental regulations, of overkill. Any good engineer knows that perfection or even near perfection (called zero risk by engineers) can be twice as expensive, or more, than accepting some degree of risk. The cost for those last few percentage points of safety or purity can often far exceed the benefits.

But Congress and an administrative bureaucracy are not well equipped to make cost-benefit judgments. Thus environmental regulations often have set air and water purity standards far higher than a reasonable cost-benefit judgment would have put them, with the result that consumers were loaded with unnecessary costs, or the regulators were confronted with strong resistance or evasion from those industries they were trying to regulate.

Some critics of the regulatory explosion see other serious defects. Murray L. Weidenbaum, director of the Center for the Study of American Business at Washington University in St. Louis, believes that it is slowing down the rate of innovation and scientific progress in the United States. In a paper delivered to the Manufacturing Chemists Association in Washington in October 1977, he said:

"The slowdown in research and development that has been occurring in this nation is pervasive and can be measured in many ways. In real terms (1972 dollars) R&D spending in the United States has been on a plateau of slightly under $30 billion a year since 1965. Private sector R&D—which rose at an annual rate of over 7% in the period 1953–67—has been increasing at a modest 2% a year since.

"The employment of scientists and engineers in industry in 1975 . . . was lower than in 1968—1,031,000 versus 1,046,000. This compares to a 19% increase in the 1964–65 period. In 1973, the Patent Office issued fewer patents to U.S. nationals than in 1963 but patents issued to foreign nationals more than doubled during the same decade. . . ."

Mr. Weidenbaum said that the longer it takes for a new product to be approved by a government agency, the less likely that it will be introduced. He noted that Professor Sam Peltzman of the University of Chicago had estimated that the 1962 amendments to the Food and Drug Act are delaying the introduction of effective drugs by about four years, leading to higher prices for drugs.

In addition, large and rising shares of corporate R&D budgets are being diverted from traditional efforts for product and process improvement to meeting regulatory requirements. He quoted a GM research executive as saying, "We've diverted a large share of our resources—sometimes up to half—into meeting government regulations instead of developing better materials, better manufacturing techniques and better products."

Senator Lloyd Bentsen of Texas blames increasing government interference and overregulation in large part for reducing formations of new companies. Observing that the number of new companies issuing stock for sale to the public plunged to 38 in 1976 from 418 in 1972, the Senator told the Financial Analysts Federation in Washington in June 1977: "I have learned from painful experience, both as a businessman and a Senator, how the current tendency to resolve problems by edict and regulation from Washington can undermine the initiative, the innovative thinking and the willingness to accept risk that has made ours the most prosperous, advanced and powerful nation in the world."

Still another spin-off of the regulatory explosion is a rise in litigation. Carol H. Falk, writing in the *Wall Street Journal* of September 30, 1977, noted that a large proportion of the cases the Supreme Court was hearing during the current term involved disputes over federal regulatory statues. Naturally, there are costs for the consumer in all that litigation along with all the other costs associated with regulation.

President Carter, having heard the swelling chorus of complaints about federal regulation while he was on the campaign trail, came to Washington with a promise to do something about it. He won, very quickly, congressional approval for a reorganization of the federal government in which he proposed to reduce sharply the overlap and numbers of federal agencies. There are skeptics who say that this won't necessarily mean less regulation.

And indeed, some of the other initiatives the President launched during his first year—the energy bill, a proposed cap on hospital cost increases, and a new act signed by the President in 1977 to extend federal control over strip-mining—look like more, rather than less, intervention by government. Proposed deregulation of the airlines and trucking also bogged down for one reason or another in Mr. Carter's first year. The Senate prepared a bill to require the President over an eight-year cycle to submit reform proposals for each major regulatory agency, but that too got bogged down in the tangle over Mr. Carter's energy package and Social Security program.

In short, the deregulation issue is in doubt, despite the brave promises of the President and Congress. Some observers are pessimistic. Professors Michael C. Jensen and William H. Meckling of the University of Rochester, whose paper, *Can the Corporation Survive?*, was quoted in Chapter Four, are among the pessimists: "We see no forces which are likely to curb the gradual encroachment of government. Moreover, we believe the era of dramatic economic growth is over—not because of new source or technological constraints not because we are running short of energy, we are not; not because we are confronted with environmental or ecological disaster, we are not; but because government is destroying the individual incentives which are the wellsprings of economic growth."

That assessment may well prove to be far too gloomy. An economy with the power of the United States economy will undoubtedly stand up to a great deal of abuse, and democracy does have ways of sorting out its problems. But thinkers throughout history have said that democracy is particularly vulnerable to the process of centralization and conflicts for special advantage. We'll all know the answer if someday, in a true Kafkaesque nightmare, we can't even get the bureaucrats on the phone.

CHAPTER SIXTEEN

CAPITAL AND CONFIDENCE

This could develop with the passing months as the biggest ripoff in history.—President Carter, at a press conference on October 13, 1977.

IF PRESIDENT CARTER HAD DELIBERATELY SET OUT TO DESIGN A sentence that would weaken the confidence of businessmen and investors in his administration, he could hardly have done better than the chapter-opening remark, which was broadcast on television and widely printed in the morning newspapers the next day. He was, of course, expressing has views of oil industry lobbying against his energy bill and for deregulation of oil and natural gas prices.

It is certainly not unprecedented for a President to use strong language in the heat of combat. President Carter was by then strongly committed to the energy "package" his energy aides had designed in the first few weeks of his administration, and he wanted to try to force it through a balky Senate.

But his use of a counterculture idiom, "ripoff," and his opposition to letting the marketplace determine prices and profits conveyed a clear impression that he had become an antagonist not only of the oil companies but of business and the market system in general.

Free prices and profits are, after all, the core of the market system. If prices and profits rise, they attract capital to a sector of the economy where there is strong demand and thus a need for expansion. A better example than energy of a sector that needs expansion could hardly be found. The assumption of market economists is that when capital is attracted and production expanded, prices and profits then adjust themselves to the norm and here is no "ripoff." This is Economics 101. Mr. Carter's contention that in the absence of government controls there would not be a free market in energy is not very impressive, considering the hundreds of different sources of energy available to mankind. It didn't help much when the President quoted totally misleading figures about the past and potential profits of the oil and gas industry, substituting gross volume numbers for income and giving exaggerated estimates of gross volume at that.

Under ordinary circumstances, the President's performance might have been passed off as a mere exercise in excessive political rhetoric. But these are not ordinary times. Many economists believe that the number one problem of the American economy is its difficulty in generating capital and the reluctance of businessmen to make capital commitments. That means, purely and simply, that insufficient provision is being made for future economic growth. If you translate that into human terms, it means that job opportunities and living standards in the future will be lower than they are today.

Mr. Carter and his economic team have shown that they recognize the problem. It has been frequently discussed in their press conferences and speeches. But somehow they have had trouble translating their concern into policy. That failure has been based in part on a certain ambivalence. The administration wants capital investment but it doesn't want profits or, to quote the President again, "ripoffs."

It wants to encourage business and stockholders with various tax breaks, but it wants to take some of that encouragement away by heavier taxes on capital gains. Raising taxes on capital is hardly an effective way to encourage capital formation.

That this ambivalence was being read in negative terms by a broad public that makes investment decisions could be seen on every hand in 1977. The Dow Jones industrial averages fell nearly 200 points in the first 10 months of the Carter administration. That says simply that millions of actual or potential stockholders were not optimistic about future business profits. And direct outlays by business for new plants and equipment since the 1975 recession had shown the slowest rate of recovery for any postwar recovery.

In the August 29, 1977 *Wall Street Journal*, University of Michigan economist Paul W. McCracken wrote: "The fact is that for whatever reason thus far in this expansion the rise in capital outlays (in real terms) has been only about half that during other comparable periods. The problem seems to be less one of inability to finance than of reluctance to commit.

"This shortfall in investment is raising fundamental questions about our economic prospects. How can the American economy's historical capability to double real incomes every generation (every 33 years, on the average) continue if the process of putting to work new and more efficient and advanced technology remains so sluggish? Will the new factories and stores and mines and generating plants, whose opening creates added job opportunities, be built in sufficient volume to get the unemployment rate back down to more nominal levels?"

Indeed, it was evident in 1977 that firms were cautiously trying to build up their balance sheets by reducing their heavy debts and increasing "liquid" assets such as cash and government securities in much the same way that an individual attempts to do when he is uncertain about his future earnings. Businessmen were still tending, as they had been for two years, to look only for investments that offered a quick payoff, unwilling to make heavy commitments to long-term projects. Spending for basic research with long-term prospects for new products and processes had been curtailed in favor of efforts to develop products that could be brought onto the market quickly at a profit.

The reasons for this lack of confidence go considerably deeper than the mere words of a President. Corporate earnings after taxes (in real dollars after adjusting for inflation) dropped steadily in the decade 1965–1975, with the exception of an upward blip in 1971–1972. Reginald H. Jones, chairman and chief executive officer of General Electric Company, observed in a 1976 speech to the American Assembly that such profits dropped to 1.6% of the GNP in 1975 from 5.3% in 1965.

Return on investment, expressed in terms of after-tax profits as a percentage of the replacement costs of new plant, equipment, and inventories, plummeted to 2.4% in 1975 from 9.9% in 1965.

This is not a case of a businessman playing with numbers. The stock market, with its uncanny knack of placing a value on real and future earnings of business corporations through millions of individual investment judgments, has confirmed those numbers. The Dow Jones industrial average dropped to an average monthly level of 803 in 1975 from 911 in 1965. If you take account of the diminished value of the dollar, using the dollar's value in 1967 as a base, the decline was to 499 from 964. And after the market recovery in 1976 and subseqent slump in 1977, the market was even lower in real terms in the closing months of 1977, despite the economic recovery, than in the 1975 recession.

This decade of declining real profits and real share values had a particular effect on corporations. They found it relatively undesirable to try to sell shares in such a weak market, since to do so would merely dilute the value of existing shares. This would have the effect of further weakening the confidence of their shareholders and lenders. So they turned to borrowing to meet their capital needs. Some companies even chose to use some of their surplus funds to buy back shares to try to strengthen their market value.

As Mr. Jones of GE noted, sales of new equity shares by nonfinancial corporations in the 20 years 1955–1975 supplied only 3.5% of the new funds raised. Borrowing was used to meet 42% of corporate financial needs in the first half of the 1970s compared with only 33% in the first half of the 1960s. And because of the lower earnings rate in the 1970s, corporations were having slower going at generating capital internally through the earnings surpluses left over after paying all their bills and dividends to shareholders.

There is one fundamental difference between raising capital through selling shares and raising it through debt. The buyer of shares takes his chances, but a lender expects to be paid back. And if you don't pay him back, he can, if he is desperate enough, throw you into bankruptcy.

In 1975, when the recession hit, exactly that happened to a good many debt-heavy companies. The number of commercial and industrial failures jumped to 11,432, involving current liabilities of $4,380,000,000, from 9,915 with liabilities of $3,053,000,000 in the preceding year. Such big names as W. T. Grant Company, the retail chain, were among the casualties.

The lesson was clear to corporate executives. Rather than applying the improved earnings of 1976 and 1977 toward new projects, many of them applied them toward putting their balance sheets into sounder condition by reducing debts and building surpluses. Some took advantage of the improved stock market in 1976 to sell shares, but here, too, the funds obtained were often applied toward retiring debt rather than new projects.

That was the background against which Mr. Carter accused the oil and gas companies of attempting a ripoff. It is indeed true that the oil companies had fared somewhat better than industry at large during the preceding decade, but the difference was not impressive. In 1976, a Citibank study showed, their return on net worth was 15.1%, compared with 15% for all industry. And the steel industry, which had suffered presidential price jawboning even longer than the oil companies, was in dreadful shape relative to industry as a whole, which helps account for its demands for import protections in 1977.

As would seem to be evident from the statistics above, an important part of the problem of American corporations in the decade 1965–1975 was inflation. During an inflationary period corporations pay out a larger share of their gross earnings as taxes. This is partly because inflation raises the nominal value of their inventories; those illusory gains are added to gross profits and taxed. Some corporations caught on to this during the 1970s and switched to a different accounting method for inventories called the "last in–first out" system or LIFO, whereby the prices of the latest materials purchased rather than the prices of the oldest items in their materials inventories are used in determining production costs. This cuts gross profits and taxes during an inflationary period and thus allows the corporation to retain more money, even though it is reporting smaller earnings.

The other way corporations lose from inflation is through inadequate depreciation allowances. The amount of money corporations can set aside free of taxes under the tax laws is based on the original cost of a piece of equipment, not on what it would cost to replace it. Thus when inflation raises replacement costs, corporations have to dip into taxed earnings merely to maintain their existing plant and equipment when the old items wear out. Industries with expensive, long-lived facilities, such as the steel industry, are particularly hard hit by this.

The investment tax credit, which allows companies to credit a percentage of new equipment costs against their federal income taxes, has relieved this a bit, but it still has resulted in an inflation tax on corporations. The Department of Commerce estimated excess taxable profits caused by underdepreciation at $24.7 billion in 1976.

When both phantom inventory profits and underdepreciation were taken into account, the effective corporate-tax rate in 1976 was estimated at 51.2% compared with the nominal rate of 48%. That is not as high as the 59.7% in 1974 when inflation was rampant and many corporations had not adjusted their inventory procedures, but it remains a problem for capital accumulation and will become one again if the inflation rate rises.

Despite the economic recovery, a lower rate of inflation, and the efforts of corporations to restore the health of their balance sheets, there were signs in late 1977 of a renewed weakness. Alfred L. Malabre, Jr., writing in the *Wall Street Journal* on November 2, quoted Dimitri N. Balatsos, a corporate analyst at Manufacturers Hanover Trust Company in New York, as saying that corporations are beginning to "eat up their liquidity again."

Mr. Balatsos arrived at this conclusion by comparing corporate cash balances and assets quickly convertible into cash (such as government securities) against debts due within 12 months. He noted that this cash-to-debt ratio had fallen to 27.6% by midyear 1977, down some seven points from late 1976 and the lowest since the 1975 slump, when it had hit 23%. It was far below the level of 1971, when it stood at 44.2% at the end of the year. The decline in the ratio in 1977 resulted from both a drop in cash-type assets and a rise in debts coming due. "Looking ahead," wrote Mr. Malabre, "analysts mostly foresee a further deterioration in corporate liquidity." Costs were rising and profit gains slowing, he noted.

Of course, it is true that debts coming due can be refinanced, and it may have been true that the cash-to-debt ratio was mainly further evidence that corporations were choosing to bring down their debt burdens rather than refinance them. This possibility was also suggested by the weak relative demand for business loans in much of 1977. But nonetheless, it did not suggest that capital spending for new plants and new jobs was likely to be robust in the months ahead.

In fact, it suggested just the opposite, that the feeble recovery in capital spending that finally got underway in 1977 might prove to be short-lived. And the negative implications of this would be nothing short of enormous.

Now, of course, it is possible to overreact to economic statistics. The United States economy is a complex structure, and it is difficult to see it as a whole. One reason for the relative weakness of capital spending, for example, could be that the economy has been moving from an industrial phase to what Herman Kahn has described as the Post Industrial phase. This means that more and more of the GNP is accounted for by services, such as teaching students or selling insurance. Services accounted for nearly half of personal consumption expenditures in 1977. And it does not require the same level of capital expenditure to provide services as to make, say, automobiles.

But industry still remains the core of the economy, and it is hard to shrug off evidence that industry is no longer expanding and contributing its share to economic growth. A 1977 Congressional Budget Office study, for example, showed that the growth rate of plant and equipment spending per worker in the 1975–1977 period was likely to be only about 1%, well below the level in the late 1960s and the early 1970s.

This low rate of investment growth also means a low rate in the growth of worker productivity, or the economic output of each individual worker. New equipment, because it employs improved technology and is less likely to break down, is a major factor in improving productivity. And rising productivity is central to improved economic efficiency, which means the ability of an economy to get the most out of its inputs of labor, land, and investment. Improved economic efficiency, in turn, is the key to real economic growth, which is the source of rising living standards. It is also the key to full employment, because with improved real incomes workers can buy more things, with the result that more and better jobs are created. The attempt to achieve this same thing by simply printing more money is

one of the favorite illusionary games of twentieth century policymakers, but, as we have seen above, that won't work if the result is to lower
the propensity to innovate and invest.

Innovation, in fact, is another concern of the mid-1970s. There is
evidence on every hand that it is slowing, which means that even the
purchase of new equipment may not necessarily bring large productivity gains. In 1976 Jerome Wiesner, president of the Massachusetts
Institute of Technology, wrote that "The United States has moved in
recent years from a situation in which all our forces, commercial and
public, encouraged the innovation which created our spectacular scientific and industrial capabilities to a situation in which there are
ever-increasing deterrents to creative change."[1]

Indeed there are, and both the slowdown in investment and innovation have to do with a lot more than merely corporate-balance-sheet
blues. In recent years a new expression, "regulatory risk," has come
into vogue in business and scientific circles. That means, in the
simplest terms, that in planning a major investment or introduction of a
new product it is necessary to take account of the time delay and cost
of getting clearance from governmental agencies. To build a nuclear
power plant, for example, it is necessary in some states to get clearance
from 40 or so federal, state, and local agencies. The nuclear power
industry estimates that regulatory delay lengthens the time required to
build such a plant by about four years to a total of 12 from the time the
decision is made to build to the time when it starts producing power.
That is, of course, assuming that it is allowed to be built at all.

Dealing with the regulatory red tape not only costs a lot of money
in lawyers' fees and paperwork but also, in inflationary times, raises
the cost of the project. The Alaskan oil pipeline, for example, increased
in cost from a projected $900 million when it was conceived in the late
1960s to $9 billion when it was finally completed in 1977. Drug
companies find that to get a new drug cleared and put on the market
can require literally a ton of paperwork and years of haggling with the
federal Food and Drug Administration.

These added risks, imposed mainly by environmental and consumer product safety laws, have a very simple effect on investment and
innovation decisions. By raising the cost of a new project they lower
the expected return on the necessary investment. Businessmen make
their investment decisions, just as everyone does, on the basis of comparative expected returns. Is the return to be expected from building a
new power plant more than the return to be expected from plowing the

same amount of money into a government bond? If not, there will be a great reluctance to make it.

Writing in *The Economist* of August 6, 1977, Alan Greenspan, former chairman of the Council of Economic Advisors under President Ford, blamed the shortfall of private investment in the economic recovery on the uncertainty that plagues the investment commitment process today, which he said was "far more pervasive" than a decade ago. "This uncertainty is embodied in investment calculations in the form of higher risk premiums and prevents a normal package of capital projects from meeting acceptable financial criteria," he said, noting that long-lived investments are particularly affected by this, in particular, long-lived investments where the payout is in the later years of the investment's life. He pointed out, for example, that much of the pickup in equipment investment in 1977 had involved not new plants but relatively short-term assets such as cars and trucks.

He attributed the uncertainty to inflation and escalating regulation. These two factors, he said, are particularly thwarting the industrial world's adjustment to sharply higher energy prices. "If risk premiums were low, development of long lead-time synthetic fuels would already be well advanced (without government subsidies), and nuclear plant construction would be at very high levels. Given enough lead-time and investment, expected future shortages would turn into welcome energy surpluses, but the payoffs are too far away on such projects to gain support at current levels of risk.

"Under normal risk conditions, energy saving equipment would likewise be highly profitable, and, in anticipation of large profit payoffs a decade and more hence, vast new research and development efforts in the area of energy conservation would move forward."

In short, he complained that high risk premiums were "blindsiding" the market system and preventing it from addressing the distant future.

There could hardly have been a bigger "blindsiding" than President Carter's energy package. What businessman is going to make an energy investment when such a bundle of regulation and subsidy and penalty is lying on the table? First there was the long pause while everyone tried to figure out what the package was all about. It was finally concluded that what it was all about was mainly higher taxes on the production of oil and gas. Then there was another long pause while Congress tried to figure it out and set about to change it to suit the many constituencies that bring their influence to bear on Capitol Hill.

In short, the continuing tinkering with economic processes by succeeding administrations and Congresses leaves investors in a state of suspended animation. Some quit in disgust and put their money into Iowa farmland or Rauschenberg paintings. By the mere creation of constant uncertainty it is possible to slow economic growth down to a crawl or even send it into a tailspin.

Which leads us to yet another problem. There is a sizable group of people in the American society who seem to have it as their principal object to do exactly that. And a good many have found their way into government posts. They are, of course, the "limits to growth" people, who feel, in all seriousness, that constant expansion of economic processes is spinning the world toward its own destruction.

We have discussed this philosophy in other chapters and have tried to make it clear that it is neither new nor valid. There is always resistance to change in any age. The familiar and most often cited example is when the Luddites tried to throw a monkey wrench into the beginnings of the Industrial Revolution in England out of fear that it would throw all the artisans out of jobs. The modern Luddites fear that economic growth will ultimately destroy the "quality of life", although this philosophy takes little account of the "quality of life" of the many people, in slums and African villages, who have not yet benefitted much from the world's economic growth but would have every reason to hope to if it is allowed to continue.

It should not be said that the no-growth ethic is the same as the environmentalist ethic. There are certainly values to be yielded by concern for the environment, for protecting the purity (within reasonable limits) of the air and water, and for simply cleaning up the mess that some industrial processes make. But that is entirely different from the doomsday philosophy that the world will exhaust its resources if economic growth continues at the rate of, say, the 1960s.

If the normal processes of investment and innovation are allowed full play, there will be substitution for scarce resources and new technology to meet new problems, just as there always has been through history in those periods in which the mind of man has been given relatively free play. One of the most troublesome things about the Carter administration in the early months was the emphasis on just the opposite—its focus on conservation of resources rather than the management of resources to achieve economic growth, its worries over someone perhaps making "too much money" through application of initiative and effort. In other words, the kind of negative conservatism that refuses to recognize that the individual judgments of a free people are more likely to bring good results than the paternalistic judgments of a President.

Even though the no-growth ethic is not the same thing as environmentalism, there is a vocal segment of the population in which the two concerns overlap each other. The result is often a sort of radical environmentalism that is not willing to settle for a cleanup of the environment but instead insists on trying to completely block the construction of new power plants, factories, or mining processes.

Economist Murray L. Weidenbaum of Washington University in St. Louis estimated in 1976 that perhaps as much as 10% of business investment today is being devoted to attaining various social objectives.[2] A further share is being used to replace facilities shut down because of environmental and other regulatory restrictions.

As we have said before, cleaning up the environment and installing improved safety equipment have social value and thus do not necessarily represent misuse of the nation's finite supply of capital. The problem with such social applications, however, is efficiency. Is the capital allocated in such a way as to get an optimum level of benefits from the total sum expended? There is a substantial body of evidence to suggest that the political process is less efficient at allocating capital than the market process. The political process is, of course, a kind of market process itself, in that it involves a great deal of bargaining among the various interests represented in the legislatures at all levels, but there can be serious doubts about the efficiency of such a market in representing the interests of *all* the people, even in a democratic society.

In an undemocratic society there can be no doubt at all. Professor Abram Bergson, a leading Sovietologist at Harvard, has noted that one of the central problems of the Soviet Union is its inefficient use of capital. It generates about twice the amount of capital relative to the size of its economy as the United States—largely because its disincentives to consumer spending, represented in large part by an absence of goods, create a higher rate of personal savings. Yet, in recent years it has been achieving only a very slow rate of economic growth. Professor Bergson attributes the inefficiency in large part to the absence of incentives for managerial or technical innovation in the Soviet system.

In the United States government does not control capital to the almost total degree of the Soviet Union, of course. But the extent is probably greater than most people realize. First of all, there is the share of the nation's savings that goes to finance federal, state, and local debt, which rose by something like $106 billion in fiscal 1976 from fiscal 1975 to a total of over $860 billion. Then there is the share of private debt that is guided to certain specific uses by federal loan guarantees, such as through Federal Housing Administration mortgage guarantees or student loan insurance. That amounted to over $218 billion in 1976. In short, government debt and government-guaranteed debt represents about one third of all debt outstanding in the United States.

In addition to these direct and indirect forms of government involvement in the allocation of credit, there is, of course, allocation through regulation—not only regulation that forces business to make investments in pollution-control equipment or safety devices but also regulations that apply to how much interest on savings accounts banks may pay or state rules with regard to the size of loans and the terms that may be offered by finance companies, to cite two of many examples. The Federal Reserve Board has tried over the years to apply various pressures to member banks to guide lending policies, something it has the power to do, although it has not been particularly active in the use of its powers in that sense in recent years except to caution banks a couple of years ago about some of their riskier-looking loans, to real estate investment trusts, for example.

But there are always latent pressures in Congress for government to take an even stronger role in guiding the allocation of credit. In 1975 Representative Henry Reuss of Wisconsin attempted to get a bill passed in Congress that would legislate lending priorities. The bill listed priority sectors, such as "low- and middle-income housing" and "small business and agriculture" as well as areas where credit would be curtailed, such as loans for "purely financial activities."

Fortunately for the Federal Reserve Board, which would have had to try to administer this regulatory mishmash, and for the economy, which would have suffered the consequences of all this attempted meddling in millions of borrowing transactions, the bill did not pass. But it will no doubt be back at some point.

The savings available for investment in the United States are finite, of course, consisting of personal savings, corporate savings in the form of retained earnings and depreciation allowances, capital imported from abroad, and depreciation allowances of noncorporate entities. In recent years this total has been running plus or minus $200 billion; depending on such variables as the propensity of individuals to save, the level of corporate earnings, and whether there is a net out-flow or inflow of capital from abroad.

Government deficits cut into this sum, and the other forms of government credit allocation mentioned above guide it to various uses selected by government. It should become fairly obvious that in a world where talk in terms of billions has become commonplace ($10-billion pipelines, $2-billion nuclear power plants, etc.), $200 billion is not a massive sum.

When large federal deficits cut into this capital supply and the money represented by those deficits does not go into capital projects but into income transfers that merely expand consumption, it is something akin to a farmer eating up his seed corn. The neo-Keynesian stress on government "stimulation" of demand and consumption through deficit spending has never quite come to terms with that truth. There is simply less left over for building and replacing all the factories, highways, schools, airports, and modern machines the economy will need for the future. And, as we have said before, inflating the money supply to meet these needs only serves to weaken the dollar, discouraging investment from abroad and savings and investment at home.

The government can follow policies that attempt to reduce inflation and direct taxation and thus encourage savings and investment. It can move toward less interference with investment decisions, so as to reduce time lags, regulatory risks, and regulatory waste, thus improving economic efficiency.

Or it can move in the way it has been moving, toward continued large federal deficits, expanded regulation, and chronic inflation. Mr. Carter may have intended to reverse the direction, and he certainly was being advised to do that by his best economic advisers. But so far he has not succeeded. There is every appearance that government is moving faster along its dangerous path than ever before. And that is why investors have shown so little confidence in the President.

CHAPTER SEVENTEEN

THE WORLD ECONOMY

Nationalism is an infantile disease. It is the measles of mankind.—Albert Einstein, 1921.

IT CANNOT BE SAID THAT THE UNITED STATES WAS OVERLY afflicted with nationalism in the 1970s, certainly not in comparison to the nineteenth century, when poet and essayist Ralph Waldo Emerson averred that "The less America looks abroad, the grander its promise." In the aftermath of World War II, the nation moved easily and naturally into a world role of political and economic leadership—naturally, because it emerged from the war as the world's strongest nation.

It took the lead in setting up a world monetary system and in encouraging freer trade through the dismantling of protective tariffs and other trade barriers. It gave its encouragement to the formation of the European Coal and Steel Community and the European Economic Community which were later merged to form the European Communities, better known as the Common Market. It took a heavy responsibility for extending economic aid to the world's underdeveloped nations, unilaterally and through such postwar institutions as the International Monetary Fund and the World Bank. Conquered Japan began its remarkable postwar economic recovery under American guidance and through the aid of American trade.

American efforts on behalf of an open world economy reached a high point in 1967 with completion of the Kennedy Round of trade negotiations, which resulted in a one-third reduction in tariff barriers by 49 nations. A growth in world trade and world prosperity went hand in hand in the 1960s and has continued, although at a slower pace, in the 1970s. In 1976 world trade, measured in exports, exceeded $1 trillion for the first time.

But despite the American leadership role in this process, its implications have never been fully appreciated by American Presidents and, more especially, by American Congresses. The fundamental implication is that a clear distinction between the world economy and the American economy can no longer be made in an open world. The tendency of American leaders to strike a dividing line between what they regard as domestic economic policy and what they see as international economy policy has become less and less valid—one might even say totally invalid.

There is a simple reason for this. To accept the truth that government interventions into the domestic economy will be influenced in their success or failure by international market forces requires acceptance of a major restraint on such interventions. That restraint can only be relieved by trying to persuade other nations to follow consistent policies, and that is not easy to do. The Carter administration learned that in its efforts in 1977 to persuade Germany and Japan to go along with its economic stimulus policies, with unhappy results that we discuss later.

Failing success at policy coordination, a United States government has the option of either going ahead or backing off from market interventions. The recovery from Professor Einstein's nationalistic measles has not yet reached the point where the United States government is inclined to back off. In fact, there are some disturbing signs of a relapse into the nationalistic economics of yesteryear, something which, if it comes about, could have very serious consequences for the world and United States economies.

The fundamental premise of an open world economy is the acceptance of world markets, along with the competition in prices and wage costs, among other things, that this implies. Interventionist policies of national governments to try to control prices, wages, or capital flows are inconsistent with a free world market. And yet, those are exactly the type of policies that the United States and some other national governments have tried to follow in the 1970s.

We have already discussed the failure of the wage and price controls imposed by Richard Nixon and John Connally in 1971, a failure brought about in large part by their inability to control world markets along with the United States market. Canada, overcome with a spirit of nationalism, also had a fling at economic controls in 1975, with similar adverse effects on its national economy. It finally decided in October 1977 to phase out controls in 1978 to try to restore economic growth and relieve inflation.

The mistaken United States economic intervention in 1971 had been followed with a policy of "Energy Independence," which had some merits on national security grounds. The national security problem could have been, and in fact has been, addressed with an oil storage program in which the United States buys oil to store away in underground salt domes as an emergency supply in case of another attempt at oil blackmail by the Arabs.

But the "Energy Independence" program failed to recognize that, aside from security questions, there is no particular merit in United States independence from the international market in oil or any other commodity if we believe in an open world economy. Even if there were such merit, the precisely wrong way to go about it was to hold down prices on domestic energy production, thus discouraging producers from developing domestic energy resources, increasing United States production, and bringing price pressure to bear on the OPEC cartel. "Project Independence" produced the opposite results from those intended. It expanded United States dependence on imported oil and diminished our capacity to participate in world energy production.

President Carter's energy program offered little correction for this fundamental mistake because of his insistence on continuing to try to thwart the market by maintaining domestic energy controls. Some of his other programs showed a similar obliviousness to the degree to which economic policy options are limited by world markets.

For example, his agriculture program, designed to quiet complaints about low prices from Western wheat farmers, moved toward higher federal price supports. As past Presidents who have wrestled with this problem could have told him, attempting to use price supports to counter an international grain surplus is simply an instrument for pricing United States farmers out of the world market. The only way it can be made to work is to also provide an export subsidy to allow farmers here to meet the international price or to try to manipulate the world supply-demand balance by giving wheat away, through foreign aid programs, to nations that otherwise would not be buying wheat.

Agriculture Secretary Beigland showed some recognition of this problem by trying to organize an international commodity program among wheat-producing nations, or in other words, an OPEC-type wheat cartel. Failing this, the United States, if it persists in its market-rigging efforts, will soon be back to the expensive export subsidies and wheat giveaway programs of the 1960s—in other words, large income transfers from American taxpayers and consumers to American farmers and to consumers abroad. The American Farm Bureau Federation, incidentally, did not want to return to high supports, with their potential damage to the huge American food exports and the ill will they engender from consumers against American farmers. But the Farm Bureau's willingness to preserve free, world-market competition was overruled by the pressures on the President and Congress from other farm groups.

A similar "domestic" policy decision with international market repercussions was the Carter administration's acquiesence to demands from organized labor for an increase in the minimum wage. On October 31, 1977, the President signed a bill raising the $2.30 hourly minimum to $2.65 on January 1, 1978, and through stages to $3.35 on

January 1, 1981. He called the bill "a step in the right direction," the same expression he used for the expanded jobs program Congress had forced upon him in the spring, suggesting that he reserves this comment for programs he is not entirely sure about.

There were good reasons not to be sure about the minimum-wage expansion. Although the minimum wage, as with most economic interventions by government, has a surface plausibility—in this case, as a way to help the nation's weakest wage bargainers—most economists think it does exactly the opposite by pricing them out of the job market. And as with the oil and farm programs, it ignores international factors.

Labor, as with wheat or oil, is an international commodity. Workers themselves cross national boundaries; a good many have been coming into the United States both legally and illegally to compete for jobs in the American economy. And so do jobs. In an open world economy, manufacturers go looking for the best sources of labor, in much the same way that they go looking for the cheapest raw materials and other factors of production. By setting a minimum price for labor, the government is encouraging American and foreign producers to build plants somewhere other than in the United States. Organized labor's main purpose in seeking a higher minimum is to raise overall pay scales in this country. Otherwise, there would be little point, since most organized workers earn wages above the minimum. To the extent this happens, the United States is discouraging domestic production in a way not altogether different from the way it discourages domestic energy production by artificially suppressing prices.

As with the farm program, there are further pressures to remedy this effect. Organized labor is increasing its demands for government to apply penalties to American companies to discourage them from going abroad. The result: further interference with international markets, a government-induced income transfer from American consumers to organized labor, further victimization of low-productivity workers, and further demands for "jobs" programs to help these unfortunates at public expense.

These examples illustrate how "domestic" economic programs cannot escape international realities. The United States performance with regard to policies more generally recognized as having international implications does not look any more promising. Outright protectionism is once again rearing its head, despite the Carter administration's efforts to fight such a trend. The President has from the outset of his administration declared a firm commitment to free trade. Indeed, his Treasury Secretary, Mr. Blumenthal, was the chief United States negotiator in the Kennedy Round discussions that were so important in promoting that cause. And the man the President appointed as his own chief trade negotiator in 1977, Ambassador Robert S. Strauss, was ardent in his advocacy of free trade.

Before going to the seven-nation economic summit meeting in London in May 1977, Mr. Carter and his economic team told the press that it was in the enlightened self-interest of the United States to look outward, even though protectionism and economic nationalism were rising throughout the world. They noted that one out of every six manufacturing jobs in the United States is dependent upon the export market; one out of every three acres of American farm land produces for export; nearly one out of every three dollars of American corporate profits comes from international activities, including both foreign production and exports; the United States depends on imports for over 25% of 12 key industrial raw materials, out of a total of 15 that fall into the essential category.

The President rejected early in his administration some demands for import protections, from shoe manufacturers, for example. But the pressures continued to build. The President gave ground on pressures for sugar import tariffs, a subject dear to the hearts of important Congressmen, including Senator Russell Long of Louisiana, from cane sugar country. He imposed a 6.1-cent-a-pound tariff to raise imports to the 13.5-cent domestic support level. Then he came under intense pressure from the American steel industry, which began shutting down some of its oldest steel plants and laying off workers in the fall of 1977, primarily blaming foreign imports. The steel companies complained that foreign producers, mainly Japan, were "dumping" steel in the United States at prices lower than they charge at home, in violation of the international trade rules set under the General Agreement on Tariffs and Trade (GATT). The industry insisted that it didn't want to thwart free trade; it just wanted to be treated fairly.

Indeed, the United States steel industry does have problems, for many of the same reasons that the energy industry has problems. Because of either direct price controls in the United States or political pressures to hold down prices, the United States steel industry has had difficulties for 20 years or so in taking advantage of peaks in world steel demand by raising prices and profits to balance against periods of low demand. As a result, its earnings have been anemic compared with other industries, lowering its ability to both generate its own capital and to compete for capital in the securities markets. This weakness, combined with pressures under the environmental laws to spend money for more efficient equipment, has left it at a competitive disadvantage in its own markets. It has frequently been outmaneuvered in the United States market by the efficient and aggressive Japanese producers. Whether the Japanese price cutting in fact constituted unfair "dumping" is a controversial point. Given the complexities of world markets, with possibilities for quiet discounts and the like, dumping is hard to prove with any certainty. Sometimes a nation's decision to take countermeasures depends more on how badly its own producers are being hurt rather than on any absolute proof of unfair practices by foreign competitors.

A finding of dumping, in short, is an easy way out, a way for a government to force foreign competitors to curtail their exports without violating GATT rules or renouncing the principle of free trade. That is the course the United States at first took in 1977. Asserting that "free trade has got to be fair trade," the President told a group of steel industry executives and union officials at the White House in October that he would impose antidumping duties on foreign steel when the United States International Trade Commission finally determined that dumping existed. The Treasury had already concluded that there was dumping in a case brought by Gilmore Steel Corporation and had set the antidumping penalty at 32%. Japanese producers had begun to pull back on exports to the United States because of the political risks.

Lindley Clark, writing in the *Wall Street Journal*, noted that a key part of one Treasury antidumping finding involved adding on an 8% profit to the Treasury's computation of the Japanese firms' costs. "If steelmakers have to get an 8% profit on everything they sell, many steel companies in the United States and elsewhere have been dumping quite a lot of steel," Mr. Clark wrote.

Later in the year, after it seemed that some of the pressure had subsided, the administration opted surprisingly for an even broader attack on steel imports. It went to work on a plan for "reference" pricing of imported steel, which simply meant that importers would not be able to sell their steel at prices below certain floors set by the government.

Although reference pricing has certain similarities to attacks on dumping, there is a certain political difference. Dumping is recognized by GATT and by national laws as being outside accepted trade rules, and to take action against dumping does not invite general retaliation.

But reference pricing is a broad, unilateral control on imports and runs the risk of touching off countermeasures in other countries that would escalate protectionism around the world. It also runs the risk of bringing demands from other industries for similar protection. The copper industry also was seeking reference pricing and was next in line after steel. Of course, as with other forms of protection, reference pricing raises prices to American consumers.

Another source of pressure was the textile industry, which has had difficulties for years in competing with textiles produced abroad and was again complaining that it was being forced to close plants. The Carter administration's response to that was to try to work out bilateral trade agreements to "constrain growth of imports in areas which have high job impact."

In puzzling contradiction to administration protectionist moves, Trade Ambassador Strauss spoke to the Conference Board's Conference on International Trade Policy and American Industry at New York's Waldorf-Astoria hotel on October 11, 1977. He made a strong pitch for greater business support for the "Tokyo Round" of trade talks that had been under way in Geneva since 1973. Ninety nations were participating in the talks, which were attempting to lower both tariff and nontariff trade barriers and to improve trading rules.

Mr. Strauss admitted that "very few results have, quite honestly, been achieved." But he said the administration would keep on trying and that he felt history was on the side of a continued movement toward free trade. He noted that the United States, in the midst of the Depression, embarked on a series of bilateral trade agreements with more than a score of countries. "We did that because our excursion during the twenties and earlier thirties into increased protectionism had been a dismal, frightening failure."

Indeed, it was a frightening failure. The crash of the stock market in 1929 probably was caused in part by a clear signal that fall that the Smoot-Hawley tariff bill would pass Congress. Smoot-Hawley raised tariffs on more than 1000 items and set some agricultural tariffs as high as 49%.

The liberalization Mr. Strauss was referring to occurred under the Reciprocal Trade Agreements Act of 1934 but was largely offset by internal tax increases, with the result that the Depression was eased but not fully relieved until World War II.

There can be little doubt that overt protectionism—or even covert protectionism, if it is successful—is like playing with fire. When one nation raises its tariffs to protect a domestic industry, other nations retaliate by doing the same thing, with the result that trade slows and prices of the protected items rise. This, of course, is a prescription for slowing down the world economy, which was what the stock market was afraid of in 1929 and was what in fact happened. There is no guarantee that it cannot happen again if the Carter administration weakens further in its resolve to resist protectionist pressures.

Indeed, there were widespread fears in late 1977 that protectionist forces were gaining new power in the world economy. In a speech delivered at the Trade Policy Research Centre in London in October, Professor John H. Jackson of the University of Michigan School of Law, described the pessimism. Said Professor Jackson, who had been general counsel to the United States GATT mission: "Many perceptive observers feel that we are currently undergoing the greatest challenge to the liberal trade system, including GATT, since the formulation of that system in the immediate post-World War II period. . . . Little progress has been made in more than four years of international trade negotiations; formidable domestic political forces are organizing coordinated campaigns for greater limitation of imported competing products; and national governments have been taking actions in blatant disregard of their legal and moral obligations concerning international trade. Where it will end we don't know—everyone present can easily conjure up a doomsday scenario, some relying on analogies of the disastrous policies of the 1920s and 1930s. . . ."

Professor Jackson said he didn't think such pessimism was warranted "yet," but he did cite some interesting reasons to worry. One of them was the one we mentioned earlier in this chapter, the tendency of free trade to constrain national political leaders in the making of "domestic" policy, a constraint that they tend to resist. Said Professor Jackson: "It becomes increasingly clear that economic interdependence does in a realistic sense reduce national sovereignty. This means that issues formerly religiously reserved for national control—such as interest rates, monetary supply, government budget policy, unemployment assistance, now become accepted agenda items for summit and other international meetings. It also means that a nation has less scope for experimenting with various models of structuring its economy or society. This is inevitably a source of frustration for national politicians, particularly at a time when citizens tend to impose greater responsibilities on their governments for their material well being and their quality of life. For example, how can environmental protection or consumer protection policies be developed in the context of international competition?"

Professor Jackson's proposed solutions to the problem, involving mainly improving GATT procedures and the like, leave doubts as to their potential efficacy. But he could not have stated the central problem more clearly. There is a fundamental conflict between free trade and attempts by governments to intervene in their own national markets.

As a *Wall Street Journal* editorial noted on November 2, 1977, the most interventionist major governments of all, Russia and China, are also the ones most isolated from the world economy. "To do so they have had to hold their own people captive." In short, excessive sovereign power and economic isolation go hand in hand.

There were few places where the conflict between sovereignty and interdependence showed more clearly in 1977 than in the Carter Administration's troubles with the monetary system. Even after the breakdown of the Bretton Woods monetary system, the United States still bears a special monetary responsibility. The dollar remains as the world's basic currency, with international transactions and external bank balances of individuals, businesses, and governments all over the world frequently denominated in dollars.

Since money is a storehouse of wealth in addition to being a medium of exchange and a measure of value, this means that the United States government and its Federal Reserve Board governors bear a responsibility not only for the monetary stability of the United States but also, to a large degree, for the monetary stability of the world. A weakening of the dollar relative to other currencies or more fundamental measurements such as gold or commodities in general is a more serious matter for the world than, say, a weakening of the Italian lira or the British pound. It means that all those people holding dollar balances around the world are having their wealth eroded by dollar inflation. They don't like it, and those that can are inclined to want to flee from the dollar into some other currency such as Swiss francs or German marks, which, of course, only weakens the dollar further.

If the strong-currency countries, like Germany, are concerned about this, and they usually are, they have it in their power to issue marks to buy up dollars to support the price of the dollar in the foreign-exchange markets. The German central bank, or Bundesbank, in Frankfurt, can put its surplus dollars to work—beyond what it needs for balancing its international accounts—by investing in United States government securities.

(It might be useful to keep in mind that these kinds of bank transactions are bookkeeping entries or, more precisely, computer transactions; banks leave exchanges of actual paper currency mainly to tourists and business travelers. Most money in the world is computer-entry money, but it is money nonetheless, and it originates, by and large, with the central banks of each individual nation. A form of international money, called Special Drawing Rights, is created through the International Monetary Fund, but it is only used by central banks as a supplement to the foreign-exchange reserves they maintain for balancing international accounts.)

The Germans might want to support the dollar for several reasons. There is a widespread conception in the world—although it is not very well supported by experience—that a weak currency gives the country issuing that currency a trade advantage. The widely held theory is that buyers will leap at that country's goods because they can exchange their own currencies for the currency of the seller at a favorable rate and thus, in effect, buy marked-down goods. This theory has long been popular with politicians, particularly the British, because it is a way to argue that a weak currency is really a good thing. "We'll sell more goods abroad, thus we'll have more jobs and a better trade balance," goes the rationale. "Best of all, we can go on creating money at a fast clip to finance government-spending schemes here at home."

This rationale has grown less and less plausible, particularly in Britain, which has used it throughout a postwar period of relative economic decline marked by a slippage in the relative value of the pound. It is a little like the retailer who thinks he makes up for in volume what he loses on each individual item. Britain may temporarily sell more cars and woolens, but in terms of international money it is merely shipping away its resources and labor for less return. The price of what it imports goes up in terms of its own currency.

In short, currency devaluation can hardly be said to be a boon for a national economy. It is simply another word for something everyone knows is *not* a boon: currency inflation. The British end up earning less and paying more in real terms.

Despite the newfound doubts about devaluation as a general economic prescription, the theory that it can promote trade and jobs still is widely held. And since most nations are concerned about maintaining their exports and the jobs represented by those exports, they are reluctant to see a major trade partner devalue his currency to any marked degree. This is one reason why such a country might buy the trading partner's currency to support it.

Another reason the Germans might want to support the dollar is simply to help maintain some stability in exchange rates, which is a matter of some importance to major trading nations. The costs to businessmen in such nations for hedging against currency swings—by buying "futures" contracts allowing them to buy a needed currency at some future time at an agreed-to price—can be a significant business expense.

But there is one fundamental problem for Germany or any other nation that chooses to support the dollar. It then suffers inflationary pressures itself. It is, after all, issuing its own currency to acquire the dollars, which is very much like the Fed creating money in the American economy through the process of issuing dollars to buy government securities from the banks. The Germans, by issuing marks for dollars and using the money to buy United States securities, become, in a sense, a part of the United States money-creation system.

That, in fact, was very much a part of the problem that led to the breakdown of the Bretton Woods money system, which placed an obligation on members to hold the parity between their currencies and the dollar at fixed levels that could be adjusted only through a formal process. When, in the 1960s, United States money creation became excessive to finance the budget deficits associated with the Vietnam war and the War on Poverty, Europeans complained that the United States was "exporting" inflation. France, which under Charles de Gaulle was only a reluctant follower of United States leadership and which had little sympathy for the United States role in Vietnam, was a particular objector. As we have said before, the system finally broke down because of periodic flights from the dollar.

In the early months of the Carter administration it became evident that a similar sort of problem could occur even with currency parities floating. The Federal Reserve, which had managed to hold money growth relatively stable under the Ford administration and thus reduce the inflation rate substantially, came under pressure from both the new administration and Congress to maintain an easy-money policy so as to hold down short-term interest rates. Here again, the Fed and the country were victim to an economic myth. Speeding up money creation may hold down short-term interest rates for a time, but since this is an invitation to inflation, it very often raises long-term interest rates as lenders hedge against their inflation expectations.

The Fed knows this, and theoretically it is an independent agency with legal protections against political interference in its management of monetary policy. But it also knows that if, through a tight money policy, it should ever be subject to accusations that it killed off an economic recovery, it might be in some political jeopardy. So even though it had demonstrated to the satisfaction of many observers in 1976 that a firm monetary policy was not inconsistent with economic recovery, it chose to become more liberal in money creation in 1977 to be on the safe side.

The result of this more rapid rate of money growth began to show up, as it usually does, in the dollar's value in international exchange. The dollar began to slip in value against the German mark, the Swiss franc, the Japanese yen, and, surprisingly, even against the British pound, which had taken a big beating in 1976 and was showing some signs of recovery. The dollar's strength wasn't helped at all when it became apparent that the United States would run a very large trade deficit for 1977, perhaps as much as $30 billion.

This trade deficit could be attributed to several possibilities. Certainly it suggested that United States demand was growing rapidly, as its economic recovery proceeded at a faster rate than the recovery in Europe. There was a special factor: worldwide crop surpluses had reduced growth in the biggest United States export, farm products. And, of course, United States oil imports were continuing to grow.

Trade deficits are not a serious problem, per se. If a national economy is growing rapidly relative to other economies, it attracts foreign capital to offset some of the trade deficit. But if it is running a deficit in all its transactions, including both capital and trade, its currency will almost certainly weaken in foreign-exchange markets by mere virtue of the fact that a lot of its currency will be in foreign hands.

There were fears in 1977 that the mere observance by Congressmen, business, and labor of the huge United States trade deficit would further stimulate protectionist demands. The idea that a trade deficit justifies protection doesn't make a great deal of sense, since it suggests that domestic demand is relatively vigorous and thus that domestic industries, unless they are grossly uncompetitive, should be faring reasonably well. But political rationality being what it is, the fears about protectionism were justified.

What the weak dollar indicated most of all—and this was borne out by money growth figures supplied by the Fed itself—was that the United States was running an overstimulative monetary policy. This claim was pooh-poohed at first by the Carter economic team, which continued to urge Fed chairman Arthur Burns to keep the money flowing. By fall, the administration could say with truth that the faster money growth that began in the spring had not affected the consumer price index, which in October was rising at the relatively low rate of 3.6% a year.

The White House issued a statement in October, saying that there was no need to worry about fast money growth because money "velocity" was down. Velocity represents the number of transactions taking place in the economy, and indeed it was down. But that was hardly reassuring to monetarist economists, who equate money expansion with inflationary potential regardless of where the velocity statistic might be at any given time.

And indeed, Treasury Secretary Blumenthal began saying when the dollar weakness first began to appear in 1977 that the United States was not particularly concerned about the dollar, that it would find its normal level. That might have been fine had the money markets not been able to see that the United States was not adopting a hands-off attitude; it was, in fact, pumping out dollars at a rapid rate. The result of Mr. Blumenthal's disclaimers was to knock further points off the dollar as dollar holders hurried to get out of a currency whose weakness didn't seem to concern its principal managers.

Mr. Blumenthal's statements were more than simple irresponsibility. He and Mr. Carter were trying to pressure the Europeans and Japanese into greater stimulus of their own economies in order to expand demand and bring about a faster world recovery. Indeed, the European recovery was lagging in 1977, but the Europeans saw things in a different light. As had so often been the case in the past, Europe had political worries that were curbing investment and growth. France seemed threatened, at least in the early part of the year, with a socialist–communist election victory in 1978. The Germans were worried about political terrorism and whether the Carter administration would maintain its NATO defense commitments. Britain, although showing some signs of revival, was hardly a well patient. Italy also showed such signs but still had the threat of a communist takeover lurking in its future.

The Germans and the Japanese, in particular, felt that the recommendations from the Carter administration were simply a prescription for a new outbreak of inflation. And this time, with the pressure from the left and the tendency of inflation to cause social upheaval (a risk particularly well known to the Germans, who hadn't forgotten the trauma of the 1920s), they might not be so lucky as they were in 1975.

Mr. Blumenthal backed off a bit with a speech in Houston in October, saying that a stable dollar was "essential to both the United States and the world at large." His remarks gave courage to the markets for a while, as did the appearance of more stringent efforts by the Fed to control the money supply in October. But by November 1 Mr. Blumenthal was again saying that the United States didn't intend to intervene to support the dollar, and the Fed still seemed to be having trouble getting money growth under control. The dollar fell to record lows against the German mark and Swiss franc and a record postwar low against the Japanese yen.

All this suggested a very low level of confidence around the world in the quality of United States economic management. The same thing was being suggested by the American stock market, which had declined nearly 200 points in the first 10 months of 1977.

It certainly should not be said that the United States administration was necessarily wrong and its critics abroad necessarily right. Europeans and the Japanese are not always kindly disposed toward international interdependence and cooperation either. The Japanese, in fact, have traditionally kept a tight rein on foreign investment and have tended to support export industries through subtle and effective means.

But there is every reason to believe that the new administration's pressures on the Fed for easy money were a serious error, particularly at a time when the world was looking with considerable skepticism and even amazement on the Carter energy policy and some of his other domestic initiatives. There was a feeling abroad that the United States was again acting unilaterally, as it had under Lyndon Johnson and the Nixon-Connally regime, telling its economic and political partners, in essence, that their views were not likely to change the United States approach to economic management. That is not a particularly wise leadership stance, given the experience the Europeans and Japanese have had with inflation in the last few years and in their not forgotten pasts.

The new administration was trying, they felt, what so many United States administrations had done in the past: to exercise its own sovereignty at the expense of less powerful nations. The conflict between sovereignty and interdependence was very much at the center of the question.

The new administration might have done well to pay more heed to Henry Kissinger, the former Secretary of State, who made some remarks about the future of international business at a conference in Washington in June 1977 sponsored by Georgetown University's Center for Strategic and International Studies. Though Professor Kissinger has admitted that his grasp of economics leaves something to be desired, and though we would not agree with all of his economic analysis, his political analysis is always worth listening to. He said:

"The future of business is inseparable from the future of industrial democracy. Western Europe, North America and Japan produce 65% of all the goods and services generated in the world. They account for 75% of its trade. Their economic performance drives international commerce and finance; their investment, technology, managerial genius and agricultural productivity are the dynamic force of prosperity everywhere. They are the world's bankers and the world's inventors. Critics of the West, in the Communist world and elsewhere, have disparaged our system for decades, but they have not solved any of their own problems. Ironically they now turn to the industrial democracies for the technology, the techniques of analysis, planning and management, the industrial systems and marketing skills which their own system seems incapable of generating.

"But this relative success story is no guarantee for the future. Realism impels us to note the signs of strain. The political future in several nations of the West may well be clouded by shortfalls in the output of goods and services, or breakdowns of the financial system. In too many countries, demands for real increases in wages, coupled with the insistent pressures to expand public services and public sector expenditures, have generated nearly unmanageable inflationary pressures at the very moment when the increase in the cost of imported energy has added its own impetus to both inflation and recession. These demands cannot possibly all be met simultaneously. An attempt to do so is bound to disrupt and ultimately to demoralize the political system. There is a grave danger of an erosion of the legitimacy of government and a prospect of basic changes in the domestic structure in Europe and perhaps even in Japan.

"It is not beyond the realm of possibility that one or more of the Communist parties of Western Europe will gain entry into national governments—an event which would mark a watershed in postwar relationships. It is not beyond imagination either, that some nations will find the discipline required to manage their levels of demand too great to permit their continued adherence to the liberal trading system, and that they will instead revert to protectionism and isolationism. Finally, it could happen that because of disparities in growth rates, balances of payments positions and international competitiveness, the momentum of European unification will further decelerate and that the political cohesion of the West in international negotiations and institutions would break down. A process of atomization could take over. The consequences for business would, of course, be ominous. . . ."

"As a nation we must understand that we can neither dominate the world nor escape from it. For the first time in our history we are permanently involved in international affairs."

Indeed we are, and the growth of world trade, which slowed sharply in 1977 after a vigorous 11.5% recovery in 1976 from the 1975 world recession, should be regarded with just as much concern in the United States as domestic trade. Similarly, the soundness of the dollar in world markets should be a matter of greater concern to the U.S. administration and Congress if they want to generate greater confidence in our reliability as an economic leader.

CHAPTER EIGHTEEN
MONEY ARGUMENTS

. . . press reports of disharmonies or arguments or lack of friendship or cooperation between me and Chairman Burns are completely erroneous. . . . I don't think I have any inclination to criticize the actions that have been taken by Mr. Burns.—President Carter.

PRESIDENT CARTER'S ASSURANCES TO THE WORLD ON November 10, 1977, that he and Arthur M. Burns, chairman of the Federal Reserve Board, were on the best of terms were greeted with surprise and a little bit of incredulity. For months before that announcement, high administration officials, both anonymously and publicly, had been sniping at the Fed for not providing enough monetary stimulus to the economic recovery.

These complaints, from Secretary Blumenthal, former Budget Director Bert Lance, and Chief Economic Adviser Charles Schultze, had been puzzling but unsettling to the money markets. The Fed had been consistently overshooting its own money-growth targets by a large margin through most of the year. As Lindley H. Clark, Jr. had noted in the *Wall Street Journal* on October 7, the Fed had, over the preceding six months, been expanding M1 (the most commonly used measure of the money supply, consisting of currency plus bank checking accounts) at an annual growth rate of 9.6%. Its target had been 4% to 6.5%.

The combination of the Fed's overshooting its targets and the administration's demanding more money had been seriously weakening public confidence in both the dollar and in the administration's grasp of monetary policy. Aside from the direct effects the rapid monetary expansion was having on the dollar in foreign-exchange markets, the strange conflict between the administration and the Fed was also having a psychological effect. The dollar was weak in world markets; gold prices were up some 20% from a year earlier; whosesale prices were beginning to rise again; and, horror of all horrors, some Arab oil sheiks were beginning to show a preference for keeping their large cash balances in British pounds rather than United States dollars.

The consumer price index, which had dropped to a more comfortable level in the third quarter from the 8%-plus growth rate in the first half, was still holding steady. A good many economists were predicting that it would not go soaring again in response to the rapid money growth. It has not, they pointed out, always followed the lead of the wholesale index, which had just gone above a 9% annual growth rate after a period of relative stability. But other economists were worried, noting that there is normally a lag of several months between a period of rapid monetary expansion and a pickup in the consumer price index.

And indeed, there were signs in the fall that the expansionist forces in both the administration and Congress were beginning to get worried too. Mr. Blumenthal promised to stop making remarks that might upset the currency markets, although he didn't entirely succeed in that. Mr. Burns increasingly publicized his determination to bring money growth under control, come what may in the way of flak from the administration or Congress, or, although he did not say so publicly, of difficulties inside the Fed's own Board of Governors in reaching agreement on money policy. And Mr. Carter began to sound more conciliatory toward the chairman, a trend that culminated in his November 10 press-conference remark.

Along with these signs of harmony, an interesting thing happened in Congress in the fall, suggesting that there was some softening up on Chairman Burns there as well: the Joint Economic Committee issued its *Midyear Review of the Economy* on September 26.

The Democratic majority of the committee seemed to be making its usual attack on the Fed for not expanding the money supply rapidly enough, and it also seemed to be calling into question Mr. Carter's goals of full employment, a balanced budget, and reduced inflation by the end of his term in 1981. Said the report: "This target is beyond reach unless monetary policy becomes sharply more expansionary and this would make it most unlikely that the inflation target could be reached. . . ."

The majority seemed to be opting for monetary stimulus. Noting that there was a danger of the recovery being interrupted, its report said: ". . . it is therefore entirely appropriate to reiterate that stimulative measures that go well beyond the budget for fiscal year 1978 or that are contained in present monetary policies, are very likely to be needed in the near future."

The committee's report was widely publicized in the press, which emphasized both the doubts about the President's economic goals and the encouragement of even more rapid monetary growth. But there was one thing wrong: on money growth, the "majority report" did not represent a majority of the committee, as was clear when you read the various dissents and caveats.

To no one's surprise, the 8 Republicans on the 20-member committee disagreed with the majority report. They accused the Democrats of committing one of the common errors of monetary expansionists (one that, incidentally, led Great Britain into a period—in 1974—when inflation exceeded 25%). This is the belief that money should be expanded at a rate *faster* than the current rate of inflation to add to "real balances" in the banking sector. Said the minority report:

"If the Federal Reserve is supposed to fund real growth and

existing inflation, when do we start to reduce the inflation? If we have 5% real growth and 6% inflation, must the Fed supply 11% more money as the Majority implies? This monetary growth works to keep inflation at present levels. And this is directly opposed to the Majority's supposed desire to reduce inflation. If that 6% inflation is to be rationally reduced, the Fed must move gradually toward 10%, 9%, 8%, 7%, 6% and finally 5% growth rates of the money supply. . . ."

As it turns out, the "majority" was not a majority on this issue. Senator Sparkman (D., Ala.,) chose not to "identify myself with all its conclusions and recommendations" because he had not been present at some of the hearings. Representative William S. Moorhead (D., Pa.) said in "Additional Views" that "it is far from clear that monetary policy during the two years of recovery has been 'too restrictive' as the report says. . . ."

Senator Proxmire wrote a separate opinion saying that "the monetary officials may receive somewhat more blame than they deserve. In the past year, for example, the money supply has increased at a rate in excess of 7%, which is more than the top of the 4% to 7% rate set by the Federal Reserve Board itself. I doubt that the monetary policies would have been more than marginally different whoever had been in charge. . . ."

And finally, Representative Henry S. Reuss (D., Wis.), one of the Fed's severest critics over the years, added, "I am not persuaded at this time that the Federal Reserve should significantly raise its present target range for the post-October, 1977, growth of the monetary aggregates, but actual future growth should be aimed at the upper part of the range for the present."

Add to this the fact that two other Democrats, Gillis Long of Louisiana and Lee Hamilton of Indiana, joined with the Republicans in urging tax cuts and spending restraint as the best course for economic policy. Although they made no specific comment on monetary policy, they could hardly have been further away from the alleged "majority" prescription. Thus the "majority" report was only agreed to, and tacitly at that, by 6 members of the 20-member committee. Chairman Richard Bolling (D., Mo.) didn't have much company.

Whether this disarray in a committee that can usually be expected to nag the Fed had some bearing on Mr. Burns' renewed boldness in the fall and on the administration's increasing caution can only be guessed. But it was becoming apparent that the weakness of the dollar and the simultaneous threat of a new round of stagflation were beginning to concern both the administration and Congress. They had reason to be concerned, because inflation is not only the number-one worry of the American people, as reflected in numerous polls, but also a phenomenon that has become chronic in the American economy in both recession and recovery. It had also become chronic through most of the world, including the socialist as well as the nonsocialist states.

The "slumpflation" of 1975 had wiped out one of the popular notions about inflation, that it can only occur when an economy is operating somewhere near the peak of its capacity. Some inflation, in the old way of thinking (which has not been entirely abandoned, by the way), was the price to be paid for full employment and a high rate of economic activity.

The experience of 1975 taught that the problem was by no means so simple. The truly simple definition of inflation is that it arises when there is too much money chasing too few goods, or, to put it another way, an imbalance between supply and demand. But the trouble arises in trying to determine whether the key problem to be attacked by public policy is supply or demand. It is fairly easy, at least in a theoretical sense, to attack the demand problem by tightening up the money supply. But it is by no means simple in either a technical or a political sense.

It is not because it means the Federal Reserve Board must do some naysaying to the banks and the United States Treasury, raising short-term interest rates and trimming down bank reserves. The Treasury doesn't like the higher interest rates because it raises the cost of financing and refinancing the huge federal debt, which now costs the Treasury some $30 billion a year in net interest. The banks, although in general opposed to inflation, are unhappy when their lending powers are curtailed too stringently, particularly if loan demand is high. Even if the Fed does curtail bank reserves, it has no control over the "velocity" of the money supply, which simply means the number of times the same dollar changes hands in a given period.

Despite these difficulties, it is usually conceded that the Fed can indeed reduce inflation by clamping down on money growth. Exactly that happened in 1975 and 1976 when the Fed brought the money-growth rate (M1) down to below 5% a year and the consumer price index growth rate fell from the alarming 12%-plus level it had hit in 1974 to a more comfortable 5-to-6% range.

But by the beginning of 1977, the Fed was allowing M1 growth to climb again to above 6%, and inflation was climbing too, up to the

8%-plus level. The Fed clamped on the money brakes in May and June and inflation cooled in the third quarter, but then money growth got out of hand again in the third quarter, leaving everyone to wonder whether (1) the Fed really was managing the money supply or it was in fact managing itself and (2) inflation would take off again at some inopportune point.

In short, there was a distinct correlation between money-supply growth and inflation, just as monetarists have always claimed. But both the desire and the ability of the Fed to control money growth and inflation were in doubt. And the doubts were not helped at all by the administration's pressure on the Fed to keep the money gates open.

The Fed is, of course, supposed to enjoy a certain degree of independence from political pressures, on the sound principle that someone in every economic system should be in a position to say no to the historical tendency of governments to want to spend more than the real output of the economy permits. Britain's central bank, The Bank of England, was even a private institution until it was nationalized in 1946, and there are those who would say that England's money troubles date from then, although that is a gross oversimplification. The Fed has undergone no such trauma since its founding in 1914, but its governors and their chairman can never forget that the Fed is a creature of Congress and that what degree of independence it has can be curtailed by the mere passage of a law.

With that thought in the back of their minds, the governors take some considerable pains to avoid putting themselves in a position where they could be accused of aborting an economic recovery. If they should err, they would prefer to err on the side of too much money growth rather than too little, particularly in a time when Democrats control both the Congress and the White House.

And indeed, an argument can be made that avoiding such a danger would be prudent policy, even if the Fed had total independence of action, since an economic slump is no more attractive as a prospect than inflation. But after the experience of 1975 a good many of the more forward-looking economists were asking themselves whether there was as much difference between the slump and inflation as everyone once thought.

In a March 1977 speech[1] economist John W. Kendrick of George Washington University noted that the productivity of the American economy had grown less rapidly in the last decade than in the preceding 50 years. The growth rate from 1966 to 1976 had been only 1.7% a year compared with an average of 2.25% in the preceding half-century. As we said in the preceding chapter, productivity, meaning how much output you can get out of a given level of input, is a key statistic to a nation's economic well-being because it translates directly to how much improvement the nation is making in its overall living standards. Every great innovation of mankind, from the bow lathe used by primitive man to start fires, to the plough, the joint stock company, and the nuclear power plant, has had as one of its foremost objectives to make work more productive and thereby make the necessities and luxuries of life more plentiful.

Professor Kendrick believes that one reason productivity growth has declined has been the accelerating inflation that has brought about misallocations of resources and squeezed the real rates of return on investment, a process we described in the preceding chapter. Or, if you would want to put it another way, the structure of the economy, its efficiency in converting savings and surpluses into new capital assets, has been weakening.

Now, it could be argued that inflation is a symptom as well as a cause, which indeed it may be. Inflation is only one of five factors listed by Professor Kendrick as reasons for lagging productivity growth. He also listed the "bulge" of youthful entrants into the labor force, meaning that a larger proportion of the working population is relatively inexperienced; a decline in the ratio of research and development expenditures to GNP to 2.2% in 1976 from 3.0% in 1966; a slower growth of productive capital goods per worker, "due in part to an increased proportion of capital outlays devoted to environmental protection and other mandated social programs;" and "certain negative social tendencies, and a loosening of the work ethic and attachment to the business system."

In other words, lagging productivity from these other possible causes could reduce the economy's productive power and thus make it more likely that in periods of high demand goods and services would become relatively scarce and prices rise. And rising prices create the distortions we have mentioned before that further inhibit the expansion of productive capacity—a vicious circle.

Two economists at the St. Louis Federal Reserve Bank, Robert H. Rasche and John A. Tatom, believe that one component of the general inflation, energy prices, has had a particular and direct influence on the nation's total economic capacity. Writing in the bank's monthly *Review* in June 1977, Messrs. Rasche and Tatom argued that the quadrupling of OPEC petroleum prices in late 1973 permanently reduced the economy's potential output by about 4%. Energy, they contended, was a factor of production the same as capital and labor, and a sharp increase in its cost and scarcity would have the same effect on potential economic output as a scarcity of those other two factors.

We won't go into the economic argument for this theory except to say that the two St. Louis Fed economists concluded their treatise with a warning: Any assessment of the economy's potential capacity based solely on the unemployment rate and estimates of unused industrial capacity might be highly misleading. "Attempts to achieve an unattainable potential output rate through stimulative policy will not only fail, but will add to inflationary pressures."

Indeed, attempting to assess the potential output of the United States economy is a task fraught with peril, given the uncertainties among economists over this question. We have already dealt with the vagaries of the unemployment rate deriving from possible reporting error and from the expansion of job demand from individuals not formerly a part of the labor force. Measurement of plant capacity is equally treacherous because of the difficulties of determining truly economical capacity under given circumstances of taxation, inflation, and profitability in all the various industries that make up the United States industrial plant. An ancient steel-industry coke oven might be capacity in a sense, but not if the steel company finds it uneconomical to use it at current costs and prices.

Another economist, Ms. Kathryn Eickhoff of Townsend–Greenspan & Company, tends to confirm the St. Louis Fed warning with what the *Wall Street Journal*[2] called the Eickhoff Curve. Ms. Eickhoff believes that there is a "trigger point" in every business recovery. At a point when operating rates reach a certain level of plant capacity, businessmen sharply increase their capital spending to add new plant and equipment to meet demand. But she notes that as the normal rate of capacity expansion has moved lower, the "trigger point" of capacity utilization at which businessmen go on a rapid expansion binge has been moving to a higher level.

The reason for this, she believes, is the high rate of inflation, which creates the inhibitions we have already discussed; worries that a sudden further rise in the inflation rate will bring government price controls that will destroy the value of new investment; increasingly burdensome regulation; and the new propensity of courts and regulators to block capital projects.

The reluctance to invest, which was certainly obvious in the most recent business recovery, has serious implications for government policy. It means that business is more likely to reach the practical limits of its capacity before new plant and equipment can be brought into play; thus the very thing feared by businessmen, a new outburst of inflation, will be self-fulfilling. This is another way of describing the vicious circle.

All of this, of course, raises serious questions about the efficacy of monetary stimulation in promoting economic recovery and growth. It is fairly certain that by restraining monetary growth, it is possible to curb inflationary tendencies. And indeed, the above arguments would suggest that this is the most important single action policymakers could take to put the economy on a more vigorous long-term growth track.

It is a great deal less certain whether rapid expansion of the money supply has any real stimulative effect. Economists have described this problem as like "pushing on a string" in which nothing happens in response to the push. And the evidence of recent years suggests that monetary stimulation is simply a way to create both inflation and inflation expectations, seriously damaging the economy's prospects for genuine growth.

When the Carter economic team first arrived on the scene its members displayed an understanding of some of the do's and don't's of inflation fighting. Mr. Carter did some jawboning of the steel industry on prices—even before he became President—but he foreswore any return to wage and price controls, which is definitely a don't. At a news conference on December 3, 1976, the President-elect said: ". . . I have no intention of asking the Congress to give me standby wage and price controls and have no intention of imposing wage and price controls in the next four years. If some national emergency should arise, and I think that's a very remote possibility, that would be the only indication I can see for a need for wage and price controls . . .".

Mr. Carter also talked of his plans to relieve the regulatory burden imposed by government. Mr. Blumenthal talked about the "structural" problems of the American economy, suggesting that he understood something, as a former businessman himself, about the forces that were inhibiting capital investment and productivity growth. Mr. Schultze had expressed himself on the limits of government's powers to manipulate the economy in any constructive way. And, of course, the administration promised certain tax cuts for business to try to stimulate a more rapid rate of investment.

The problem with these prescriptions, and no doubt one reason the economic team was itself soon eclipsed by other members of the administration, was that they were essentially a call for less government. And it was hard for a President to resist the persistent demands in Washington that he "do something" to deal with economic problems or, in other words, that he expand government intervention in the economy.

The result, as we have said before, was that in the first year there was very little of that early promise fulfilled. First came the energy bill with its vast expansion of taxation and federal regulatory power and its promise of further increasing energy costs. Then came the jawboning of the Fed to expand the money supply more rapidly. And in the summer of 1977 there were even noises coming out of "reliable sources" in the White House that a contingency plan for wage and price controls was being prepared. A better prescription than this for killing off the feeble capital-spending recovery could hardly have been devised. Mr. Carter denied that there were any such plans, but it was unsettling nonetheless. Everyone knew that there were still Congressmen who would vote for wage and price controls and who actually still seemed to believe in them, despite the disastrous experience of the early 1970s.

The friendlier attitude toward Arthur Burns in November was a note of encouragement, suggesting that maybe the President didn't want rapid monetary growth after all. But by that time there were a lot of people wondering what sort of economic policy the President really wanted. Thus the main reaction was confusion, not reassurance. The confusion was not relieved when, on December 28, Mr. Carter, still espousing deep respect and friendship for Dr. Burns, fired him.

CHAPTER NINETEEN

CONCLUSION

JIMMY CARTER WAS A VERY FORTUNATE PRESIDENT IN THE FIRST year of his administration. The American economy expanded vigorously in 1977, continuing its recovery from the 1974–75 recession. The political problems that Mr. Carter suffered were largely of his own making, the result of too much haste and too much faith in technocracy in the design of sweeping economic policies. But those kinds of problems are not as serious as those that arise when there is a genuine threat—economic recession, for example.

We hope that Mr. Carter will continue to be as fortunate through the remainder of his administration. After all, his good fortune is ours as well. But we fear that the odds will be stacked against him as he serves out the remainder of his term.

The economic recovery is three years old, which means that if history is any guide, some sort of economic adjustment, and possibly a recession, will be due in 1978 or 1979. The President did not use his first year in office to bring either inflation or the federal budget under better control, which means that even with a tax cut in 1978, the combined burden of inflation and taxation is likely to keep rising. An especially large burden is due in 1979, when the economy must start paying sharply increased Social Security taxes.

There is evidence that Mr. Carter understands the prospect he faces. Although he was a relatively easy mark for Congress in 1977 when it was expanding the fiscal 1978 budget, he has made efforts to hold the 1979 budget, prepared by his own administration, within stricter limits. As he prepared to submit his 1979 budget, he still seemed serious about his goal of bringing the federal budget within approximate balance by 1981, despite claims from both conservative and liberal economists that this is impossible. It certainly is not impossible, but meeting the goal could very well require Mr. Carter to go to the mat with Congress, something he showed a reluctance to do in his first year.

There can be little doubt that a smaller federal deficit would ease inflationary pressures. And this in turn might encourage business confidence and prolong the economic expansion. Without a doubt, Mr. Carter's greatest problem in the months and years just ahead will be inflation. The 6% inflation of 1977 was certainly less severe than the average of 12% in 1974, but it remains high by United States historical standards. And with the American economy's large debt burdens, which the Fed must finance in some way if it is not to risk a credit market "crunch," the economy will remain poised on the brink of serious inflation for some time to come. Mr. Carter is absolutely right in wanting to reduce some of the inflationary pressure by reducing the federal deficit, providing he can do it by reducing federal spending rather than heaping new tax burdens on the economy.

Although neo-Keynesian economists might dispute this, a cut in federal spending will do far less harm to the national economy than further increases in effective taxation. There is a simple reason for this. Federal spending, by almost anyone's measure, involves a great deal of economic waste, meaning that a large component goes to support people who produce either nothing at all or nothing that is useful. Lower tax burdens will go to buy what individuals see as their true needs.

If the President tries to balance the budget with increased taxes, which certainly seemed to be the thrust of his 1977 policies, there is a different problem. Increased tax rates can actually be counterproductive, in terms of budget revenues, to the extent that they discourage production of valuable and useful goods and services. If less is produced, taxes yield less. The government still has its deficit to contend with, and there still are inflationary pressures.

Trying to reduce federal spending, even as a percentage of the GNP, is an arduous political task. Mr. Carter gave indications as his first year drew to a close that he was turning inward toward the business of managing the government rather than attempting programs designed to manage the general economy. That was a healthy sign. A government that cannot even manage itself can hardly manage a $2-trillion economy.

With authority from Congress for government reorganization, Mr. Carter has the means of achieving certain marginal efficiencies. It is hoped that he will make the fullest possible use of them.

But even for marginal changes in spending, he will face heavy flak from liberal spenders in his own administration, in Congress, and in the lobbies. The real test of his seriousness may ultimately be whether he is willing to veto appropriations bills, something he has so far been unwilling to do.

If Mr. Carter can indeed cut relative spending, the relative federal tax burden, and the federal budget deficit, he has a chance to preserve a healthy national economy through his term and will have an excellent chance for reelection. If he is not able to do this, his chances look a lot dimmer.

The President will also be plagued with his damaged credibility, the result of his fumblings in the first year of his administration. This will weaken his hand in bargaining with Congress and will cost him some public support he might otherwise have received for his efforts to cope with the spending pressures in Washington.

Finally, there are the problems that the President would suffer if the economy should turn sour. If this should be accompanied, as in 1974–75, by a new outbreak of serious inflation, the President will come under heavy pressures to install wage and price controls. He has stated publicly that he will never do such a thing, but Mr. Carter has shown himself to be a highly flexible President, not at all inhibited by past policy declarations.

If he does fall prey to this temptation—and it is a very powerful temptation for a government faced with serious economic difficulties—the American economy will be in for an extended period of erratic movements. As in 1972, there will most likely be an initial appearance of economic recovery as consumers take advantage of artificially controlled prices. Then the combined effect of rising prices of imported products and the squeeze on domestic producers will begin to be felt once more. The government will have the choice of either relaxing controls or seeing a lot of businesses fall into bankruptcy, so it will relax controls. The pent-up inflation will then be translated into sharp price increases just as in 1974, and the recession will hit again just as in 1974–75.

Except for one thing. This time around, it is likely to be more serious. Inflation will start from a higher base. There will be new cries from the left that capitalism doesn't work, that the system is at fault for brutal economic swings, that big business is rapacious in its quest for higher prices—and finally, that government should not relax its economic grip but should go to the ultimate extreme and seize the economy.

Mr. Carter will avoid this kind of trauma if he follows a steady policy in the months and years ahead, ignoring all advice that he try new government "innovations" and attempting as best he can to do the hard, slogging business of government management: eliminating bureaucracy, reducing federal regulation, trying to balance the budget. He will not show any dramatic successes this way, but he also is unlikely to experience any dramatic failures.

If the people come to feel that they can trust this President, that he is not going to dump any more big "energy" or "welfare" programs in their laps, confidence in the economy will return. If the President keeps his head in the face of economic setbacks and does not start grabbing for controls, confidence will be preserved. Inflation in the United States and the Western world can be managed, but it will not be a dramatic process and it will not be through the superficial application of wage and price controls. It will be through the prudent management of money and debt.

We wish the President good luck. We all may need it.

NOTES

CHAPTER TWO

1. Cited by Marcus Cunliffe, *American Presidents and the Presidency* (American Heritage Press, 1972), p. 213.
2. William Watts and Lloyd A. Free, *America's Hopes and Fears—1976* (Potomac Associates, Washington, D.C., 1976).

CHAPTER THREE

1. *Wall Street Journal,* September 23, 1977.
2. *Ibid.*
3. Robert Shogan, *Promises to Keep* (Thomas Y. Crowell Co., New York, 1977), pp. 66–67.
4. *New York Times,* May 22, 1977.

CHAPTER FOUR

1. John Maynard Keynes, *General Theory of Employment, Interest, and Money* (Macmillan, London, 1936), p. 00.
2. Sir Arthur Robinson, *Keynes V. the Keynesians* (Institute of Economic Affairs, London, 1977), p. 58.
3. Ben J. Wattenburg, *The Real America* (Capricorn Books, G.P. Putnam's Sons, New York, 1976), p. 68.
4. *Wall Street Journal,* September, 30, 1977.
5. Harry Magdoff and Paul M. Sweezy, *The End of Prosperity: The American Economy in the 1970s* (Monthly Review Press, New York, 1977), p. 136.
6. Herbert Stein, *Economic Planning and the Improvement of Economic Policy,* (Domestic Affairs Study 38, American Enterprise Institute for Public Policy Research, Washington, D.C., September 1977), pp. 6–7.
7. Friedrich A. Hayek, *The Road to Serfdom* (The University of Chicago Press, 1944), pp. 34 ff.
8. Paul Johnson, *The Enemies of Society* (Atheneum, New York, 1977).
9. Alan A. Walters, *The Politicization of Economic Decisions* (The International Institute for Economic Research, Los Angeles, 1976), p. 9.
10. Michael C. Jensen and William H. Meckling, *Can the Corporation Survive?* (The International Institute for Economic Research, Los Angeles, 1977), p. 1.

CHAPTER FIVE

1.   Christine Ammer and Dean S. Ammer, *Dictionary of Business and Economics* (The Free Press, New York, 1977), p. 321.
2.   *Newsweek,* June 28, 1976, p. 59.
3.   *New York Times,* February 6, 1977.
4.   *Wall Street Journal,* December 15, 1976.
5.   *Dun's Review,* December 1976.
6.   *National Journal,* March 5, 1977, Vol. 10, p. 363.
7.   *Fortune,* June 1977, p. 100.
8.   *Wall Street Journal,* September 6, 1977.
9.   *New York Times,* May 8, 1977.
10.   *Washington Post,* July 10, 1977.

CHAPTER SEVEN

1.   Cited by Emmet John Hughes, *The Living Presidency* (Coward, McCann & Geoghegan, New York, 1972), p. 208.
2.   *Ibid.,* p. 49.
3.   Cited by Arthur Bernon Tourtellot, *The Presidents on the Presidency* (Doubleday & Co., New York, 1964), p. 224.
4.   Cited by Huges, *op. cit.,* p. 195.
5.   *Ibid.,* p. 199.
6.   Lawrence H. Chamberlin, "The President, Congress, and Legislation," *Political Science Quarterly,* **65**, 1 (March 1946), 42. Reprinted in Aaron Wildavsky, Ed., *The Presidency* (Little, Brown and Co., Boston, 1969), p. 440.
7.   Wildavsky, *op. cit.,* p. 441.
8.   Michael Andrew Scully, "Reflections of a Senate Aide," *The Public Interest,* No. 47 (Spring 1977), p. 41.
9.   *Ibid,* p. 42.
10.   *Ibid.,* p. 17.
11.   *Ibid.,* p. 26.
12.   *Business Week,* January 31, 1977.
13.   *Wall Street Journal,* January 24, 1977.
14.   *New York Times,* May 25, 1977.
15.   Sanford J. Ungar, "Bleak House—Frustration on Capital Hill," *The Atlantic,* July 1977, p. 32.
16.   *Wall Street Journal,* August 18, 1977.
17.   *Wall Street Journal,* August 4, 1977.
18.   *Wall Street Journal,* August 5, 1977.
19.   *Ibid.*

CHAPTER EIGHT

1.   Alan Greenspan, "The Price of Oil: Is It a Threat to World Stability?", presentation before the 1977 Financial Conference, The Conference Board, New York, February 24, 1977.
2.   *Federal Energy Administration Regulation Report of the Presidential Task Force,* Paul W. McAvoy, Ed., 1977, p. 18.
3.   *Ibid.,* p. 143.
4.   *Ibid.,* p. 146.
5.   *Wall Street Journal,* September 28, 1977.
6.   *Wall Street Journal,* April 27, 1977.
7.   *Wall Street Journal,* May 20, 1977.
8.   *Wall Street Journal,* September 14, 1977.

CHAPTER NINE

1.   *Wall Street Journal,* August 3, 1977.
2.   *The National Energy Plan,* issued by the White House, Washington, D. C., April 29, 1977, p. 36.
3.   Milton Friedman, "Energy Rhetoric," *Newsweek,* June 13, 1977.
4.   Lewis H. Lapham, "The Energy Debacle," *Harper's,* August 1977, p. 59.
5.   *Ibid.,* p. 60.
6.   *Ibid.,* p. 64.

CHAPTER TEN

1.   Will Durant, *The Life of Greece, The Story of Civilization,* Vol. 2 (Simon and Schuster, New York, 1939), p. 283.
2.   *Ibid.,* p. 282.
3.   Robert J. Lampman, "Growth, Prosperity, and Inequality Since 1947," *The Wilson Quarterly,* Autumn 1977, p. 148.
4.   Paul W. McCracken, "What Our Society Should Be All About," *Across the Board* (Conference Board magazine), July 1977, p. 5.
5.   Bette K. Fishbein, *The Journal of the Institute for Socioeconomic Studies,* July 1977, p. 54.
6.   F. A. Hayek, *The Mirage of Social Justice* (University of Chicago Press, 1976), p. 23.
7.   *Ibid.,* p. 83.
8.   Robert Nisbet, "Where Do We Go From Here?", from *Income Redistribution* (American Enterprise Institute for Public Policy Research, Washington, D.C., 1977), p. 180.
9.   *Ibid.,* p. 181.

CHAPTER ELEVEN

1. *The Public Interest,* No. 47 (Spring 1977), p. 87.
2. *New York Times,* July 15, 1977.
3. *New York Times,* July 17, 1977.
4. *New York Times,* July 23, 1977.
5. *U.S. News & World Report,* August 8, 1977.
6. *Ibid.*
7. Associated Press, June 22, 1977.
8. *U.S. News & World Report,* July 11, 1977.
9. *U.S. News & World Report,* August 8, 1977.
10. *Time,* August 29, 1977.
11. Courier–News, Bridgewater, N.J., July 1, 1977.
12. "Poverty Status of Families Under Alternative Definitions of Income", Congressional Budget Office, Background Paper No. 17, Revised June 1977, p. xiv.
13. *Congressional Quarterly,* September 3, 1977, p. 1865.
14. *New York Times,* September 16, 1977.
15. *New York Times,* May 22, 1977.
16. *Washington Post,* September 22, 1977.
17. *New York Times,* September 24, 1977.
18. *ibid.,* July 31, 1977.
19. *The Public Interest,* No. 47 (Spring 1977), p. 63.
20. Backgrounder, *Analysis of Carter's Welfare Reform Proposal* (The Heritage Foundation, Washington, D.C., No. 30, August 8, 1977).
21. *New York Times,* OpEd article, November 4, 1977.
22. Courier–News, Bridgewater, N.J., May 19, 1977.

CHAPTER TWELVE

1. *New York Times,* November 4, 1977.
2. *Time,* October 10, 1977.
3. *New York Times,* October 30, 1977.
4. *Time,* October 10, 1977, p. 18.
5. J. Douglas Brown, *Essays on Social Security* (Princeton University, 1977), p. 4.
6. *New York Times,* May 27, 1977.
7. *New York Times,* May 11, 1977.
8. Cited by Robert L. Schuettinger in *Saving Social Security* (Council on American Affairs, Washington, D.C., 1977), p. 19.
9. Martin Feldstein, "Facing the Social Security Crisis," *The Public Interest,* No. 47 (Spring 1977), p. 93.

10. Schuettinger, *op. cit.,* p. 36.
11. *New York Times,* November 26, 1977.
12. *Wall Street Journal,* October 28, 1977.
13. *New York Times,* August 19, 1977.
14. *Wall Street Journal,* October 26, 1977.

CHAPTER THIRTEEN

1. Martin Feldstein, "The High Cost of Hospitals," *The Public Interest,* No. 48, Summer 1977, p. 47.
2. *Wall Street Journal,* August 2, 1977. Excerpted from Eric J. Cassell, *The Healing* (J. B. Lippincott Co., Boston, 1976).
3. "The Race to Cut Medical Costs," *Dun's Review,* May 1977, p. 50.
4. "Uproar Over Medical Bills," *U.S. News & World Report,* March 28, 1977, p. 36.
5. Feldstein, *op. cit.,* p. 42.
6. *New York Times,* October 30, 1977.
7. *Expenditures for Health Care: Federal Programs and Their Effects* (Background Paper, Congressional Budget Office, August 1977), p. 18.
8. Harry Schwartz, *The Case for American Medicine* (David McKay Co., New York, 1972), p. 92.
9. Feldstein, *op. cit.,* p. 47.
10. *New York Times,* November 9, 1977.
11. Cited in *Debating National Health Policy* (American Enterprise Institute, Washington, D.C., 1977), p. 92.
12. Charles L. Schultze, *The Public Use of Private Interest* (The Brookings Institution, Washington, D.C., 1977), pp. 63–64.
13. Feldstein, *op. cit.,* p. 52.
14. Feldstein, *op. cit.,* p. 53.
15. *New York Times,* October 30, 1977.

CHAPTER FOURTEEN

1. Fabian Linden, "The New Army of the Unemployed," *Across the Board* (Conference Board Magazine), February 1977.
2. Kenneth W. Clarkson and Roger E. Meiners, *Inflated Unemployment Statistics,* Law and Economic Study Center, University of Miami, March 1977.
3. James M. Rosow, *Changing Attitudes to Work and Life Styles,* paper presented at the Sperry Rand International Press Symposium, March 22, 1977.
4. Edward M. Gramlich, "New York: Ripple or Tidal Wave?" *American Economic Review,* **66,** 2 (1976), 415–429.

CHAPTER FIFTEEN

1.   Franz Kafka, *The Castle* (The Modern Library, New York, 1969), p. 94.
2.   Anne Brunsdale, *Regulation* (American Enterprise Institute, Washington, D.C.), July–August 1977.
3.   Louis Lasagna, *Perspectives in Biology and Medicine* (University of Chicago publication, Summer 1976), p. 548.

CHAPTER SIXTEEN

1.   Jerome B. Wiesner, "Has the U.S. Lost Its Initiative in Technological Innovation?" *Technology Review,* July–August 1976.
2.   Murray L. Weidenbaum and James McGowon, "Capital Formation and Public Policy," *Electric Perspectives* (Edison Electric Institute), May 1976.

CHAPTER EIGHTEEN

1.   John Kendrick, *The Changing Productivity Environment,* paper presented at Sperry–Rand symposium on The Changing Environment for Industrial Enterprise, New York, March 22, 1977.
2.   *Wall Street Journal* editorial, April 4, 1977.

INDEX